THE CHALLENGE TO URBAN LIBERALISM

Twentieth-Century America Series

Philip J. Funigiello

The Challenge
to Urban Liberalism

Federal-City Relations during World War II

THE UNIVERSITY OF TENNESSEE PRESS : KNOXVILLE

ᏏᏉ *Twentieth-Century America Series*

DEWEY W. GRANTHAM, GENERAL EDITOR

Library of Congress Cataloging in Publication Data

Funigiello, Philip J
 The challenge to urban liberalism.
 (Twentieth-century America series)
 Bibliography: p.
 Includes index.
 1. Federal-city relations—United States—History—
20th century. I. Title.
HT123.F86   309.2′0973   78-2670
ISBN 0-87049-228-4

TO MY WIFE, *Joanne*

Contents

Tables

Introduction

The process of urban growth in the United States and the origins of characteristically urban problems have come under scrutiny from historians only in the years following World War II and largely in response to the urban "crisis." A few pioneering scholars wrote from the urban vantage in the 1930s, but the preponderance of the literature of urbanization then and since has been the fruit of political scientists, economists, sociologists, and city planners.[1] Their writings were, and continue to be, important for identifying areas of urbanism that need to be investigated, for showing the historian of the city the kinds of questions he has to ask at each stage of his research, and for their analysis of contemporary urban problems. In few instances, however, have social scientists gone back to the raw data—to the archival and agency records, to the manuscripts and personal papers of the participants—to lend historical perspective to their findings. Most likely, this is attributable to the social and behavioral sciences' preoccupation with the contemporary metropolitan community.

On the other hand, thanks largely to the social sciences, we know a great deal about the tortuous path of urban policy making since the landmark Housing Act of 1949. Historians over the past decade have contributed to our understanding of urban growth in the early twentieth century. The pre-World War I era of progressive reform has been extensively investigated, as have the Great Depression and New Deal experiences. The period

---

1. Among the early studies interpreting American history from the urban viewpoint are Albert B. Hart, "The Rise of American Cities," *Quarterly Journal of Economics* 4 (1890), 129–57; Charles A. Beard, "The City's Place in Civilization," *National Municipal Review* 17 (Dec. 1928), 726–31; Arthur M. Schlesinger, "The City in American History," *Mississippi Valley Historical Review* 27 (June 1940), 43–66; Carl Bridenbaugh, *Cities in the Wilderness: The First Century of Urban Life in America, 1625–1742* (New York, 1938).

from 1940 to 1945 has, by and large, been given short shrift, conveying the impression that the war years were either unimportant or an aberration in the overall development of urban America. Where the war years are discussed, the tendency of writers has been to concentrate on the spectacular and ephemeral aspects of the wartime experience and to ignore the routine but perhaps in the long run more significant developments for urban growth.[2] This study is intended to call attention to the policy-making aspects of the war period for future urban development and to close still one more gap in our knowledge of the urban process and policy making.[3]

Before examining the war years, one must first analyze briefly the condition of the cities in the preceding decade. By every available index, the Great Depression had a devastating impact upon the cities and dispelled forever the myth of urban economic self-sufficiency. The problem for the cities was basically financial, and as local municipal and state efforts failed to relieve the distress urban officials individually and collectively approached the national government for assistance. Their inability to cope with mounting economic hardship caused Washington to move gradually toward a cooperative federalism that took account of the states but also encompassed the cities in their own right. The pattern of relationships among levels of government changed in the 1930s but without causing violence to the essential sovereignty of the states and localities.[4]

Besides plunging the cities and states into financial chaos, the

2. See, for example, Charles N. Glaab and A. Theodore Brown, *A History of Urban America* (New York, 1967), William H. Wilson, *Coming of Age: Urban America 1915-1945* (New York, 1974), and Richard Polenberg, *War and Society: The United States 1941-1945* (Philadelphia, 1972). A recent exception is Mark I. Gelfand, *A Nation of Cities: The Federal Government's Response to the Challenges of Urban America, 1933-1965* (New York, 1975), chs. 3, 4.

3. This monograph should logically stand on the one side between J. Joseph Huthmacher's *Senator Robert F. Wagner and the Rise of Urban Liberalism* (New York, 1968) and Joseph L. Arnold's *The New Deal in the Suburbs* (Columbus, Ohio, 1971) and, on the other side, Richard O. Davies's *Housing Reform During the Truman Administration* (Columbia, Mo., 1966).

4. See Joseph D. McGoldrick, "The Cities Cannot Act Alone," *National Municipal Review* 37 (Jan. 1948), 7-9; Paul V. Betters, *Recent Federal-City Relations* (Washington, D.C., 1936), 137-38.

Depression coincided with the Democratic party's achieving majority status. Its launching of the New Deal as a governmental response to the massive economic and social problems of a society more than half urban brought a great expansion of federal programs. Some of these were in response to municipal and state pressures; others were designed by urban reformers eager to stimulate city and state action. In either case, the Depression eroded much of the earlier resistance to federal aid, and the great acceleration of governmental activity made cooperative federalism all-pervasive.[5]

It was not until 1936 that the New Deal achieved a modicum of financial stability for the cities. Partly through emergency relief and welfare activities, partly through housing programs, and partly through urban planning, the Roosevelt administration assisted the states and municipalities in the same spirit of partnership that motivated other forms of intergovernmental cooperation. The Works Progress Administration (WPA) program provided made work for the urban unemployed, while the Public Works Administration (PWA) enabled cities to resume public construction programs. But why the delay? Why did it take the administration nearly four years to achieve financial stability for the cities? And what was being done in the interim? The answers to these questions must be found in part in the character, personality, and preferences of the President, Franklin D. Roosevelt.

In the years before he entered the presidency, Roosevelt personally was indifferent to the needs and problems of urban America. As state senator and governor he was quite willing to cultivate an urban constituency, but Roosevelt had little interest in the programs of housing reformers concerned with clearing the slums and improving the cities. He strongly believed that the future of American society lay in maintaining the strength of the countryside. Thus in the early years of his presidency, Roosevelt supported the back-to-the-land movement—not because he was

5. Daniel J. Elazar, "The Shaping of Intergovernmental Relations in the Twentieth Century," in *The Annals of the American Academy of Political and Social Science* 359 (May 1965), 10–22.

concerned about the welfare of the city dweller per se but because he believed that the return of the population to the countryside would save the nation's rapidly declining rural civilization. It took the collapse of the land movement and continual prodding from influential urban liberals in Congress and inside the administration—men and women who had accepted large-scale urbanism as a permanent condition of American life and were trying to cope with it—to persuade a reluctant President to reorient his policies, if not his beliefs.[6]

One of the first indications of a reevaluation of policy toward urban problems occurred in 1935, when Rexford G. Tugwell, a member of the original "Brains Trust," persuaded Secretary of Agriculture Henry A. Wallace and Roosevelt to allocate some of the emergency unemployment funds to the Resettlement Administration (RA), a branch of the government chiefly concerned with farm communities, so that it could undertake a demonstration of new town construction. The hope of the RA's new town program was to effect a fundamental change in the wasteful and unhealthy pattern of urban growth; to demonstrate that urban expansion by the construction of complete new towns could provide superior safety, convenience, and beauty; and to foster a deep sense of community spirit—all at a low cost.[7]

The federal government built only three greenbelt towns before opposition from entrenched private realtors and industrial

6. Roosevelt's attitude toward the city has been the subject of scholarly disagreement. Alfred Rollins, Jr., in a review of Huthmacher's study of Senator Wagner in the *American Historical Review* 74 (June 1969), 1744, states that FDR "stood for the new politics of the city." Several other historians have endorsed this point of view, arguing that FDR was fully aware of the voting power of the urban masses and therefore supported all proposals calling for additional housing, transit, and recreational facilities for the cities. (See David Burner, *The Politics of Provincialism: The Democratic Party in Transition, 1918–1932* [New York, 1968], 248, and George E. Mowry, *The Urban Nation, 1920–1960* [New York, 1965], 88.) Another group of historians has argued that FDR was apathetic to the city because he firmly believed that country life was better. (See Daniel Fusfeld, *The Economic Thought of FDR and the Origins of the New Deal* [New York, 1956], 84, and Paul Conkin, *The New Deal* [New York, 1967], 4.) The most comprehensive study of FDR's attitude toward the city is Howard S. Zavin's "Forward to the Land: Franklin D. Roosevelt and the City, 1882–1933" (Ph.D. diss., New York Univ., 1972). Zavin's evidence supports the latter judgment, and it is the one which this author has accepted.

7. The most recent comprehensive treatment of the greenbelt new town program is Arnold's *The New Deal in the Suburbs,* cited earlier.

mobilization in 1940–41 cut short the program. The lessons and dreams that inspired the experimental new towns were not forgotten, however. The program served as an inspiration to urban reformers and city planners who, in the turmoil of war, dreamed of the future in an era of peace. Despite wartime dislocations, urban liberals redirected part of their energies away from the suburban communities to rehabilitation of the urban environment. Against all odds, they hoped to create in the city the warm community of the small town while maintaining the superior economic, social, and cultural advantages of an urban location.

A second indication that a reconsideration of policy was under way came when, in 1937, Congress legislated the National Housing Act sponsored by urban reformers, notably Senator Robert F. Wagner of New York. Though the bill was not an administration measure in the first instance, President Roosevelt eventually came to its support and deserves credit for its passage. This legislation, establishing the United States Housing Authority (USHA), was the urban counterpart of the suburban new towns program of the New Deal. Of course, the Wagner Act did not fully resolve the housing needs of low-income families, but the federal government did make a basic commitment to housing for its own sake. From 1937 on, decent housing for the urban population was a recognized national goal. The National Housing Act of 1937 established the groundwork for action and a permanent policy for future urban renewal.[8]

That same year, the administration spelled out the rationale for its new approach to urban America in the report of the National Resources Committee entitled *Our Cities: Their Role in the National Economy.* This study, prepared under the direction of Clarence A. Dykstra, former city manager of Cincinnati, was the counterpart of the report of the Country Life Commission which had examined rural society three decades earlier. The report identified the city's unsolved problems and presented a series of recommendations. The solutions proposed were not

8. The definitive study of the National Housing Act of 1937 is Huthmacher's *Senator Robert F. Wagner and the Rise of Urban Liberalism,* cited earlier.

new, but the fact that the federal government itself was proposing them was new and marked a new era in the nation's urban development. The National Resources Committee had stated explicitly that urban problems were national problems and required consciously directed national efforts for their solution.[9]

To some extent, however, the urban programs of the Roosevelt administration were a snare and delusion. They encouraged municipalities to expand social service activities and physical plants without guaranteeing the means to continue them. A matching grant toward construction was very tempting, but there was no similar federal grant for maintenance and upkeep. Some of the cities were just beginning to realize this when World War II diverted attention. Moreover, the same New Deal programs that initiated a broadly based direct federal-city relationship also precipitated serious political and ideological controversies, centering usually on the nature of American federalism. Practically speaking, the struggle between conservatives and liberals defined the parameters of New Deal reform.[10]

Following immediately upon the Depression, World War II altered in several fundamental aspects the values and character of American society. These were the critical years that saw a restructuring of economic arrangements, the birth of the modern civil rights movement, the reform of the educational system, the liberation of women into the labor force, and the federal government's establishment of a network of institutional arrangements in fields that it had not entered before. The war caused a reexamination of the relationship of government to the individual and of individuals to each other.[11] Mobilization and war also left their imprints on the urban landscape. The organization of civilian protection, dislocations in housing, transportation, and morale resulting from population shifts, the diversion

9. National Resources Committee, Urban Section, *Our Cities—Their Role in the National Economy* (Washington, D.C., 1937), esp. vi.

10. See, for example, James T. Patterson, *Congressional Conservatism and the New Deal: The Growth of the Conservative Coalition in Congress, 1933–1939* (Lexington, Ky., 1967).

11. See, for example, Polenberg, *War and Society,* 239–44, and Geoffrey Perrett, *Days of Sadness, Years of Triumph: The American People, 1939–1945* (New York, 1973).

of city and state resources for defense purposes, employment shortages attendant upon selective service, financial strain on municipal budgets, and overseeing military personnel in a civilian urban environment were among the difficulties for which the cities, states, and federal government were expected to devise solutions.[12]

It seems, therefore, all the more desirable to examine how the war years influenced the process of urbanization in the United States, the quality of urban life, and what Americans thought about their cities. By focusing upon federal-urban relationships (which necessarily means to talk also about the states), we may be able to determine whether World War II disrupted traditional thinking about urbanism and the nature of urban society, whether the war years afforded the Roosevelt administration and urban reformers a unique opportunity to move away from the past and evolve new plans and programs for the orderly growth of cities in the future, and whether there existed certain constraints upon New Deal reform (such as the American tradition of private property which was so fundamental in shaping the early history of the cities) that made a national urban policy to reconstruct American cities a chimera.

Within these broad areas, the research and writing have been organized around more narrowly focused questions. How effectively did the federal system serve the cities in time of crisis? How did demographic changes wrought by mobilization affect the cities, states, and rural areas, as well as the federal-city relationship? How did the cities and states adjust to the stresses placed upon them as a result of wartime dislocations, and what was the impact of the federal government upon the daily lives of urban dwellers? Who were the principal figures and which were the major organizations concerned with urban planning? What were the aspirations, attitudes, and assumptions of each? What methodological techniques, programs, and policies did they formulate to cope with urbanization under wartime and postwar conditions? What problems were identified, and what com-

12. Arnold Miles and Roy H. Owsley, *Cities and the National Defense Program* (Chicago, 1941), 103.

promises of a political, economic, or social nature were made? Finally, did the Roosevelt administration pursue contradictory policies that negated the hopes for meaningful urban rehabilitation after the war?

The answers to these questions will, it is hoped, illuminate the urban policy-making process of more recent decades. For the questions address themselves to the broader issue of whether the roots of our contemporary urban problems—the waning sense of community, inadequate housing, urban congestion, racial antipathy, suburban sprawl—are to be discerned in this period of the 1940s, when decisions affecting the long-term well-being of the cities might have been made but were not.

Acknowledgments

In the course of writing this book I have become indebted to many people and institutions whose encouragement and information have enabled me to accomplish my task. Their words and thoughtful comments have been most helpful and greatly appreciated.

My debt—intellectual and personal—to my mentor and friend, Vincent P. Carosso of New York University, is profound; his integrity and professionalism exemplify the highest ideals of academic life. Professor Bayrd Still of New York University and Professor Richard Lowitt of Iowa State University shared their extensive knowledge of urban and recent American history with me and tendered encouragement well beyond the obligations of friendship and scholarship. Professor Dewey W. Grantham of Vanderbilt University subjected the manuscript to a thorough and searching reading. Maggie Potts, Patricia C. Blatt, Anne Kimber, and Pat Smith rendered yeoman's service in typing the manuscript. Finally, I wish to thank my colleagues at the College of William and Mary who encouraged me to complete this undertaking.

A substantial portion of the research support and a grant toward the publication of this study were subvened by the Committee on Faculty Research of the College of William and Mary. The award of a J. Bruce Bredin fellowship, allowed me to devote my full attention to this project. An earlier version of chapter 5 appeared as an article in the June 1972 issue of *Social Science Quarterly*.

I particularly want to acknowledge the assistance of the staff of the Franklin D. Roosevelt Library, Hyde Park, New York, and the staff of the National Archives, in Washington, D.C. The personnel of the Federal Records Center in Suitland, Maryland, and the Municipal Archives Center in New York City generously guided me through their considerable collections of records pertaining to civilian defense. The resources of the Library of Congress, the New York Public Library, the Fordham University Library, and the libraries of New York University also were made available to me. Special thanks must go to the professional staff of the Earl Gregg Swem Library of the College of William and Mary for its cooperation and diligence in attending to my many requests.

Beyond the academic field, the confidence and interest of my wife, family, and friends have been an inestimable source of strength.

Abbreviations

AFofL	American Federation of Labor
AIP	American Institute of Planners
ASPO	American Society of Planning Officials
AWVS	American Women's Volunteer Service
CWS	Civilian War Services
DDHC	Division of Defense Housing Coordination
DSLC	Division of State and Local Cooperation
FEPC	Fair Employment Practices Committee
FHLBB	Federal Home Loan Bank Board
FHA	Federal Housing Agency
FSA	Federal Security Agency
FWA	Federal Works Agency
NAHB	National Association of Home Builders
NAHO	National Association of Housing Officials
NAREB	National Association of Real Estate Boards
NCHE	National Committee on the Housing Emergency
NDAC	National Defense Advisory Commission
NHA	National Housing Agency
NRPB	National Resources Planning Board
OCD	Office of Civilian Defense
OCWS	Office of Community Welfare Services
ODHWS	Office of Defense Health and Welfare Services
OEM	Office of Emergency Management
OPA	Office of Price Administration
OPM	Office of Production Management
PBA	Public Buildings Administration
PHC	Public Housing Conference
PWA	Public Works Administration
RA	Resettlement Administration
RFC	Reconstruction Finance Corporation
USES	United States Employment Service

| USHA | United States Housing Authority |
| WPA | Works Progress Administration |

THE CHALLENGE TO URBAN LIBERALISM

I. The Great Defense Migration

In the spring of 1940 the House of Representatives, pursuant to H. Res. 63, established a select committee "to investigate the interstate migration of destitute citizens." Congressman John H. Tolan, Democrat of California, the committee's chairman, had first introduced the resolution in February 1939, one month before *The Grapes of Wrath* was published to critical acclaim. As befitted the subject of the novel of the year, the focus of the hearings was a direct response to the economic depression of the 1930s, particularly to the plight of the thousands of tenant farmers of the South and West, like the Joads.[1] The committee's final report in 1942 confirmed what many people knew or suspected: that the migration of the 1930s had been symptomatic of two major problems, displacement in agriculture and unemployment in industry. Thousands of jobless men and women had set out as families or alone in search of a new beginning elsewhere. Unable to locate steady employment, they never sank roots in any community but instead joined the ranks of habitual migrants who followed seasonal employment in farming and industry.[2]

What began as a belated inquiry into the economic problems of the thirties took on enhanced significance as the full force of the Nazi war machine was demonstrated to the world. On May 16, 1940, while the invasion of France was in full swing, President Roosevelt sent a message to Congress calling attention to the blitzkrieg tactics and asked for appropriations of $1 billion to enable industrial production to gear up to a capacity for

1. See U.S. House of Representatives, *National Defense Migration,* Hearings before the Select Committee Investigating National Defense Migration pursuant to H. Res. 113, 77th Cong., 2d sess. (34 parts, 1940-42). Cited hereafter as *National Defense Migration Hearings.*
2. See "Interstate Migration of Workers," *Monthly Labor Review* 52 (June 1941), 1347-50.

fifty thousand aircraft a year. He followed this with additional requests for funds, totaling in excess of $15 billion. The rapid acceleration of defense activities through the fall of 1940 once again focused attention on the interstate migration of workers, but this time they were migrant workers gravitating toward defense industries located in urban centers. The Tolan Committee had first taken account of this phenomenon in November 1940. Confronted with a drastically altered situation, Congress in March 1941 extended that committee's mandate to enable it to investigate all aspects of the national defense migration. It instructed the committee to report back no later than January 3, 1943.[3]

In its quest for data, the Tolan Committee relied extensively (but not exclusively) upon WPA surveys requested in 1940 by the Federal Security Agency. The completed and tabulated information encompassed fifty-one urban centers of industrial activity, each having a population of 25,000 or more. When this is supplemented with census figures, knowledge of the geographic distribution of the sugar ration book of 1942, and the testimony of expert witnesses, an urban profile of defense migration may be composed. The data provide a base from which to make observations concerning (1) the impact of wartime migration upon population distribution; (2) the sources, destinations, and characteristic traits of the migrants; (3) the effect of the special status of minorities upon their specific patterns of migration; (4) the extent of occupational shifting resulting from migration; (5) the migrants' effect upon the composition of both the receiving-city populations and their places of origin; and (6) the long-range demographic, economic, and social impact of war upon urbanization and the sense of community. This knowledge is requisite to understanding how the federal government coped with urban change under wartime stress.

3. Samuel I. Rosenman, comp., *The Public Papers and Addresses of Franklin D. Roosevelt*, 13 vols. (New York, 1938–50), IX, xxvii; John J. Sparkman, "Two Years of Work by the Tolan Committee," in *Proceedings of the National Conference of Social Work, New Orleans, Louisiana, May 10–16, 1942* (New York, 1942), 176–85. See also Henry S. Shryock, Jr., and Hope Tisdale Eldridge, "Internal Migration in Peace and War," *American Sociological Review* 12 (Feb. 1947), 27–39.

Industrial Mobilization and Migration

The surveys disclosed unmistakably that while no geographical section or urban community escaped the impact of defense mobilization, the effect was by no means universal. The principal factor accounting for the differences was the degree to which a community participated in the defense effort. This in turn was significantly influenced by the location policies of the Plant Sites Division of the War Production Board (WPB), as well as the form of contract letting. In the period of mobilization prior to Pearl Harbor, the government awarded to fifty-six corporations an average of 75 percent of all war contracts by dollar value. After 1942, the pattern of contract allotments produced further concentration of population and industries in a limited number of older urban metropolitan areas and established several newer metropolitan centers of imposing stature in the Southwest and on the Pacific Coast. This process occurred within a matter of weeks and months, so that the growing pains of urbanization were compressed into a relatively brief span of time.[4]

Too often the decision where to locate a factory or let a contract was made on a basis other than economic, so that the migration during the early months of mobilization was smaller and more concentrated than many of the frenzied newspaper and magazine articles suggested. Howard B. Myers, the WPA director of research, drove home this point before the Tolan Committee. The points of destination of defense migrants, he testified, were (1) army cantonments, camps, and other military establishments; (2) powder and shell loading plants in or near rural areas; (3) shipbuilding and aircraft communities in urban metropolitan areas such as Seattle; and (4) older centers of steel, machine, tool, brass, and other heavy industries. Because of the lingering, massive unemployment of the thirties, the industrial movement was less spectacular through 1941; factories were still in the process of tooling up for defense production. In the long run, how-

---

4. Louis Wirth, "The Urban Community," in William F. Ogburn, ed., *American Society in Wartime* (Chicago, 1943), 67; *National Defense Migration Hearings,* pt. 16, 6545–47; 6576–81.

ever, industrial employment was destined to be of greater duration and both socially and economically much more important than the movement to large construction jobs. The latter, while impressive in 1940–41, was mostly temporary.[5]

Both the census data for 1940 and the number of registrants for Ration Book Number 4 in November 1943 (by which date industrial production had attained its peak) illustrate the major flow patterns created by the new job opportunities. These were the movement of people from interior to seacoast states or to states bordering on the Great Lakes, the interchange between the South and North, the flow of hundreds of thousands of people to the West and Southwest, and by 1943 the vast movement from rural to metropolitan areas. Nineteen states, including the District of Columbia, experienced a net population gain of about 3.7 million, while thirty states recorded losses.[6]

More importantly from the perspective of demography, the pattern of interstate migration between 1940 and 1943 was similar to that of the preceding five years and almost identical to the population shifts of the 1920s. This continuity was broken temporarily only in the period 1930–35, when the Depression in the heavily urban-industrial states precipitated a back-to-the-land movement.[7] Thus, of the nineteen states experiencing net population gains in the years 1940–43, sixteen also had recorded increases during the 1920s, and fourteen experienced gains in the period 1935–40. Only ten states that profited from defense migration also showed increases in the depths of the Depression. Conversely, of the thirty states with net losses in the early years of defense and war mobilization, twenty-eight also had lost population in the 1920s, and twenty-four during the years 1935–40, when recovery seemed probable. Again in contrast, only nineteen of the lesser urban-industrial states lost popula-

5. *National Defense Migration Hearings*, pt. 27, 10318–24; pt. 11, 4323, 4441, 4445–65; pt. 17, 6758. See also Howard B. Myers, "Defense Migration and Labor Supply," *Journal of the American Statistical Association* 37 (Mar. 1942), 69–76.

6. See especially *Sixteenth Decennial Census of the United States* (Washington, D.C., 1944), Ser. P–44, No. 17 (Aug. 28, 1944), *passim*.

7. For the impact of this phenomenon on a city like Detroit see *National Defense Migration Hearings*, pt. 18, 7171–73; 7198, 7203.

tion in the period 1930–35. Thus, between 1940 and 1943, interstate migration was adhering closely to the traditional pattern characteristic of periods of industrial expansion in the United States, as shown in Table 1.

That the national defense migrants were moving along trails blazed long before the war, and in the same direction in which millions had gone before them, is also evident from an analysis of the thirty states that suffered population loss through out-migration. Only two of the states in this category had experienced population increases in the 1920s: New York, because of the influx of immigrants from abroad, and Texas, as a result of the tremendous growth of the oil industry. Virginia, Delaware, and Utah, net losers in the 1920s, were by virtue of their strategic locations as centers of shipbuilding or munitions production the only states to record population gains during the period of mobilization. This trend was altered temporarily during the worst years of the Depression; between 1930 and 1935 the industrial states of Michigan, Illinois, Indiana, Ohio, New Jersey, Massachusetts, and Rhode Island recorded net losses of population as people hurried back to the agricultural states.[8]

Neither the Great Depression nor the back-to-the-land phenomenon, however, could halt the long-range shift of population. At most, hard times slowed down or reversed temporarily the direction of the migrations. In the later 1930s the trends that prevailed in the preceding decade were partially resumed: Michigan and Indiana regained population; the losses in Ohio, Illinois, and Massachusetts subsided; and Minnesota, Tennessee, and Maine once more sent their sons and daughters to the urban industrial states.[9]

But there was a difference between the Dust Bowl wanderers who harvested lettuce in the Imperial Valley in the 1930s and the newer refugees from the anthracite mines of Scranton, Pennsylvania, who migrated to work in the defense factories of Bridge-

8. Wladimir S. Woytinsky, "Interstate Migration During the War," *State Government* 19 (Mar. 1946), 81–84.

9. Warren S. Thompson, *Research Memorandum on Internal Migration in the Depression* (New York, 1937), ch. 3.

TABLE 1. Interstate Migration Before and During World War II, Showing Net Gain and Loss.

State*	Civilians only Apr. 1940– Nov. 1943	Total population		
		1920–30	1930–35	1935–40
California	+ 1,368,600	+ 1,738,000	+ 387,300	+ 664,900
Michigan	+ 280,800	+ 595,000	− 81,400	+ 76,000
Washington	+ 244,900	+ 82,000	+ 26,200	+ 80,400
Maryland	+ 235,400	+ 13,000	+ 49,300	+ 61,300
Ohio	+ 231,000	+ 282,000	− 61,500	− 9,800
Dist. of Columbia	+ 205,300	+ †	+ 121,600	+ 22,500
Florida	+ 186,700	+ 349,000	+ 188,300	+ 146,800
New Jersey	+ 184,900	+ 477,000	− 76,600	+ 29,400
Virginia	+ 154,700	− 231,000	− 36,400	− 27,200
Oregon	+ 138,200	+ 96,000	+ 18,600	+ 77,400
Connecticut	+ 127,400	+ 84,000	+ 6,100	+ 24,900
Indiana	+ 79,000	+ 35,000	− 14,100	+ 26,300
Arizona	+ 76,700	+ 27,000	− 12,000	+ 37,800
Illinois	+ 68,600	+ 488,000	− 59,200	− 19,100
Massachusetts	+ 37,000	+ 49,000	− 74,000	− 32,200
Utah	+ 32,400	− 30,000	+ 50,900	− 12,400
Rhode Island	+ 29,500	+ 18,000	− 5,900	+ 400
Nevada	+ 26,900	+ 5,000	+ 8,600	+ 8,000
Delaware	+ 19,400	− 18,000	+ 49,300	+ 61,300
Wyoming	− 8,700	− 1,000	− 2,600	+ 2,700
New Hampshire	− 12,000	− 7,000	+ 2,800	+ 6,100
Texas	− 15,700	+ 288,000	+ 48,700	− 22,100
Louisiana	− 19,000	− 22,000	+ 40,100	+ 8,600
Colorado	− 22,800	− 15,000	+ 12,400	+ 9,100
Maine	− 30,400	− 35,000	+ 6,800	− 8,600

*States are arrayed by net gain or loss of civilian population through interstate migration from April 1940 to November 1943.

†Data not available.

SOURCES: Derived from Wladimir S. Woytinsky, "Interstate Migration during the War," *State Government,* 19 (Mar. 1946), 83. Figures for 1940–43 are from Bureau of the Census, *Special Report,* Ser. P–44, No. 17 (Aug. 28, 1944), and the estimate is based on registration for Ration Book No. 4. Figures for 1920–30 are from C. Warren Thornthwaite, *Internal Migration in the United States* (Study of Population Distribution,

State*	Civilians only Apr. 1940– Nov. 1943	Total population 1920–30	1930–35	1935–40
Vermont	− 31,400	− 19,000	− 14,100	− 5,700
New Mexico	− 44,400	− 20,000	+ 23,100	+ 13,800
Idaho	− 44,900	− 51,000	+ 7,400	+ 16,400
Kansas	− 54,100	− 95,000	− 95,400	− 111,100
Montana	− 69,000	− 71,000	− 13,200	− 11,100
Tennessee	− 70,800	− 117,000	+ 95,100	− 38,800
South Dakota	− 89,100	− 42,000	− 60,800	− 61,200
Nebraska	− 96,300	− 81,000	− 76,800	− 106,600
North Dakota	− 100,400	− 72,000	− 59,200	− 66,500
Wisconsin	− 102,900	− 7,000	− 13,400	− 31,800
Pennsylvania	− 112,400	− 69,000	− 251,800	− 103,700
Alabama	− 116,400	− 150,000	− 85,400	− 73,500
Missouri	− 116,900	− 60,000	+ 72,900	− 85,500
Georgia	− 130,900	− 416,000	− 61,700	− 33,200
South Carolina	− 137,900	− 258,000	− 38,200	− 16,000
West Virginia	− 139,600	− 53,000	− 36,400	− 27,200
Minnesota	− 192,000	− 113,000	+ 20,300	− 17,900
Iowa	− 192,600	− 168,000	− 44,200	− 60,900
Mississippi	− 194,200	− 103,000	− 72,800	− 28,400
New York	− 223,000	+ 1,229,000	+ 37,100	− 57,100
Arkansas	− 225,400	− 214,000	− 38,400	− 75,500
Kentucky	− 262,700	− 203,000	− 16,400	− 54,800
North Carolina	− 262,800	− 8,000	− 47,500	− 14,900
Oklahoma	− 303,500	− 49,000	− 118,000	− 183,900

Univ. of Pennsylvania Press, 1944), and the estimate is based on comparison of age composition of the population of each state in 1920 and 1930. Migration of children under 10 is not taken into account. Figures for 1930–35 are the balance of net gain or loss in 1930–40 over net gain or loss in 1935–40 (for 1930–40 data see paper of W.S. Woytinsky, *Internal Migration during the War,* Social Security Board, spec. rpt., Nov. 27, 1944; for 1935–40 data see the last column of this table). Estimate is based on the number of births and deaths in each state in 1930–39. Figures for 1935–40 are from Bureau of the Census, Census 1940, Population, Internal Migration 1935 to 1940, p. 18.

port, Connecticut. The "Okies" went west to escape certain economic death on barren farms. Nothing could have been worse than what they left behind. For the miners what they had was fair, but the urban industrial centers might offer something better.[10]

Most public and newspaper attention in 1940, though, concentrated upon the few cities that were experiencing a hectic, mushroom-like growth. Twenty-seven percent of San Diego's population, for example, was composed of in-migrants lured to the shipyards and aircraft factories. San Diego was growing so rapidly that city manager Walter Cooper predicted twenty years of future population growth would be compressed into the next two years. In Wichita, Kansas, a center of aircraft production, 20 percent of the population had originated elsewhere; more than 150,000 workers had migrated to Los Angeles, 40,000 to Seattle, and 50,000 to Washington, D.C. Statistically, however, these cities did not conform to the more general pattern of 1940. For, in more than half the central cities for which WPA data were available, the migration rate was still below 5 percent, and in only nine cities had it exceeded 10 percent. Their hothouse growth obscured a more fundamental development in the urban pattern: the deconcentration of population throughout the metropolitan area and into suburban districts.[11]

Almost entirely the product of migration, this phenomenon originated in the early twenties, had been partially obscured during the Depression, but was renewed and accelerated in 1940–41. As population moved from the central city toward the periphery, industry followed closely behind, abandoning old manufacturing sites within the central business district for underdeveloped, less heavily taxed suburban locations. One out of six Americans in 1940 was a suburban dweller, and there existed one suburbanite for every two inhabitants still living in the central city of the metropolitan area.[12] When the War Production

10. Blair Bolles, "The Great Defense Migration," *Harper's Magazine* 183 (Oct. 1941), 460; *National Defense Migration Hearings,* pt. 11, 4289, 4295.

11. *National Defense Migration Hearings,* pt. 12, 4830; pt. 27, 10318–24.

12. See Amos H. Hawley, *The Changing Shape of Metropolitan America: Deconcentration Since 1920* (Glencoe, Ill., 1956), 12ff.

Board chose to allot contracts to new plants in the outlying metropolitan areas in order to relieve the strain on central city facilities, it was unwittingly encouraging the dispersal that left the central cities moribund. Louis Wirth, the distinguished urban sociologist and consultant to the National Resources Planning Board, predicted that the acceleration of population loss by the central cities would result in blight, physical decay, civic irresponsibility, and impotence.[13]

The continuing phenomenon of massive gains by metropolitan areas during the war years was confirmed by census authorities in 1943. After analyzing population returns for selected metropolitan counties, they concluded that the metropolitan areas of the United States as a group were gaining population at a rate that exceeded the loss of civilians to the military. This conclusion was based on a survey of 137 counties conducted between April 1940, the start of industrial mobilization, and its completion in May 1943. Eighty-eight metropolitan counties had recorded population gains attributable primarily to inmigration; forty-three showed a decline, and six no appreciable change. In counties in which population increased the total was 2,639,000, or about 6.8 percent above 1940 figures, which compared favorably with a net gain of 1,853,000, or 2.8 percent for all the counties surveyed.[14]

The distribution pattern of states having a high rate of inmigration also confirmed that wartime population concentration was selective. It occurred in the metropolitan counties of large central cities. The population gain of Mineral and Clark counties (which encompassed the naval ammunition depot at

13. Edgar M. Hoover, Jr., and Glenn E. McLaughlin, "Strategic Factors in Plant Location," *Harvard Business Review* 20 (Winter 1942), 1933–40; Louis Wirth, "The Metropolitan Region as a Planning Unit," in *Proceedings of the National Conference on Planning, May 25–27, 1942* (Chicago, 1942).

14. However, in order to keep the magnitude of their growth in historical perspective, we should compare these figures with the growth rate of the preceding two decades. The average annual rate of increase in the 137 metropolitan counties from 1940–42 was 1.3 percent, which was significantly *below* the annual rate of 2.7 percent that prevailed in the twenties when metropolitanization advanced most rapidly. See "Preliminary Estimates of Civilian Population in Selected Metropolitan Counties: May 1, 1942," in *Sixteenth Decennial Census of the United States* (Washington, D.C., 1943), Ser. P–3, No. 31 (Dec. 1, 1942), 1–2.

11

Hawthorne and Las Vegas) exceeded Nevada's gain as a whole, indicating that there was indeed a disequilibrium in favor of metropolitan areas. The counties within which were located the cities of Los Angeles, San Diego, and San Francisco recorded population gains of 131,000, 97,000, and 95,000 respectively; the Detroit metropolitan counties (and to a lesser extent Kalamazoo and Muskegon) registered a greater population increase (about 336,000) than the state of Michigan as a whole. Chicago's Cook County was swollen by an influx of 149,000 war workers and their dependents. A similar pattern prevailed in the South. More than 90 percent of Maryland's growth occurred in the Baltimore-Washington metropolitan corridor. In Virginia, traditionally a rural state, growth also centered in the metropolitan counties: the Norfolk-Hampton Roads military-industrial complex (107,000); the suburban Washington counties of Alexandria and Fairfax; Henrico County, which included Richmond; and the Petersburg and Lynchburg metropolitan areas.[15]

The District of Columbia, the fulcrum of government, politics, and war-making, was of course in a class by itself. Apart from being the only city in a large metropolitan complex that did not have extensive manufacturing, it probably had the highest percentage of newcomers. The city experienced a population explosion of nearly 231,000 government workers, secretaries, "dollar-a-year" men, and blacks between 1940 and 1943. This tremendous influx of humanity in so brief a time strained every urban amenity to the breaking point.[16]

Despite heavy out-migration, the population of the metropolitan counties of the South exhibited relatively the largest rate of increase.[17] The figure was approximately 3.9 percent for the

15. Henry S. Shryock, Jr., "Internal Migration and the War," *Journal of the American Statistical Association* 38 (Mar. 1943), 23ff.; Philip M. Hauser, "Population and Vital Phenomena," *American Journal of Sociology* 48 (Nov. 1942), 301–22.

16. See the diary entries of Feb. 13, 1941, and Jan. 5, 1943, John Ihlder Diary, John Ihlder Papers, Franklin D. Roosevelt Library (FDRL), Hyde Park, N.Y.

17. Despite ongoing industrialization and the large number of military installations, the South as a region was the major *loser* by wartime migration. Between 1940 and 1943, almost 900,000 people left Dixie for the North and West, offsetting an in-migration of 500,000. By 1945, nearly 1.6 million Southerners had gone elsewhere. See "Civilian Migration in the United States: Dec. 1941 to Mar. 1945," in *Sixteenth Decennial Census of the United States* (Washington, D.C., 1945), Ser. P–5, No. 5 (Sept. 2, 1945).

region as a whole in 1940–43, a growth rate that compared favorably with the West's 2.7 percent, the North Central section's 2.0 percent, and the *decrease* of 0.6 percent for the Northeast. The most dramatic gains occurred in selected Southern cities favored by the presence of manufacturing or military activity and resulted primarily from an intraregional flow from rural to urban counties. Within three years Mobile had grown by 33 percent, as had Norfolk; Montgomery registered a 30 percent gain; Corpus Christi, 28 percent; Charleston, 25 percent; and Jacksonville, 23 percent. The population growth of these cities exceeded the figures for any previous decade, including the twenties, when urbanization and industrialization were extremely rapid in the South and cities such as Baltimore, Dallas, Birmingham, Atlanta, Memphis, and New Orleans had made great advances.[18]

Metropolitan urban growth within the region must be kept in perspective, however, for the increase was not uniformly shared. Just as population accretion varied from one Southern state to the next, so too were marked differences to be found among the counties. While the nonmilitary population as a whole increased more than 10 percent, Virginia, with a growth of 32 percent, and North Carolina (excluding Durham), with a decline of 7.1 percent, represented the extremes. Alabama, Georgia, and Florida came closer to the average. Moreover, despite the spectacular population growth of a few cities, a comparison of the annual rates of change in the metropolitan counties of Tennessee, Alabama, Mississippi, Louisiana, and Arkansas with the two prewar decades indicates that the boomlike effect of national defense upon Southern urbanization needs to be qualified. For the growth rate in these counties was 1.9 percent, which was actually less than two-thirds of the rate of increase from 1930 to 1940. The pre-Depression level of metropolitan growth in these urban counties was not attained until 1944.[19]

18. Philip M. Hauser, "Wartime Population Changes and Postwar Prospects," *Journal of Marketing* 8 (Jan. 1944), 238–48; Robert K. Lamb, "Mobilization of Human Resources," *American Journal of Sociology* 48 (Nov. 1942), 323–30.

19. Rudolf Heberle, *The Impact of the War on the Population Redistribution in the South* (Nashville, 1945), 26–30.

In contrast to the metropolitan counties of the South and the West, some of the more heavily populated industrial sectors of the Northeast received relatively few in-migrants. This was largely a consequence of the WPB's policies. Most communities involved in defense production, of course, did report to the Tolan Committee some interchange of skilled, semiskilled, and even unskilled workers with other localities. Metropolitan Boston managed to meet production demands by drawing upon workers from within a twenty-five-mile radius. Conditions were less favorable elsewhere in New England. As workers deserted communities on the fringes of the defense program for the more lucrative jobs in the industrial cities, they threatened to throw the region's economy out of normal equilibrium. In far northern New Hampshire, the Brown Company paper mill lost employees to the better-paying jobs in Portsmouth's shipyards. The local labor market in Hartford was so tight that the Pratt and Whitney Machine Tool Company sent labor scouts across the border to Springfield, Massachusetts, to lure workers to the city.[20]

Where urban communities lacked the good fortune by virtue of strategic location or political influence to become focal points of war production, they also lost population. This again underscores the fact that the population shifts between 1940 and 1943 were more complex than simply a rural to urban movement. For nearly one-third of the 137 metropolitan counties studied by census officials had lost population, the decline in some instances being as high as 10 to 12 percent. Metropolitan Topeka and St. Joseph, for example, suffered a 12 percent population decline during the first two years of industrial mobilization; Oklahoma City and the chronically depressed mining communities of Scranton and Wilkes-Barre, 11 percent. The New York and northeastern New Jersey metropolitan counties suffered the largest absolute loss in population (nearly 305,000

---

20. *National Defense Migration Hearings,* pt. 17, 6731; Bolles, "The Great Defense Migration," 466; "In Bridgeport's War Factories," *Fortune* 24 (Sept. 1941), 86–92, 156–62.

by May 1943) as a consequence of being passed over in the early stage of contract letting.[21]

The fear of becoming a ghost town was in most instances unwarranted, but the frequency with which witnesses before the Tolan Committee repeated the tale of a particular community that vanished during World War I indicates that the dread of urban atrophy was real. The same fears might also have been expressed about the postwar future of central cities being bypassed by the WPB's policies, or of the metropolitan counties when the boom ended.[22]

The Pattern of Defense Employment

In the absence of a coherent, well-articulated national employment policy, the in-migrants, when viewed in the aggregate, were remarkably successful in finding defense-related employment. WPA statistics for fifty-one urban centers, entered into the Tolan Committee's records, bear out this conclusion.[23]

In nearly half the defense centers surveyed during 1941, the unemployment rate for in-migrants was less than 8 percent; in another fourth about 5 percent; and only one city in seven experienced unemployment reaching 15 percent of the newcomers. Fort Smith, Arkansas, to which large numbers of workers had flocked prematurely in anticipation of the building of an army base, recorded the highest unemployment rate of 17 percent. Elsewhere, St. Louis and Los Angeles, among the largest metropolitan agglomerations, registered 16 percent unemployed in-migrants—a figure that rapidly approached zero, or full employment, once defense production shifted into high gear.[24]

The migrants' ability to locate employment was certainly a welcome contrast to the tragic experiences of the destitute and shelterless wanderers of the thirties. But the early date of the sur-

21. See *Sixteenth Decennial Census,* Ser. P-3, No. 31 (Dec. 1, 1942), *passim.*
22. Joyce Campbell and Catherine R. Harris, "Migration and National Defense," *Social Security Bulletin* 4 (Sept. 1941), 12–19.
23. *National Defense Migration Hearings,* pt. 27, 10324B.
24. Myers, "Defense Migration and Labor Supply," 69; Lamb, "Mobilization of Human Resources," 325.

vey and the differential impact of mobilization upon communities suggest that the in-migrants were perhaps less "strikingly successful" than they appear to have been. This was particularly true in cities where the newcomer had difficulty adjusting to unfamiliar surroundings, where a large resident labor pool was present, or where it took industry somewhat longer than anticipated to expand plant capacity. The Seattle metropolitan region was a prime illustration of one where the ability of newcomers to find work was only moderately successful. On the other hand, where the newcomer did find employment, he often moved into a relatively better economic position. Howard B. Myers, of the WPA, indicated that manual workers were shifting in sizable numbers from unskilled to semiskilled and even skilled positions. The proportion of in-migrants employed in unskilled occupations was surprisingly small, constituting less than 10 percent in the majority of cities canvassed.[25]

In sum, the patterns of migration during the war years were not inconsistent with those of earlier periods. They represented an acceleration of the population shift resulting from basic forces which have operated in population distribution during much of the nation's recent history, rather than exceptions that could easily be reversed when the war ended. Large numbers of migrants went to the cities of the West Coast, the Gulf Coast, the Great Lakes, and the South Atlantic seaboard. The West gained about twice as many migrants as during the prewar period, and the (nonmetropolitan) South lost about five times as many. The annual losses in the North were about three-fourths as great as during the prewar period. To the degree that occupational shifting and upgrading meant a steady progression in income, the national defense emergency functioned as a catalyst for the upwardly mobile.

Composition of Migrants: Sex and Race

Although most wanderers in pursuit of defense jobs did find

25. *National Defense Migration Hearings*, pt. 12, 4865; pt. 17, 6729, 6763; pt. 27, 10321; Clark Kerr, *Migration to the Seattle Labor Market Area, 1940–1942* (Seattle, 1942), 163.

employment, the ancient prejudices of sex, race, and age did not disappear readily and continued to offset the specific patterns of migration of women, blacks, and other minorities. Young adult males generally were more successful in attaining employment than the elderly, except for youths under twenty with no previous work experience. Skilled manual workers, professionals, and technicians had the lowest unemployment rates among in-migrants. The least successful continued to be domestics. A similar pattern held for minorities, notably women and blacks. These two groups were inextricably linked with one another whenever the subject of additional manpower arose.[26]

In the first year of industrial mobilization, women constituted a relatively small proportion of the in-migrants. They ranged from 10 percent in Johnstown, Pennsylvania, to an atypically high 45 percent in the District of Columbia.[27] (See Table 2.) Similarly, black migrants totaled fewer than 0.5 percent to about 20 percent in Macon, Georgia, which prompted Howard B. Myers to tell the committee: "Even in the South, migration rates for the Negroes are much lower than for whites. This is understandable, in view of the widespread discrimination against Negroes in war industries."[28] (See Table 3.)

In both cases the rate of unemployment was triple that of adult white males. The Women's Bureau, extrapolating from figures provided by the United States Employment Service and the number of women appearing on WPA rolls, calculated that nearly three million women were immediately available for defense employment and another half million were not being fully utilized. This corroborated the findings of one survey of forty defense industries in the autumn of 1940, which concluded that women "could be employed to a much greater extent." The same could have been said—and was—of black Americans in 1940–41.[29]

The delay in hiring women has generally, and correctly, been

26. *National Defense Migration Hearings,* pt. 27, 10313; pt. 15, 6003–4.
27. *Ibid.,* pt. 27, 10327.
28. *Ibid.,* pt. 27, 10313.
29. "Employment of Women in Defense Industries," *Monthly Labor Review* 52 (May 1941), 1147–51.

TABLE 2. Percentages of Male and Female Workers in the Migrant Force. (Ranked by the proportion of female workers)

City and State	Female	Male	City and State	Female	Male
Washington, D.C.	45	55	Glendale, etc., Calif.	17	83
Muskogee, Okla.	30	70	Bristol, Conn.	17	83
Atlanta, Ga.	28	72	Augusta, Ga.	17	83
Macon, Ga.	28	72	Detroit, Mich.	17	83
Greenville, S.C.	28	72	Pittsburgh, Pa.	17	83
Nashville, Tenn.	28	72	Corpus Christi, Tex.	17	83
Newburgh, N.Y.	28	72	Oakland, Calif.	16	84
Quincy, Ill.	27	73	Indianapolis, Ind.	15	85
Kalamazoo, Mich.	26	74	South Bend, Ind.	15	85
Los Angeles, Calif.	25	75	Portland, Me.	15	85
Des Moines, Iowa	25	75	Bloomfield, N.J.	15	85
Washington, Pa.	25	75	Portsmouth, Va.	14	86
San Francisco, Calif.	25	75	Marion, Ohio	14	86
Lafayette, Ind.	24	76	Newport News area, Va.	13	87
Appleton, Wis.	23	77	Wichita, Kans.	13	87
Terre Haute, Ind.	22	78	Saginaw, Mich.	13	87
Oklahoma City, Okla.	22	78	Warren, etc., Ohio	13	87
Philadelphia, Pa.	22	78	Hackensack, N.J.	13	87
Seattle, Wash.	22	78	Dayton, Ohio	12	88
St. Louis, Mo.	21	79	Fort Smith, Ark.	12	88
Brockton, Mass.	21	79	San Diego, Calif.	12	88
Battle Creek, Mich.	20	80	Wichita Falls, Tex.	11	89
Norfolk, Va.	20	80	Burlington, Iowa	10	90
Houston, Tex.	19	81	Baltimore, Md.	10	90
Bridgeport, Conn.	18	82	Johnstown, Pa.	10	90
Long Beach, Calif.	18	82			

SOURCE: National Defense Migration Hearings, pt. 27, p. 10327.

TABLE 3. Percentages of Migrants in Racial Categories. (Ranked by the proportion of blacks)

City and State	Black	White	Other	City and State	Black	White	Other
Appleton, Wis.	0	100	0	St. Louis, Mo.	3	97	0
Bloomfield, N.J.	0	100	0	Newburgh, N.Y.	4	96	0
Des Moines, Iowa	*	100	0	Indianapolis, Ind.	4	96	0
Portland, Me.	*	100	0	Detroit, Mich.	4	96	*
Seattle, Wash.	*	100	*	Warren, etc., Ohio	4	96	0
Burlington, Iowa	*	100	0	Hackensack, N.J.	4	96	0
San Francisco, Calif.	*	100	*	Dayton, Ohio	5	95	0
Marion, Ohio	*	100	0	Greenville, S.C.	5	95	0
Brockton, Mass.	*	100	0	Wichita Falls, Tex.	5	93	2
Bristol, Conn.	*	100	0	Philadelphia, Pa.	6	94	0
Fort Smith, Ark.	1	99	0	Corpus Christi, Tex.	6	84	10
Long Beach, Calif.	1	99	*	Johnstown, Pa.	6	94	0
Glendale, etc., Calif.	1	99	*	Washington, D.C.	7	93	0
San Diego, Calif.	1	99	*	Houston, Tex.	7	93	*
Bridgeport, Conn.	1	99	0	Battle Creek, Mich.	7	93	0
Terre Haute, Ind.	1	99	0	Pittsburgh, Pa.	8	92	0
Oklahoma City, Okla.	1	99	*	Nashville, Tenn.	8	92	0
South Bend, Ind.	2	98	0	Muskogee, Okla.	10	90	0
Wichita, Kans.	2	98	0	Washington, Pa.	10	90	0
Saginaw, Mich.	2	98	0	Baltimore, Md.	11	89	0
Quincy, Ill.	2	98	0	Norfolk, Va.	14	86	0
Los Angeles, Calif.	2	97	1	Atlanta, Ga.	16	84	0
Lafayette, Ind.	2	98	0	Newport News area, Va.	16	84	0
Kalamazoo, Mich.	3	97	0	Augusta, Ga.	17	83	0
Oakland, Calif.	3	97	*	Portsmouth, Va.	18	82	0
				Macon, Ga.	20	80	0

*Indicates less than half of 1 percent.

SOURCE: *National Defense Migration Hearings*, pt. 27, p. 10327.

attributed to sexual discrimination on the part of a male-dominated corporate hierarchy, as well as an inexplicable tardiness in recalling the labor shortages of World War I. To these explanations must be added two other considerations: private employers continued throughout 1941 to draw from a reservoir of unemployed men, while the Women's Bureau initially adopted a cautious approach to female employment. The bureau confined its early activity to exhorting employers to hire women who could perform relatively simple defense work; the result was that conversion to defense production did not precipitate any definite trend toward greater employment of women before the fall of 1942. External circumstances forced the change, and the first breach in the wall of male prejudice occurred in January 1942, when President Roosevelt requested that governors place state employment services under federal jurisdiction in order to integrate them into a unified national system of employment. In November 1942 the National War Labor Board issued General Order Number 16, which required equal pay for equal work in federal employment.[30]

As the pool of available adult white male laborers diminished, the barriers gradually crumbled in the defense industries, although they did not wholly disappear. The first stage saw the wider employment of women in fields that were customarily open to them. As men went into factories in search of higher-paying jobs, women replaced them in office, clerical, and sales positions (thereby creating a shortage of domestics). The next stage brought women into light mass production industry to perform work requiring a high degree of manual dexterity, speed, and accuracy; repetitive tasks requiring patience; and jobs demanding careful observation rather than unusual physical strength or long apprenticeship. Employers hired single women initially, then married women with young children. It was not until the labor crisis of the last quarter of 1942 that employer

30. "Women in Democracy's Arsenal," *New York Times Magazine* 6 (Oct. 19, 1941), 10–11; "War Work of the U.S. Women's Bureau," *Monthly Labor Review* 55 (Dec. 1942), 1170–84.

resistance finally broke down, and older women (aged forty to fifty) and especially black women were hired.[31]

From being called upon to supplement the skills of men in war establishments, women were soon substituting for men in a steadily widening variety of tasks. Voight-Sikorsky of Bridgeport, Connecticut, manufacturers of aircraft, cooperated with the United States Employment Service (USES) in tapping the regional New England supply of female workers. It sent scouts out to the villages and towns of New Hampshire and Vermont, calling young single women to rallying points by radio and newspaper advertisements that played up high wages, a guaranteed place to live, patriotism, and the glamour of building planes. Boeing in Seattle concentrated on the local market, appealing to nonworking women through spreads in the local newspaper and window displays of pretty girls in smart slacks outfits demonstrating how easy it was to work on a wiring board. In Detroit, the USES mailed out voluntary registration cards that were returned by 300,000 women. Nearly 146,000 women without children stated that they were available for factory jobs immediately, while another 35,000 said they would be willing to work once day-care centers were established for their children. By 1945, women had come to constitute 36 percent of the labor force and had demonstrated the capacity to work as efficiently as men.[32]

When the Tolan Committee began its hearings, the migration of black Americans to the centers of defense production was not

31. Marjorie B. Greenbie, "Women Work for Victory," *Independent Woman* 21 (Jan. 1942), 8–10; "Minutes of the Meeting of the Advisory Committee on Social Protection, Office of Health, Welfare, and Related Defense Activities," June 14, 1941, National Archives (NA), Record Group (RG) 215, Records of the Office of Community War Services (OCWS).

32. "The Margin Now Is Womenpower," *Fortune* 27 (Feb. 1943), 99–103; Frances Perkins, "Women's Work in Wartime," *Monthly Labor Review* 56 (Apr. 1943), 661–65; Elizabeth Hawes, "Do Women Workers Get an Even Break?" *New York Times Magazine* 6 (Nov. 19, 1944), 13, 41–42; Helen Baker, *Women In War Industries* (Princeton, 1942), 47; Minnie L. Maffatt, "Under-Use of Womenpower Slows War Effort," *Independent Woman* 22 (Aug. 1943), 230–31, 252; "Policy on Recruitment, Training and Employment of Women Workers Established by the War Manpower Commission," *Monthly Labor Review* 56 (Apr. 1943), 669–71.

yet taking place in large numbers, even though a continuous flow of blacks cityward had been a permanent feature of the American landscape since the close of the Civil War. Although the bulk of the black population in the South in 1940 was still largely rural (63.5 percent), the reverse held outside the region. Blacks in the North and West were overwhelmingly urban (83.1 and 89.4 percent respectively). Moreover, the census of 1940 indicated that nearly half (48.7 percent) of the total number of blacks, estimated at 12,865,518, lived in urban localities of 2,500 residents (or more).[33]

World War II, like its predecessor a generation earlier, eventually exercised a pervasive and permanent influence upon the spatial and social distribution of the black population, although this was not immediately apparent during the tooling-up phase of industrial mobilization. The resurgence of industry in 1940 and 1941 had precipitated some black migration (chiefly of skilled labor), but the phenomenon of blacks moving en masse from the rural South, so characteristic of the years 1917–19, had not recurred. In fact, mass migration of blacks did not take place before the close of 1942. A comparative analysis of census data for black and white migrants discloses further that the beginning and peak of large-scale black migration lagged behind similar phases in the general movement of population. Whereas the zenith of migration for the entire population occurred in 1943, the black migration did not crest until two years later, in 1945.[34]

The Social Science Institute of Fisk University in Nashville worked out careful estimates for the black population, 1940–43, in forty-one cities engaged in war production. The distribution of urban centers was as follows: cities in the South and Southwest, 10; in the border states and the District of Columbia, 5; in the North, including New England, 11; in the Midwest, 13; and on the West Coast, 2. These forty-one cities included all but

33. See "Population—Special Reports," in *Sixteenth Decennial Census of the United States* (Washington, D.C., Nov. 14, 1942), Ser. P-10, No. 20, 2; Preston Valien, "Social and Economic Implications of Migration for the Negro in the Present Social Order," *Quarterly Review of Higher Education Among Negroes* 10 (Apr. 1942), 74–84.
34. Ira De A. Reid, "Special Problems of Negro Migration During the War," *Milbank Memorial Fund Quarterly* 25 (July 1947), 284–92.

eight or ten of the cities with more than 50,000 population in which blacks had in the past responded perceptibly to industrial changes. The figures showed that there was an estimated net in-migration of 457,800 blacks since 1940. If estimates for all cities of 50,000 total population or over had been obtained, they would very likely have shown that the total in-migration of blacks, 1940–43, was approximately 600,000. But—and this is the crucial point—75 percent of the in-migration had occurred since September 1942.[35]

The increase in the black population in the cities according to area was as follows: South and Southwest, 159,500; Midwest, 145,000; border states, 83,000; West Coast cities, 40,300; and cities of the North, including New England, 30,000. The estimates of Fisk University's social scientists corroborate the observations made above about the nature of the black migration.[36]

In contrast to the period of World War I and the early twenties, blacks were not yet migrating to the cities of the North in the same numbers or proportions. Indeed, several Northern cities that had recorded large black increases in the World War I migration registered small increases or a slight decline in the black population. This is partly due to the presence in those cities of an already large reservoir of black workers who were both unemployed and underemployed, and partly due to the fact that these cities did not receive major new war industries. Rather, there was an expansion or conversion to war production of those industries already in existence.[37]

Likewise, there was a proportionally larger migration of blacks to Southern cities from Southern rural areas and, consequently, less long-distance migration than in 1917–19. This seemed to reflect the larger percentage concentration of war industries in the South than in the earlier war. The shipyards of tidewater Virginia, the steel mills of Birmingham and Houston, and the various aircraft and shell loading plants in Southern ur-

35. See "Negro Internal Migration, 1940–1943: An Estimate," *Race Relations* 1 (Sept. 1943), 10–11.
36. *Ibid.,* 11.
37. New York City, for example, lost about 25,000 of its black population. See *ibid.*

ban centers provided employment and high wages for a large working force. Blacks were sharing to some extent in this general increase in employment. Such employment and high wages had not been available in the South during World War I, causing blacks to seek these advantages elsewhere—in the cities of the North and Midwest.[38]

Tables 4 and 5 show the largest estimated increases in the black population through in-migration, 1940–43.[39]

Beginning in 1943, black migration commenced in earnest, and the numbers involved were disproportionately large and the rate more intense. An analysis in 1945 by the Census Bureau of selected urban centers designated "Congested Production Areas" confirmed the magnitude of this movement. The bureau's study also indicated that the fundamental demographic change in the black population was not simply an out-migration from South to North but, more importantly, a movement from the South to the industrial cities of the Far West. Blacks, of course, continued to migrate to Norfolk and Dallas—more than 100,000 entered Southern industrial cities from other urban localities in the region in 1943–44—but whenever possible they traveled north and west to the Pacific Coast cities. Thus more than 700,000 left the South during the war years, but the bulk of the movement occurred in 1943–44 when 300,000 migrated to the border states and the resurgent industrial cities of the North and West.[40]

Though delayed, the exodus from the South was nonetheless spectacular as job opportunities opened up. In the five metropolitan centers of the West designated congested production areas (Los Angeles, Portland-Vancouver, Seattle-Tacoma, San Diego, and San Francisco), the total population of blacks between 1940 and 1944 grew from 107,000 to 230,000, an increase

38. *Ibid.*
39. See "Internal Migration of Negroes, 1940–1943: A Correction and an Addition," *Race Relations* 1 (Nov. 1943), 12.
40. Conrad Taeuber, "Wartime Population Changes in the United States," *Milbank Memorial Fund Quarterly* 24 (July 1946), 238–39; U.S. Bureau of the Census, Press Release, Mar. 4, 1945; Claude A. Barnett, "The Postwar Outlook for the Southern Rural Negro," *Journal of Negro Education* 14 (Fall 1945), 566–75.

TABLE 4. Percentage Increase and Estimated Total In-migration of Blacks for Ten Major Cities, 1940–43.

City	Black population 1940 census	Estimated black population July 1943	Numerical increase of black population over 1940	Percentage increase of black population over 1940
San Francisco	4,846	18,000	13,154	271.4
Mobile	29,046	60,000	30,954	106.6
Charleston	31,765	51,765	20,000	63.0
Los Angeles	63,774	91,000	27,226	42.7
New Orleans	149,034	196,000	46,966	31.5
Chicago	277,731	350,000	72,269	26.0
Detroit	149,119	185,000	35,881	24.1
Baltimore	165,843	200,000	34,157	20.6
Washington, D.C.	187,266	225,000	37,734	20.1
Philadelphia	250,880	280,880	30,000	12.0

SOURCE: Social Science Institute, Fisk University.

TABLE 5. Selected Cities in Which the Estimated Black Population Increase Is Greater than 20 Percent, 1940–43.

City	Black population 1940 census	Estimated black population July 1943	Numerical increase of black population over 1940	Percentage increase of black population over 1940
Utica, N.Y.	514	1,800	1,286	250.2
Warren, Ohio	2,526	4,200	1,674	66.3
Chester, Pa.	10,162	16,500	6,338	62.4
Milwaukee	8,821	14,000	5,179	58.7
Minneapolis	4,646	6,891	2,245	48.3
Waterbury	2,015	2,700	685	34.0
New Haven	6,235	8,235	2,000	32.1
Buffalo	17,694	23,000	5,306	30.0
Akron	12,260	15,000	2,740	22.3

SOURCE: Social Science Institute, Fisk University.

of 113 percent. Los Angeles, with 75,000 blacks in 1940 and 134,000 in 1944, had the largest absolute increase; but San Francisco with 4,000 blacks in 1940 and 23,000 in 1945, Portland with 1,300 in 1940 and 15,000 in 1945, and Seattle with 3,365 in 1940 and 16,000 by the end of the war had their share of growth. Other cities across the nation experienced similarly dramatic gains: New York, 25,000 black in-migrants; Cleveland, 17,000; Chicago, 50,000; and Detroit, 65,000. More significantly for the future racial composition of American cities, the percentage of blacks who indicated that they planned to reside in the receiving cities after the war was considerably higher than the percentage for all in-migrants.[41]

The delay in black migration must be attributed primarily to widespread discrimination in defense industries on the part of employers, who could select from a pool of unemployed residential white labor, and to trade unionists, anxious to protect their hard-won gains. Not even the establishment of a Committee on Fair Employment Practices (FEPC) or the threatened loss of contracts under Executive Order 8802, issued on June 25, 1941, induced employers to modify their racial hiring practices. The implications of their action were not lost upon Robert C. Weaver, the future head of the Department of Housing and Urban Development, who predicted early in 1942 that industrial mobilization and employment would peak within a year, thereby freezing the pattern of racial employment. The expansion of the war economy and the large drain on white manpower, however, eventually persuaded even conservative newspapers such as the *Baltimore Evening Sun* that discrimination must be put aside or temporarily muted.[42]

World War II was also the single most potent force transforming the rural, untutored agricultural labor force of Mexican-Americans into an urban, semiskilled, and skilled in-

41. Reid, "Special Problems of Negro Migration During the War," 287–88.

42. Myers, "Defense Migration and Labor Supply," 74; *National Defense Migration Hearings,* pt. 13, 5463–64; pt. 14, 5843–44; pt. 15, 5964, 6023; pt. 16, 6530–38; pt. 27, 10313; Robert C. Weaver, "Racial Employment Trends in National Defense: I," *Phylon* 2 (Fourth Quarter 1941), 357–59, and the same author's "Racial Employment Trends in National Defense: II," *Phylon* 2 (First Quarter 1942), 30.

dustrial population. In itself, however, the war did not create any new pattern of migration to the cities but simply accelerated a trend that was set in motion in the 1920s.[43] By 1940, there were approximately 1.5 million Spanish-speaking people in the United States, concentrated mainly in the Southwest and West, with smaller communities scattered elsewhere in cities like Pittsburgh, Toledo, and Newark. The Census Bureau had classified about 51 percent of this population as urban, in comparison with 56 percent of the total population. The 1940 census also disclosed that 25 percent of the Mexican-Americans still were located in rural nonfarm areas, in contrast to the 19 percent of the total population.[44]

Wherever he migrated in search of defense work, the Mexican-American encountered the same hostility and prejudice shown toward women and blacks. And similarly, it was the shortage of Anglo labor and their own work performance rather than any abstract appeal to justice or equality that opened the gates of opportunity to Mexican-Americans. Federal war manpower officials had prepared the groundwork for that day when the Department of Labor's Office of Education established, between 1939 and 1942, vocational schools in the urban centers of Albuquerque, Santa Fe, Las Vegas, and Las Cruces. These schools trained rural youth as skilled welders, mechanics, plumbers, and other craftsmen.[45]

In the course of their training these young men also became initiated into urban ways. They found defense jobs in the shipyards and aircraft factories of Seattle, San Diego, Long Beach, Los Angeles, Corpus Christi, and Albuquerque. Still others

43. By 1930, 97,116 Mexican-Americans were listed as having permanent residence in Los Angeles. See Elizabeth Broadbent, "The Distribution of Mexican Populations in the United States" (Ph.D. diss., Univ. of Chicago, 1941), for the period 1850–1930. There are no reliable demographic studies of the Mexican-American population for the war years, but see Robin F. Scott, "The Mexican-American in the Los Angeles Area, 1920–1950: From Acquiescence to Activity" (Ph.D. diss., Univ. of Southern California, 1971), esp. 11–12ff., 193–94.

44. *Sixteenth Census of the United States, 1940: Population, Nativity and Parentage of the White Population* (Washington, D.C., 1943), 42–73.

45. *National Defense Migration Hearings,* pt. 12, 5010; Charles P. and Nellie H. Loomis, "Skilled Spanish-American War-Industry Workers from New Mexico," *Applied Anthropology* 2 (Oct.-Dec. 1942), 33–36.

went north—to Detroit, Chicago, Kansas City, and even to New York—traversing the same well-worn paths frequented by the Spanish-speaking migrants of the 1920s.[46]

Composition of Migrants: Age

Most migrations, and the wartime movement was no exception, are highly selective of young adults in the prime of their productive years. It is the young who are both less bound to a former place of residence and more ready to respond to new opportunities. In nearly half the cities surveyed by the WPA the average age was under thirty, and in no city did it rise as high as thirty-five, reflecting both the greater mobility of young, unattached workers regardless of race or sex and the relatively low hiring age limits in many defense industries. Wichita, a center of aircraft production, was the most pronounced example of this trend. Because of unusually stringent hiring restraints imposed by employers and the exacting nature of the work, the average age of in-migrants was under twenty-five years.[47]

Although the migrants were for the most part in their twenties and early thirties, the number of "one-person families" in the receiving cities was unusually high. The percentages ranged from 30 to 50 percent in most cities to the extreme of 78 percent in Washington, D.C. These figures were somewhat misleading, however, because anywhere from one-fifth to one-half of these so-called one-person families might more accurately be termed incomplete. That is, the breadwinner had left wife and children behind temporarily while he searched for employment or suitable housing. Where entire families had migrated in advance of employment or housing, their plight was worse. Frequently they resorted to makeshift living arrangements, such as renting

46. After Los Angeles and the West Coast cities, Detroit was the destination of most Mexican-Americans. The war helped to reverse the decline of its Spanish-speaking population that had set in with the Depression. See Norman D. Humphrey, "The Migration and Settlement of Detroit Mexicans," *Economic Geography* 19 (Oct. 1943), 358–61.

47. *National Defense Migration Hearings*, pt. 27, chart 11, 10324K; Paul H. Landis, "The Loss of Rural Manpower to War Industry Through Migration," *Washington Agricultural Experiment Station Bulletin* 10 (Jan. 1943), 5, 12–14.

tourist homes or hotel rooms or camping in trailers that had become a staple of every military camp and industrial city. According to WPA sources, in most localities up to 30 percent of the newcomers were doubling up. In search of opportunities, they strained community facilities and increased the risk of health and fire hazards.[48]

As the supply of available housing dwindled in the industrial cities, the proportion of incomplete migrant families rose sharply and proved to be a source of considerable alarm to both the War Manpower Commission and witnesses testifying before the Tolan Committee. Both Myers and Lamb recalled a similar experience in the previous war. As the housing shortage intensified during the years 1917–19, the numbers of "unstable" migrants increased correspondingly. Away from home for the first time, alone and alienated in the impersonal urban environment, these young men often did not report to work on time, were inebriated when they did, left early, or quit within a few weeks or months. Their plight threatened to have an adverse effect upon industrial efficiency and productivity. A similar crisis was in the making once again.[49]

Defense Migration: Points of Origin and Destination

Not only the composition of the migrants but their places of origin and destination had a direct bearing on policies that affected the cities and the performance of the economy. In this respect, also, the migration of 1940–41 repeated earlier patterns: the greater number of migrants did not move directly from their place of origin to defense production centers but instead made either one or several moves before they finally arrived there. Migration for these individuals was a stepping-stone process involving several changes of residence before eventual settlement.[50]

Excluding the Pacific Coast cities, the average migrant trav-

---

48. For the figures on one-person families see *National Defense Migration Hearings,* pt. 27, 10329 (Table 10) and 10330 (Table 11).
49. *Ibid.*
50. *Ibid.,* pt. 27, 10328.

eled a distance of about 125 miles, although regional variations such as availability of labor, location of defense plants, and transportation often stretched the distance. Along the highly urban-industrial Northeastern corridor, defense workers traveled on the average fewer than seventy to eighty miles before obtaining suitable employment. By contrast, the exodus from the anthracite regions of Pennsylvania, where the Depression had been both severe and prolonged, was quite marked and the distance traversed to the industrial cities of Connecticut greater. But even this was puny compared with the long trail to the aircraft factories and shipyards of the Pacific slope. Migrants to Long Beach and San Diego traveled on the average 1,000 miles, and to Los Angeles 1,300 miles. This transcontinental migration persisted despite the efforts of local defense officials to discourage it, and it was more typical of people fleeing economically stagnant communities, such as in southern Illinois, southeastern Missouri, and the rural South. These beaten but not vanquished fighters uprooted their lives and taxed an already overburdened transportation network in order to escape the blight of poverty.[51]

Contrary to popular wisdom, relatively few defense workers in the urban centers had migrated directly from the farm. The average was less than 10 percent in most cities of the North and West, and even in Southern cities the proportion of former farm laborers seldom exceeded 15 percent. In Bridgeport, Connecticut, and Washington, D.C., 96 percent of the in-migrants came from occupations other than agriculture. The figures were 92 percent in Seattle and Long Beach on the Pacific Coast, and 10 percent and 14 percent, respectively, for Corpus Christi and Altanta. The Newport News metropolitan area of Virginia and Detroit with 20 and 21 percent, respectively, were clearly exceptional. These statistics seem surprising in view of the large agricultural labor reserve of the Depression-ridden thirties, but are less so when one considers other factors. For in the early stage of industrial mobilization, professional and semiprofessional workers were relatively more mobile than were the unskilled.

51. See Table 8 in *ibid.*

Also, the policy of the selective service boards (and later the War Manpower Commission) was, with some exceptions, to encourage farmers to remain on the land and grow food for national defense.[52]

For the relatively smaller number of farmers living close to the margin who did choose to abandon the soil, employment in a defense factory *might* have provided an avenue of greater opportunity. There was no guarantee of this, of course; it depended on whether the transplanted agriculturalist was able to acquire the necessary industrial skills, adjust to the discipline and monotonous routine of the factory, and accommodate his traditional life-style to an often bewildering urban culture.[53] Counterbalancing these negative factors, the appeal of patriotism, high cash wages, regular employment at a specialized job, and the lure of urban life entered into the decision of most rural (i.e., nonfarm) workers to leave the home area for urban war work.[54]

If farmers were not deserting the open country in any great numbers in 1940–41 to toil in crowded factories, where was industry recruiting its workers? From other cities and metropolitan counties, towns adjacent to urban centers, and unincorporated villages. Evidence from a cross section of the rural population— Ohio farm youth, Kentucky mountaineers, and Washington rural dwellers—corroborates this conclusion. In the thirty-three months of war and preparation for war, Ohio's farm youth population declined from 285,000 to 191,000, a decrease of

52. By the fall of 1943 nearly two million farm workers had received occupational deferments, a policy that placed an unfair proportion of the burden of providing soldiers on urban industries and encouraged inefficient use of farm labor. See *ibid.*, pt. 27, 10328 (Table 7), and Richard Polenberg, *War and Society: The United States, 1941-1945* (Philadelphia, 1972), 22.

53. The Mexican-American inhabitants of the rural villages of Sandoval, San Miguel, Taos, and Dona Ana counties of New Mexico illustrate this. Between 1939 and 1942, nearly half the adult male population aged 15–65 (c. 1,200) left their villages to engage in war work. The inhabitants of Dona Ana County journeyed to California to find work in agriculture—but Sandoval men shunned the fields for the higher-paying defense jobs of the city. See Charles P. Loomis, "Wartime Migration from the Rural Spanish-Speaking Villages of New Mexico," *Rural Sociology* 7 (Dec. 1942), 384–95.

54. *National Defense Migration Hearings,* pt. 17, 6758; Landis, "Loss of Rural Manpower," 5, 12–14.

94,000. The youths who left did not enter defense employment directly; the overwhelming majority enlisted in the armed forces, leaving the remainder to take up nondefense jobs in the home area or to move to farms in other communities. By contrast, the chronically underemployed Kentuckians leaving rural Knox County found defense jobs in industrial Detroit, Cincinnati, and Hamilton, Ohio. Of their number, only one-quarter went directly from farm to factory with no intermediate stops; the rest had originated in the villages and larger towns of Knox County. A similar pattern prevailed in the "rurban" counties of Whitman and Stevens, Washington. The common laborer in the small towns and college students without any special skills—rather than the farmer—migrated to Seattle or Spokane.[55]

These illustrations, admittedly selective, nonetheless demonstrate that the war had a differential impact upon rural America. As industry raced to full production in 1943, it drew more deeply from the rural labor pool, causing a shortage of labor, higher wages for farm hands, and protests from the farm bloc in Congress. There were very few rural dwellers, such as those living in the mountains of northeast Georgia, who were far enough removed from any large war industry, city, or military training center not to have experienced any serious effects of the war from these sources. When asked in 1943 how the war was affecting their community, they frequently answered, "This community ain't been affected much by the war."[56]

The Effects of Migration

Perhaps as significant as the effect of internal migration in altering the size, composition, and distribution of the wartime urban population was its impact on the cultural systems of the

55. Arthur Magnus, "Wartime Migration of Farm Youth," *Ohio Agricultural Experiment Station: Bimonthly Bulletin* 28 (May-June 1943), 105-7; Wayne J. Gray, "Population Movements in the Kentucky Mountains," *Rural Sociology* 10 (Dec. 1945), 380-86; Landis, "Loss of Rural Manpower," 15-17.

56. Gladys K. Bowles, *Farm Population: Net Migration From The Rural-Farm Population, 1940-1950* (Washington, D.C., 1956), 5; Frank D. Alexander, "Some Effects of Two Years of War on a Rural Community," *Social Forces* 23 (Dec. 1944), 201.

areas into and out of which the migrants came. For in the process of moving large numbers of persons, migration also performed the very important function of diffusing the culture traits of the diverse ethnic subcultures that existed, and thus it contributed to the homogeneity of the nation. But the process of cultural diffusion, the erosion of sectional and regional barriers, and the social reintegration were protracted and painful, requiring months and sometimes years before the newcomers and the residents of the receiving communities fully adjusted to each other's presence.[57]

In a number of instances, especially in medium-sized and smaller cities, the magnitude and suddenness of the influx aroused latent hostility on the part of older established residents. Louis Wirth concluded that this antipathy was deeply rooted in sociopsychological, economic, and political fears. The quality of life as older residents had known it was seemingly threatened. Wartime mobility broke down the familiar, structured, orderly community of their youth and young adulthood, replacing it with no perceptible guide to conduct or system of values. And yet in their eyes the community was necessary for the development of the individual. It offered him or her a natural opportunity to achieve personal recognition, share experiences in common, find assurances of emotional and material support, and develop some enduring friendships. The choice of whether, how many, and what kinds of strangers were thrust upon them was never really an option in the crisis atmosphere immediately preceding Pearl Harbor; and while most residents ultimately resigned themselves to the invasion, many also responded with observable manifestations of alienation and displacement.[58]

One sensitive observer, who decried the transformations being wrought in the peaceful valleys of the Merrimac and the Connecticut, described succinctly the weakening of community identity attendant upon industrial mobilization. He wrote,

57. See Sidney Goldstein, "Migration: Dynamic of the American City," *American Quarterly* 6 (Winter 1954), 338.
58. Wirth, "The Urban Community," 72-73.

"New England fears, justly, that the migrations will distend and misshape beyond prospect of future repair the coastal towns and valley cities which are their objectives. Portsmouth's 16,000 rooted inhabitants cannot swallow 10,000 newcomers without becoming a new Portsmouth. Hartford cannot remain the same if 50,000 men, women, and children are added to its population within two years." At Willow Run, the site of a mammoth bomber factory twenty-seven miles west of Detroit, long-time residents particularly resented the intrusion of strangers. "Before the bomber plant was built, everything was perfect here," observed one. "Everybody knew everybody else and all were happy and contented. Then came that bomber plant and this influx of riffraff, mostly Southerners. You can't be sure of these people." The physical as well as metaphysical community was being wrenched out of recognizable shape. San Diego's city manager testified: "This sudden growth, of course, has meant a disorganization of practically all municipal services. Our plans were laid for an orderly growth. Suddenly we find ourselves with a disordered growth, and we have to step up the tempo of every community function."[59]

Part of the difficulty, of course, was rooted in the fact that many of the newcomers were from racially or religiously heterogeneous backgrounds and seemed alien to the older residents. Some had come from economically depressed circumstances, while others, recruited from widely dispersed rural areas, had difficulty making the transition from a predominantly small-town rural to a predominantly urban-industrial culture. The fact that so many of the workers were single, unattached, or uprooted from their homes and families (and thus temporarily released from the normal societal constraints) created problems of vice and social disorganization that were difficult to contain in a boom-town atmosphere. Implicit in the anxieties of New Englanders (and city dwellers elsewhere) who asked, "Shall Portsmouth be as good a home town for 26,000 as for 16,000?

59. Bolles, "The Great Defense Migration," 460–62; Lowell J. Carr and James E. Stermer, *Willow Run: A Study of Industrialization and Cultural Inadequacy* (New York, 1952), 238.

Or shall Portsmouth decline into a sort of Roaring Camp?'' was a fear of social rebellion, loss of a sense of community, and growing uncertainty about one's role in a social hierarchy that was rapidly becoming outmoded.[60]

Beyond the desire to hold on to familiar patterns of the past in a nation and world enveloped in turmoil, these residents perceived that the newcomers posed a challenge to the economic and political status quo. The threat was more clearly seen in smaller urban communities where the government established war plants. For, despite its solemn assurances, the management team was often imported from the outside, thus depriving local residents of the more lucrative opportunities occasioned by the war. Fueling their resentment was a complicated system of rent and price controls which enabled government to intrude into the home and prevent them from turning a profit. Memories of World War I, when another generation of parvenus had required them to provide greatly expanded public services, sustained their xenophobia.[61]

Fear that the wartime prosperity would be short-lived and would be terminated suddenly once the government curtailed defense expenditures stalked both the residents of older communities and newcomers to the boom towns. To avert such a catastrophe the president of the Bath Iron Works of Maine felt compelled to urge his employees ''to save some money while you have it coming in for the ebb-tide condition that is bound to come.'' He predicted that, as the newcomers departed, residential neighborhoods would deteriorate and real estate values decline, leaving in their wake high taxation, debt, and devastation. John E. Sloane, vice chairman of New Jersey's State Planning Board, shared the view that cities and towns propped up by extraordinary government spending and influxes of outsiders would become the ghost towns of the 1940s, reminiscent of World War I.[62]

The more sensitive migrants acknowledged and made a genu-

---

60. Bolles, ''The Great Defense Migration,'' 460–62.
61. *Ibid.*
62. *National Defense Migration Hearings,* pt. 14, 5585.

ine effort to ameliorate the disruptive impact of their presence upon the local community, but too often they were few in number. Most newcomers believed that the transition to city and town was temporary; after a while they would have to find their way back into the more familiar social and economic structure of their communities of origin. They had little disposition to sink roots into their new locations or to share their experiences with the older residents. The more perceptive migrants realized that war was opening economic and psychological opportunities that might bring them into the mainstream of American society; they sought to become a part of their new environment and, in concert with older residents, to forge a new community synthesis.[63]

Conclusion: Mobilization, Migration, and Urban Growth

From the foregoing account what observations may be made? First, the war accelerated internal migration in the United States, but population movement flowed through the same major channels as in the previous twenty years. Second, the pattern of net gains and losses by states during the war years had high positive correlations with the patterns in earlier periods. There were notable exceptions, of course, but the relative size of the net in- or out-migration tended to persist from one period to another. Third, migration itself was an arduous process because of overburdened railroads, bus lines, and transfer companies. Fourth, during the early period of mobilization, white males were overrepresented on the basis of their proportion in the labor force. Migrants were young and tended to be either single men or married men who had left their families behind. As the war progressed, the pattern changed in some particulars. Female migrants, blacks, and other minorities became proportionately more numerous in defense jobs as young adult males were siphoned from the civilian labor force into the military. Fifth, even as early as 1941, the average migrant was bettering his economic position. Occupational upgrading of experienced workers

---

63. Elizabeth Gilmore, "For I May Not Live Here Long," *American Home* 27 (Feb. 1942), 18.

was frequent and incomes increased steadily, factors that would persuade many migrants to remain in their new places of residence after the war and sink social and economic roots.[64]

Finally, out of the confused and often confusing conditions of wartime mobilization, a policy approaching migration as an integral component of national defense was slowly taking shape. That policy was tempered by several considerations that neither Congress nor the Roosevelt administration could ignore. These included the widely held belief that unemployment would be rife in postwar America's industrial cities and towns and that migration must be used as a vehicle for adjusting the supply of manpower to the requirements of industry. This was a belated acknowledgment that a substantial portion of the civilian migration in 1940–41 had been unnecessary and inefficient. Few cities were equipped to receive the newcomers, which only added to the distress of both.[65]

The implications of this situation were not lost on federal policy makers. The War Manpower Commission would have to arrest the unfettered flow of migrants to congested production centers and stabilize employment therein. The War Production Board would have to modify its practice of concentrating defense contracts in a few large cities and turn to underutilized industrial areas where local labor was still available, recognizing full well that the promotion of population dispersal throughout metropolitan regions might also accelerate central-city decline in the postwar period. Above all, federal officials would have to confront the quality of life in urban neighborhoods wrenched out of shape by thousands of migrants. To protect their social fabric they would have to preserve as much of the older notion of community—wherein stabilities of place, shared intimacies over time, and enduring common involvements were maintained —as was feasible. Failing this, Congress and the administration would have to encourage localities to evolve a new community

64. Henry S. Shryock, Jr., "Wartime Shifts of the Civilian Population," *Milbank Memorial Fund Quarterly* 25 (July 1947), 279.

65. Lamb, "Mobilization of Human Resources," 327. See also Robert K. Lamb, "War Industry and Community Problems," *Public Administration Review* 2 (Spring 1942), 159.

synthesis. The latter would take time, however. In the interim, federal authorities concentrated on building a system of defense that would render the cities and their hard-pressed residents secure from aggression.[66]

66. *National Defense Migration Hearings,* pt. 17, 6762-63; "Summary of Recommendations of Mr. Robert Moses's Report Covering Report of Surveys of Congested War Production Areas for the Army and Navy Munitions Board," Mar. 2, 1943, in NARG 212, Records of the Committee on Congested Production Areas.

II. Mobilizing the Home Front: The First Lady and the Politics of Civilian Defense

The sudden eruption of war-boom communities had threatened a condition bordering on anarchy. To organize and coordinate the nation's productive capacity more efficiently, President Roosevelt declared the existence of a national emergency, and on May 28, 1940, he appointed a seven-member Advisory Commission to the Council of National Defense (NDAC). In August, the President requested that state governors gear up local and state defense machinery where, in their judgment, conditions warranted. The President's memorandum to the state executives also attempted to define the limits of the defense councils' jurisdiction, showing his concern lest the states and localities seek to tamper with New Deal domestic policies under the guise of a wartime emergency.[1]

To give formal recognition to the states' and local communities' participation in the national defense program, the NDAC established a separate Division of State and Local Cooperation (DSLC), forerunner of the Office of Civilian Defense (OCD). It was hoped that the DSLC would bring order and uniformity to the states' contributions and also alleviate the social and economic pressures on harassed localities.[2] The workings of

1. See entries in the unpublished *Daily Memoranda,* May 19, 22, 24, 25, 1940, Harold D. Smith Papers, and "Minutes of the Meeting of July 17, 1940," Records of the National Defense Advisory Commission (NDAC), Franklin D. Roosevelt Library (FDRL), Hyde Park, N.Y.; "Summary of Meeting of Liaison Committee of Advisory Commission," Oct. 24, 1940, and "Minutes of the Meeting of Nov. 20, 1940," National Archives (NA), Record Group (RG) 171, Records of the Office of Civilian Defense (OCD).

2. "State and Local Cooperation in National Defense," and William H. McReynolds to the State Governors, memorandum and cover letter dated Aug. 2, 1940, reprinted in The Council of State Governments, ed., *The Book of the States 1941–1942* (Chicago, 1941), 34–42.

both the DSLC and the OCD provide insight into how the civilian administrative agencies of the federal government affected the course of federal, state, and local relations and how the experiment in civilian defense conditioned the war's impact on the cities and the response of urban dwellers to the national emergency.

Although it was an agency of the federal government, the DSLC relied on voluntary cooperation to implement its mandate. This procedure suggested that the most striking feature of federal-state relations during the 1940s was not the omnipotence of the Roosevelt administration but the limits within which it had to operate. In theory, of course, the DSLC might have invoked federal authority derived from the war powers clause of the Constitution to coerce state and local action, but historical precedent, the background of DSLC head Frank Bane (who came to the post from the respected Council of State Governments), and the structure of cooperative federalism precluded this. Moreover, the decision to preserve state and local autonomy was logical; all comparable activities in World War I had been conducted jointly by state defense councils and local units of the Women's Volunteer Committee. To have proceeded otherwise, perhaps by erecting a federal civilian defense apparatus vested with authoritarian power over state and local governments, would have courted disaster.[3]

Of equal importance, the decision to proceed through the states retarded, even if it did not altogether reverse, a tendency that had arisen with the Depression: the federal government's practice of forging, through its various aid programs, direct ties with the cities. Washington's increasing services to and controls over local government had rendered the urban centers less dependent upon state authorities for guidance and assistance. Beginning in 1940, the expansion of the defense program contributed to the revitalization of state influence, for by operating through the DSLC and the OCD the states became the pivot of the new governmental relationship in matters pertaining to civilian

3. William Carey, "State Defense Councils, 1917 and 1941," *State Government* 14 (May-June 1941), 133–35; "Portrait" [Frank Bane], *Survey* 76 (Feb. 1940), 42.

defense. Not only did the state defense councils originate new services to the localities, but they were also the channels through which the advice and aid of federal agencies were routed to local governments. The states provided the legal foundation and administrative stimulus for regional and community defense programs, such as the coordination of communications and police and fire protection.[4]

During the summer and fall of 1940, Bane encouraged the states and cities to form defense councils, but only where community circumstances actually warranted them. This deliberate, cautious approach was born of the experience of 1917 when, without careful advance planning, local governments rushed pell-mell into setting up defense machinery. The result had been a confused and inefficient use of personnel, a consideration that caused Daniel W. Hoan, associate director of the DSLC and former mayor of Milwaukee, to urge city officials not to fall into a similar trap. His advice, unfortunately, went largely uheeded in the initial outburst of patriotism that accompanied mobilization.[5]

In the early phases of mobilization, the tasks of the municipal and state defense councils were largely of an advisory or coordinating nature. The outbreak of war in December 1941 vested the councils with greater authority to act. They could issue regulations having the force of law, a procedure which still did not satisfy some municipal and state officials who believed the councils were insufficiently flexible to cope with real emergencies such as air raids. The latter preferred to give the head of the defense council (usually the mayor of a city or governor of a state) virtually dictatorial powers to cope with every possible situation. In time of crisis, they argued, executive control was analogous to

4. Elton D. Woolpert, "Highlights of 1941," in Clarence E. Ridley and Orin F. Nolting, eds., *The Municipal Yearbook 1942* (Chicago, 1942), 1–10; National Institute of Municipal Law Officers, *One Year's Experience of American Cities At War* (New York, 1942), 6.

5. See New York Council of Defense, *Report on New York State Defense Program 1942,* in Charles Poletti Papers, New York State Defense and War Councils Folder: 1941, Columbia Univ.; Daniel W. Hoan, "The Work of the Division of State and Local Cooperation of the National Defense Council," *Public Management* 22 (Oct. 1940), 302–3.

military command, and there was no time for committee action. The New York State War Emergency Act of 1942 sought to meet this criticism by providing for a Director of Civilian Protection who would become the absolute head of all civilian forces in the area. Richmond, Virginia, and some other cities adopted a similar ordinance making the mayor virtual dictator of the city in the event of an enemy attack.[6]

One of the most serious problems encountered by state and local officials was to secure data whereby they might assess the impact of greatly expanded defense production upon local communities before taking appropriate action. Evidence of severe community dislocation was highly visible: roads, schools, police, hospitals, and recreational and sanitary facilities, as well as the supply of labor, were being strained almost to the breaking point. Norfolk, a city almost literally conscripted into the national defense program in 1940, experienced these problems in the extreme. World War II came to the Virginia Tidewater largely through the expansion of the naval shipyards and military bases. There were 6,520 workers employed in the Norfolk Naval Yard in 1940; two years later, the number had increased to 43,000. Nearly ten thousand additional dwellings were needed to shelter civilian workers in 1941; meanwhile, the commandant of the naval base was expending much time and energy bombarding Washington for funds to build housing units for enlisted men. New water lines had to be added to supply not only the city but also the growing Army and Navy facilities. Roads had to be built and improved and two new elementary schools added to accommodate the offspring of civilian and military personnel. The local hospitals—Norfolk General, Leigh Memorial, Community, and DePaul—also needed funds for expansion. The shortage of recreational facilities was another matter of concern.[7]

Under normal circumstances the handling of these problems would have been a function of state and local government al-

6. "Governors Study War and Postwar Problems," *State Government* 26 (July 1943), 175.

7. For Norfolk's difficulties see the *Virginian Pilot,* Dec. 20, 1941, Jan. 6, 1942; the *Ledger Dispatch,* Aug. 28, 1940, Sept. 17, 1940, and Dec. 31, 1941.

most exclusively, and because of a lingering feeling that they were the agencies properly empowered to act, the DSLC hesitated at first to intrude. More and more insistently, however, defense councils were notifying Bane's office of problems of coordination requiring federal attention. In response, Bane and the heads of several federal and state agencies developed legislation on civilian defense matters and suggested it to local officials, formulated plans for emergency police and fire department mobilization, and established a state Home Guard to replace the federalized militia. The communications gap between Washington and the localities was further bridged when Bane, assisted by an advisory committee of editors and publishers that included Jonathan Daniels of the *Raleigh News and Observer,* developed an eight-page weekly called *Defense.* [8]

The DSLC viewed the extension of federal authority into these local spheres as extraordinary and occasioned by the national emergency. Both Bane and Hoan went to great lengths to reassure local officials that the federal presence was not intended to be permanent and would diminish as national security policy permitted. They were not wholly successful in persuading them that the national government was seeking cooperation rather than submission. The testimony of Earl D. Mallory, executive director of the American Municipal Asociation, indicates that many state and local officers reacted cautiously to action that might lead to a further accretion of federal powers. [9]

In some clearly defined areas, however, state and local officials eagerly endorsed federal assistance. As soon as it appeared probable that the National Guard would be summoned to federal service, several governors, notably Herbert H. Lehman of New York, requested the assistance of the DSLC in developing

8. Samuel I. Rosenman, comp., *The Public Papers and Addresses of Franklin D. Roosevelt,* 13 vols. (New York, 1938–50), X, 166n.; XI, 32–35, 237–39; Frank Bane to William H. McReynolds, Sept. 20, 1940, in "Minutes of Meetings, Sept.–Dec. 1940," and "Progress Report of the Division of State and Local Cooperation," Feb. 26, 1941, NDAC Records.

9. Daniel W. Hoan, "National Defense and the Cities," *National Municipal Review* 30 (May 1941), 282; "Federal-State Conference on Law Enforcement," *Defense* 1 (Aug. 30, 1940), 7; Earl D. Mallory, "Municipal Cooperation in Local Defense," *Public Management* 22 (Oct. 1940), 304.

methods whereby local police might be utilized to supplement existing state police forces. Bane's staff drafted an amendment to the National Defense Act of 1916 removing the prohibition against maintaining state militia other than the Guard in time of peace. The DSLC followed this with a blueprint for mobilizing law enforcement authorities on a metropolitan and region-wide basis that presaged the initiation of other steps in the direction of metropolitan and regional planning. Virginia, Connecticut, New York, and New Jersey were among the states that adopted the plan experimentally.[10]

At the request of the Secretary of War, Bane also emphasized the need to study the growing problems of recreation and leisure time in communities located near military and industrial concentrations. In concert with federal health and welfare agencies, the DSLC promoted conferences in cities across the nation to focus attention and secure appropriate action on a broad spectrum of urban problems, including venereal disease, juvenile delinquency, sanitation, housing and rent control, child-care centers for working mothers in defense plants, gasoline and rubber conservation, and food rationing. These activities reached a peak in 1941 when the DSLC borrowed fifteen city managers free of cost from their communities for a period of thirty days. They were dispatched to the most important congested production areas to ascertain the need for additional community facilities, the relationship of such facilities to the effective operation of the defense program, and the availability of state and city financial resources to meet all or part of the costs. The President used their data to support his request of February 24, 1941, that Congress appropriate $150 million to relieve the most hard-pressed communities.[11]

The Community Facilities Act (popularly known as the Lanham Act, after its sponsor Representative Fritz Lanham of

10. "Home Guard Act," *Defense* 1 (Oct. 25, 1940), 8.

11. Charles Poletti, "Local Participation in National Defense," reprinted in New York State Defense Council, comp., *New York State and Local Defense Programs* (Albany, Feb. 1941), in Charles Poletti Papers, Columbia Univ.; "Defense News Affecting Cities," *Public Management* 23 (Mar. 1941), 82.

Texas) of June 1941, despite its shortcomings, aided war-boom communities and became another landmark in the evolution of federal-state-city relationships. Although deficient in some respects, especially in the opinion of urban liberals, the legislation helped ease the worst miseries of boom-town life by authorizing the Federal Works Agency (FWA) to provide money for nursery schools, child-care centers, clinics, elementary- and secondary-school expansion, the construction of recreation facilities, and almost anything else for which a war-created need could be shown. As a result of the Lanham Act, thousands of localities acquired new community centers, playgrounds, schools, and medical facilities, all completely paid for out of federal funds. The gain to each community and to the nation as a whole was enormous. Of all the countries at war, only in America was there such an extensive rebuilding of physical plant while the war was still under way.[12]

The threat of Axis aggression also caused the DSLC to look to the British Local Defence Volunteers (later Home Guard) as a model for devising "passive defense" measures to ward off domestic invasion, foil saboteurs, and minimize damage to cities from aerial bombardment. Few high-ranking military officials believed American cities would actually be bombed, but as a precaution the War Department asked Bane to send observers to Britain to acquire firsthand knowledge of how Londoners were handling the evacuation of the civilian population from the large urban-industrial centers, providing health and medical services, caring for children, and protecting transportation and public utilities. Drawing upon the British experience but modifying it to suit American conditions, Bane, the Army engineers, and the defense councils cooperated to draft plans to protect metropolitan water supplies, dams and utilities. Cities grouped closely together, such as New York, Yonkers, and Mount Vernon, risked surrendering some degree of sovereignty in order to form metropolitan-wide fire-fighting units. The process of by-

12. "Citation of the Shortages of Necessary Community Facilities—Discussion by Mr. Frank Bane," *Defense* 2 (Mar. 11, 1941), 8.

passing the artificial divisions created by political boundaries was a gradual one, however, and its difficulties should not be underestimated.[13]

The presence of hostile submarines prowling off the Atlantic Coast likewise caused Bane to initiate discussions with federal aviation officials which culminated in the formation of the Civil Air Patrol, one of the most popular "home guard" forces. The Army was only too glad to relinquish the coastal and border watches to civilian pilots because military aircraft available for this duty were in short supply and required for more pressing assignments. Inevitably, civilians undertook other paramilitary functions: local defense councils supplied thousands of volunteer spotters for the Army's Aircraft Warning Service; offered training to volunteer air raid wardens; identified protective shelters; and prepared contingency plans for the evacuation of the urban population in the event of aerial bombardment. In concert with the Materials Branch of the Office of Production Management (OPM), the DSLC also drafted plans for the collection of scrap aluminum, rubber, and household fats essential to the defense program. With a flair for detail and a view toward mobilizing the metropolitan population, Bane's staff drafted organizational charts, publicity releases, posters, and procedural instructions. With the exception of the morale-building program, which had not advanced beyond the preliminary planning stage, civilian protection was well advanced at the time the DSLC's functions were absorbed by the newly established Office of Civilian Defense.[14]

At the time Bane left the DSLC in March 1941, he asserted that "the focal point of the National Defense Program . . . is shifting more and more from Washington to the states and localities." Nonetheless, it is also true that a number of obstacles continued to block the efficient functioning of local defense ma-

13. "The Reminiscences of Herbert H. Lehman," vol. IV, 461–62, 561–63; vol. V, 677–79, Oral History Research Office (OHRO), Columbia Univ.; "Progress Report of the Division of State and Local Cooperation," Feb. 26, 1941, NDAC Records; "Fire Defense Committee Meets," *Defense* 1 (Dec. 13, 1940), 5.

14. *New York Times,* Sept. 27, 1940, June 14, 1941; "Cooperative Plan to Conserve Vital Materials," *Defense* 2 (Apr. 8, 1941), 9.

chinery. The production line of municipal action was in many instances not being retooled with an appreciation of what were the defense problems of cities, or with a knowledge of how these problems could be solved. Where this knowledge and appreciation was developed, it was not sufficiently decentralized.[15]

Despite Bane's imaginative and aggressive policies, often pursued in the face of isolationist anger and lackadaisical cooperation, the DSLC was at a disadvantage in handling some problems. On issues where the distinction between civilian and military requirements was not easily delineated, or which might fall within the purview of an already existing agency, the DSLC lacked the prestige required to command complete cooperation.[16]

By far the most serious challenge to Bane's leadership emanated from the persistence of state-city animosities. As early as the summer of 1940, there were indications that a few of the more prominent urban personalities were miffed by the President's decision to entrust civilian protection to the states rather than the cities, where they believed it properly belonged. William H. McReynolds, secretary to the National Defense Advisory Commission, conveyed to Roosevelt the substance of his conversations with Frank Bane. According to the latter, Mayor Fiorello La Guardia of New York City was unhappy over the prospect of dealing with the NDAC through the state organization, and he intended to get a number of other mayors to join him in personally presenting to the President his objections to being subordinated to state supervision.[17]

La Guardia, recalling the shabby neglect of the cities—especially his own—by upstate rural legislators, was no doubt sincere in his concern for their welfare. As president of the United States Conference of Mayors, he had the primary obligation to alert the municipalities to the imminent threat of war. Hence he submitted to Roosevelt in January 1941 a preliminary

15. Robert McElroy, "Narrative Account of the Office of Civilian Defense," unpub. ms., Nov. 1944, ch. ii, 4, NARG 171, OCD Records.
16. Arnold Miles and Roy H. Owsley, *Cities and the National Defense Program* (Chicago, 1941), 68.
17. William H. McReynolds to FDR, Aug. 8, 1940, Office File (OF) 813–A, Franklin D. Roosevelt Papers, FDRL.

report on civil defense organization and administration that was largely the handiwork of Paul V. Betters, executive director of the Conference of Mayors. The document not only ignored the existence of Frank Bane and the DSLC but also disparaged the belief that the states could possibly make any contributions to civilian protection.[18]

The report proposed to establish a new federal agency of cabinet-level status to serve in advisory and supervisory capacities in its communications with local civilian defense authorities. Although the agency would function under the aegis of a central board in Washington, the report endorsed the principle of decentralization by proposing to set up nine regional offices coterminous with the Army's designated Corps Areas. The central board would consist of representatives from the federal defense agencies plus one spokesman each for the state and local governments. This was La Guardia's only concession to the states' interest in civilian protection, and it reflected his belief and that of Betters that the federal government should deal with the cities directly.[19]

Besides the report, La Guardia and Betters peppered the White House with letters from various urban officials, such as the mayor of Tacoma, Washington, that purported to show the DSLC was not doing its job in alerting the populace to the seriousness of civilian defense.[20]

Bane was alert to the lobbying activities of La Guardia and the Conference of Mayors, and if they alarmed him, he did not show it. He knew that the administration had under consideration various recommendations for reorganizing the entire home

18. *First Deficiency Appropriation Bill for 1942,* Hearings before the Subcommittee of the Committee on Appropriations, U.S. House of Representatives, 77th Cong., 2d sess. (1942), 260–68; John F. O'Ryan to Herbert H. Lehman, Apr. 24, 1942, Herbert H. Lehman Papers, Columbia Univ.; *Boston Globe,* June 4, 1941; "Air Raid Protection," folder in Fiorello H. La Guardia Papers, Civilian Defense, Municipal Archives (MA), New York City (NYC).

19. La Guardia to FDR, Jan. 31, 1941, OF 1892, FDR Papers; *Preliminary Report for Civil Defense Organization and Administration in the United States,* submitted to the President of the United States by F.H. La Guardia, president of the United States Conference of Mayors, Jan. 31, 1941, n.p., copy in the La Guardia Papers; Paul V. Betters to La Guardia, May 29, 1940, in *ibid.*

20. Harry P. Cain to FDR, May 8, 1941, OF 1892; Paul V. Betters to Stephen Early, May 14, 1941, in President's Secretary File (PSF), FDR Papers.

defense program, although the outlines of the reorganization were not yet clear. Events beyond Bane's control in the winter of 1940–41 ultimately forced the DSLC into a larger federal structure.

Presidential adviser Wayne Coy, liaison officer in the Office of Emergency Management (OEM), and Budget Director Harold D. Smith had been analyzing the status of the civilian defense organizations to determine their readiness in the event of war. On Smith's recommendation, Roosevelt transferred the DSLC to the OEM on March 1, 1941. This administrative reshuffling did not satisfy the Conference of Mayors, which wanted a new federal agency empowered to deal with the cities directly.[21]

La Guardia, of course, stood in the forefront of these nationally known urban officials. He made known their feelings in a letter to President Roosevelt at the conclusion of the annual Conference of Mayors.[22] The mayor's passionate style and skillful politicking achieved their intended effect because they coincided with similar expressions of dissatisfaction from Secretary of the Interior Harold L. Ickes and others within the Executive Office who wanted to upgrade civilian protection.

The President soon began to think along the lines of a wholly new organization. He broached the subject to Budget Director Smith, Wayne Coy, and William Bullitt in a conference on April 4, 1941. After the meeting, Smith recorded that Roosevelt seemed to think that the job did not really require an administrator of Bane's talents, "but that someone should head it who would attract public attention as a good ballyhoo artist and speech-maker." This description fitted La Guardia, a fact that alarmed both Smith and Coy, who were opposed to transforming the DSLC into a propaganda agency. Two weeks later, they made a strong personal plea on behalf of Bane, even though they were aware that, disenchanted, he now wanted to return to the Council of State Governments.[23]

---

21. Wayne Coy to FDR, Apr. 4, 1941, Wayne Coy Papers, FDRL; Lloyd Eno to Allen More, Apr. 30, 1941; John Farley to Allen More, May 19, 1941, NARG 171, OCD Records; "Conferences with the President," Harold D. Smith Papers, FDRL.

22. La Guardia to FDR, Apr. 25, 1941, La Guardia Papers.

23. "Reminiscences of Herbert H. Lehman," vol. IV, 610; "Conferences with the President," entries dated Apr. 4, 11, 17, 22, 1941, Harold D. Smith Papers.

After another month of backstage politicking, on May 20, 1941, the President issued Executive Order 8757, which established the United States Office of Civilian Defense (OCD). Simultaneously, he announced the appointment of La Guardia as its director, a move suggesting that in Roosevelt's opinion the "Little Flower" would be a better morale builder than Frank Bane.

The duties assigned to the new organization were relatively broad in scope but stopped just short of making it the home-front watchdog. The OCD was empowered to coordinate the various levels of defense machinery; to plan and implement programs for the preservation of civilian life and property in the event of war; and to promote national morale and create opportunities for constructive volunteer participation. On the advice of Budget Director Smith, Roosevelt decided not to accord cabinet-level status to the director. He also agreed to continue the understanding that Bane had with the governors, whereby the day-to-day operation of the civilian defense program would be left to the states, and through the states to the local governments. This commitment to cooperative federalism put a crimp in La Guardia's plan to designate his fellow mayors as federal representatives. But the appointment of La Guardia himself soon proved an irritant in the close working relationship that was needed between the states and the national organization.[24]

From the beginning La Guardia devoted his attention solely to the civilian protection aspects of OCD and gave short shrift to the volunteer participation program. His budget request to Congress of $100 million for the purchase of necessary equipment confirmed the heavy emphasis which he put upon protection from the destructive effects of aerial bombardment.[25] On June 16, 1941, he publicly broadcast over radio the agency's plans for instructing the public in all phases of air raid defense. This address was consistent with La Guardia's belief that the director's office was not merely advisory but had substantive powers. Two weeks earlier, he had told Boston's city defense

24. Rosenman, comp., *Public Papers of FDR,* x, 162–66.
25. *First Deficiency Appropriation Bill for 1942,* 259–60, 263, 288.

commission that the director "must have the authority to issue orders," promising that the instructions would be brief and "as intelligently written as the English language will permit." Had OCD faithfully adhered to this promise, better results might have followed; but all too soon headquarters was flooding the bewildered regional and state officers with huge stacks of pamphlets, books, reports, and surveys.

Worse, the mayor's intention "to issue orders" raised the eyebrows of several governors who had been given to understand that all OCD communications to the cities would first pass through their hands.[26]

In view of the centrality of the civilian protection program in La Guardia's hands, the propaganda aspects of OCD often became the number one priority. The director was seen and photographed everywhere: civil defense helmet in place, spotting "enemy" planes, assisting in "evacuations," administering first aid to the "wounded," and modeling the latest in civilian defense regalia. The director was playing to packed and, on the whole, approving crowds, commented the *Saturday Review.*[27]

Behind the masquerade and the publicity there was a deadly serious purpose. La Guardia wanted to convince Americans that personal danger from abroad was not only possible but *imminent* and that an alert, mobilized civilian defense force was needed to protect the home front. Air raid defense called for a high level of community cooperation and served an important integrative function. Thus La Guardia spoke very bluntly in October 1941 when he warned that "every city is now a legitimate target of attack" and that "total war recognizes no boundaries."[28]

Toward the end of October 1941, civilian protection had made observable progress but not nearly enough to satify La Guardia.

26. "Calling All Fire Chiefs . . . —And Other Municipal Officials," *The American City* 56 (Oct. 1941), 5; *Boston Globe,* June 4, 1941; *National Defense Migration Hearings,* pt. 25, 9745.

27. "The Office of Civilian Defense," n.d. [May 1941?], La Guardia Papers; "Totalitarian War and the O.C.D.," *Saturday Review of Literature* 25 (Feb. 14, 1942), 10.

28. "Calling All Fire Chiefs," 5.

Much still remained to be done. Two thousand units were reported in the process of formation, but these were mostly located in the vulnerable coastal communities along the Atlantic seaboard; there were few units in the interior. La Guardia's testimony before a congressional committee in January 1942 confirms that the OCD had not been entirely successful in the days before Pearl Harbor in alerting the population to the danger of aggression.[29]

Indeed, under La Guardia's aegis the OCD functioned in an atmosphere of controversy, which was especially evident whenever the agency's activities appeared to overstep the fragile network of relationships that comprised the federal system. Harold L. Ickes was correct in his observation that La Guardia was not a team player but one who wanted to run all over the field with the ball. He simply could not confine himself to working through the states as the administration and the governors had agreed. Instead, the mayor complained that the state defense councils were tying his hands by insisting that the OCD should not have direct communications or dealings with the cities and local defense agencies. In a letter to novelist Fannie Hurst, a critic of the new organization, La Guardia went to great lengths to excuse his deficiencies and shift the blame to the states. "Your observations are entirely correct," he wrote. "The fault, however, is not with the central office in Washington. Specific instructions on every little detail have been sent out. The Mid-West is just indifferent. Then another great handicap I am up against is that I am compelled to deal with state officials and through the State officials down to the municipalities. The only way to do it is, of course, to deal direct with each community. The governors protested this and there is nothing else to do but go through regular bureaucratic channels."[30]

T. Semmes Walmsley, the assistant director and former mayor of New Orleans, likewise attributed the OCD's faults to an inabil-

29. *First Deficiency Appropriation Bill for 1942,* 258; La Guardia to OCD Staff, Nov. 17, 1941, La Guardia Papers.
30. Harold L. Ickes, *The Secret Diary of Harold L. Ickes,* Vol. III: *The Lowering Clouds, 1939-1944* (New York, 1953), 398; La Guardia to Fannie Hurst, Nov. 9, 1941, La Guardia Papers.

ity to persuade the states to cooperate. There was, no doubt, a modicum of truth to this, for before Pearl Harbor some states were laggard in alerting their citizens to civilian defense, especially where isolationist sentiment ran strong. But the degree of cooperation sought and attained by La Guardia must be evaluated against the President's decision, rooted in historical precedent and experience, to proceed with civilian defense through the states. Two months after La Guardia was appointed director, Secretary Ickes wrote that the mayor was a poor choice and should never have accepted. Presidential adviser Bernard Baruch had told Ickes that La Guardia was getting in the President's hair. The mayor was too spectacular to devote attention to the routine and dull but necessary tasks that had to be performed.[31]

Baruch's most serious complaint was that La Guardia had been establishing his own rival organizations in the cities, an action that infuriated the governors. The Budget Bureau was particularly critical of this practice. Even while conceding that New York City and Chicago deserved to be treated as separate civilian defense areas because of their size and complexity, Budget Bureau officials warned that "organizations of city officials should not be used as a way to circumvent the OCD-state-city channel agreed upon."[32]

This critical evaluation of the director's performance was confirmed in letters of the governors themselves. Writing to President Roosevelt on November 21, 1941, Governor Culbert L. Olson of California, a friend of the New Deal, accused the agency of blurring the lines of authority. Governor Herbert H. Lehman, the mayor's political rival in New York, likewise dispatched a telegram to La Guardia protesting "the issuance of orders and instructions by your Office direct to the numerous municipal officials of the State instead of through the State Defense Council." Governor Harold E. Stassen of Minnesota,

31. T. Semmes Walmsley, "How the OCD Is Functioning and How Local Defense Corps Can Cooperate," *American City* 57 (Feb. 1942), 35; Ickes, *Secret Diary,* III, 572–73.
32. Bureau of the Budget, "Memorandum on Program and Organization, Office of Civilian Defense," Nov. 6, 1941, OF 4422, FDR Papers.

53

speaking on behalf of the Governors' Conference, also warned La Guardia of the pitfalls of divided authority.[33]

La Guardia's persistent efforts to circumvent legitimate areas of state jurisdiction activated political waves that lapped against the White House gate itself. On February 16, 1942, for example, John J. Dunnigan, the Democratic leader of the New York State Senate, introduced a resolution criticizing the mayor for separating the civilian defense of New York City from the State Defense Council's authority. A copy was sent to the President with a covering letter which emphasized that the resolution was nonpartisan and had the support of *both* political parties.[34]

Many of the differences between OCD and the states arose from the latter's ingrained abhorrence of coercive action. In the course of administering one program or another, state officials sometimes suspected that the national headquarters was attempting to pressure them. OCD authorities, on the other hand, considered the states laggard or deficient in their perception of the essentials of jointly administered programs. The result was administrative confusion, with objectives vaguely defined and lines of authority between the OCD and the state defense councils uncertain. "We are still interested in the CD program—especially the fire protection education phase of it," wrote the head of a public relations firm to the President's press secretary. "And, try as we have, we can't find the key to Mr. La Guardia's set-up. In fact, it appears that he is it—and he is making the circuit himself."[35]

Even La Guardia's talents as an administrator were called into question. The editors of *Public Management* were disturbed by the director's misguided emphasis on quantity rather than quality and asserted that the OCD should not recruit volun-

33. Culbert L. Olson to FDR, Nov. 21, 1941, Wayne Coy Papers; Herbert H. Lehman to La Guardia, July 29, 1941; Harold E. Stassen to La Guardia, July 12, 30, 1941, NARG 171, OCD Records.
34. "Statement by Senator John J. Dunnigan, Democratic Leader, New York State Senate," Feb. 16, 1942, copy in Poletti Papers.
35. James J. Bamford, "Listen Washington! The Local Community Talks Back," *Survey* 78 (Mar. 1942), 73; Jonathan Daniels, "Organization for Civilian Defense," *State Government* 15 (Sept. 1942), 176; L.W. Hutchins to Marvin H. McIntyre, June 9, 1941, and Ambrose Burns to La Guardia, June 24, 1941, OF 4422, FDR Papers.

teers more rapidly than they could be assimilated through adequate training programs. They noted that the local units had failed to establish and adhere to training priorities. In their enthusiasm for volunteer training, the instruction of regular personnel such as firemen, police, and utility repairmen—who were the city's first line of protection—was being neglected. The editors attributed this error to national OCD officials who mistakenly emphasized the dramatic and spectacular, thereby encouraging the separation of training from management and command in violation of the canons of efficient public management.[36]

From the perspective of federal-urban relations, the OCD in 1941 was putting a strain on the structure of cooperative federalism as it had evolved in the Depression-ridden thirties. La Guardia could not work within the limits set by the President, and this was reflected in the agency's lack of clear-cut objectives. OCD headquarters exhibited ineffective and sometimes indecisive management, had a faulty organizational structure, and was torn by personality conflicts. La Guardia was unable to secure effective coordination of civil defense protection on a truly national basis or to unify direction and control of air raid protection measures. Congressional sniping, a skeptical press, and a director who spent his time shuttling back and forth between New York City and Washington added to the OCD's burdens. The problem, wrote Wayne Coy to the President in December 1941, had grown so acute it could no longer be ignored.[37]

In fact, Roosevelt was already seeking a graceful way to relieve La Guardia of his administrative duties. On December 19, 1941, the President conferred with Budget Director Smith, who was convinced that La Guardia could not handle the director's duties on any basis. Smith declared that the position warranted a full-time director. At that point La Guardia entered the Oval Office with "Pa" Watson. Roosevelt turned to La Guardia and

36. "What's Wrong with Defense Training?" *Public Management* 24 (Mar. 1942), 65–66; Lillie H. Nairne, "Effects of War Activities on Public Welfare," *The Family* 23 (Apr. 1942), 46.

37. Eleanor Roosevelt to Joseph P. Lash, Sept. 16, 1941, Eleanor Roosevelt (ER) Papers, FDRL; Wayne Coy to FDR, Dec. 13, 1941, OF 4422, FDR Papers.

indicated that the jobs of OCD director and mayor of New York City were too much for one man and that he should get an administrative assistant. The President stopped short of firing La Guardia, who spent most of the hour defending his actions and shifting the blame elsewhere.[38]

On January 2, 1942, Roosevelt cut the Gordian knot. He forced La Guardia to accept a new executive officer, James M. Landis, dean of the Harvard Law School and regional head of the New England office, to run the daily affairs of the OCD's central headquarters. His authority undercut and with the agency in deep trouble with Congress, La Guardia resigned in bitter protest in February. It was the one job in his entire career in which he was unsuccessful.[39]

During his tenure, La Guardia chose to ignore the fact that the President had given the OCD a broader mandate than simply civilian protection. The executive order of May 20, 1941, also spoke of recruiting civilian volunteers and promoting morale. La Guardia's interest in the nonmilitary aspects of civilian defense, however, had been limited to decking out women volunteers in smart uniforms without giving them any clearly defined duties, which caused Cornelia Bryce Pinchot, the wife of the former Republican governor of Pennsylvania, to complain to Eleanor Roosevelt that La Guardia had positioned a wall of bureaucrats between himself and the do-gooders [i.e., the Volunteer Participation Division], causing the latter to languish.[40]

The mayor's indifference—not to say overt hostility—toward the volunteer aspects of civilian defense clashed with the more ambitious plans of women leaders, who were thinking in terms of creating an "American Social Defense Organization." Eleanor Roosevelt, a symbol of women's emancipation for almost two decades, was among those whom the director's myopia annoyed. On July 22, 1941, she had written a note to the President requesting that he address a few words of encouragement to a group of volunteer women workers before their meeting with

38. "Conferences with the President," entries dated Dec. 15, 19, 1941; Jan. 2, 1942, Harold D. Smith Papers.
39. Charles Garrett, *The La Guardia Years* (New Brunswick, 1961), 282.
40. Cornelia Bryce Pinchot to ER, Aug. 28, 1941, ER Papers.

her in the White House. In closing, she added: "I feel that you will have to make it clear that civilian participation is important. Otherwise, the Mayor will not do much with his volunteers."[41]

Women engaged in community service, the counterpart of the one-year military draft, formed a recurring theme in Mrs. Roosevelt's speeches. "Women's role in the community is no different than the role of any citizen and that is to assume the responsibility which falls on any citizen in a democracy," she wrote in 1942 to the secretary of Syracuse's defense council. Then she added a sentence that had a direct bearing not only on the mobilization of the urban population for war work but on the quality of life in the cities, towns, and villages of America. "Each community," she said, "is a link in the chain which makes up our nation and every weak link weakens the whole chain."[42]

The First Lady looked upon the civilian defense program in a broader perspective than did La Guardia, believing that it contained the seeds of renewal for American cities and communities after the emergency. She also feared conservative pressures upon her husband to abandon New Deal programs during the war crisis, which would mean sacrificing the interests of young people, working men and women, and blacks.[43] At first, however, she hesitated to intrude publicly into what was becoming a major controversy and confined her views to a few trusted friends. But because of La Guardia's continued insensitivity to the women's volunteer groups and pressure on her from presidential adviser Harry L. Hopkins to speak out more vigorously, she soon became the most prominent critic of the mayor's indifference. The President, dissatisfied with the progress the OCD had made thus far, encouraged her along this path.

So effective a critic was the First Lady that in September 1941 La Guardia offered her—and she accepted—the position of associate director, in charge of the Division of Volunteer Participation. The Little Flower saw advantages in having the President's

41. ER to FDR, July 22, 1941, OF 4422, FDR Papers.
42. ER to Mrs. Raymond F. Piper, Mar. 3, 1942, ER Papers.
43. Robert E. Lane to ER, June 19, 1941; La Guardia to ER, June 26, 1941, in *ibid.* See also Joseph P. Lash, *Eleanor and Franklin* (New York, 1971), 823-29.

57

wife as his colleague. It meant not only enhanced prestige and publicity but unique leverage in establishing OCD within the federal bureaucracy. For Eleanor Roosevelt, acceptance of the OCD post offered a visible platform from which to fight to preserve the social gains of the New Deal which benefited the urban population and advanced the cause of community revitalization. In October 1941 she appealed to all women to advise their congressmen of the needs of their communities, observing that Congress would be enacting "a great deal of legislation" soon "without a great deal of knowledge of the community needs of the nation."[44]

Almost at once, the First Lady focused her seemingly inexhaustible energy upon the evolution of a true community program that would draw all civilians and local agencies into the total war effort. Reporting for duty on her first day at OCD headquarters, she outlined her objectives to reporters: (1) to give every person—man, woman, and child—wishing to volunteer his services in the interest of civilian defense an opportunity to train for the work he wished to do; (2) to provide opportunities to participate in work beneficial to the neighborhood or community; and (3) to prepare citizens to meet "any emergency call that may come in the future." Behind the words was a firm conviction that the successful mobilization of the home front rested ultimately with local municipalities, spurred on by the OCD. She viewed her contribution as coordinating the nonmilitary activities so as to maximize the effectiveness of civilian volunteers.[45]

With these goals in mind, Mrs. Roosevelt approached her responsibilities with a single-minded determination. Her thinking had been influenced by the British experience of 1940, particularly the network of voluntary community associations which J.B. Priestley, the novelist, called "the organized militant citizen."[46] She knew about the activities of the Local Defence Volunteers (renamed the Home Guard), the Observer Corps, and the Air Raid Wardens' Service from a pamphlet, *The Mobiliza-*

44. *New York Times,* Oct. 26, 1941.

45. *Ibid.,* Sept. 30, 1941.

46. See Angus Calder, *The People's War: Britain, 1939-1945* (New York, 1969), 121-28, 163.

tion of the Home Front, written by an American, Eric H. Biddle. The First Lady's copy, with its pencil markings and underlinings, suggested that she had carefully read and analyzed its contents. Biddle's opening sentence affirmed what Mrs. Roosevelt believed all along: "The war will be won on the home front." Another of his observations applied to La Guardia's hitherto exclusive emphasis upon the protective services. The author had written critically: "One of the things that should be understood is that civilian officials of every locality . . . will have a much more significant part to play in wartime than merely to protect communities from air raids, important as that function may be." Overemphasis on air raid precautions was the best way to cultivate a "Maginot Line" complex.[47]

Further down, the First Lady's attention was drawn to the passage that asserted "the feeling of local—even neighborhood —responsibility evoked by the system of reliance on voluntary cooperation brought about an enormous cooperative effort for the common good." One can almost imagine her nodding vigorously as she read on, for Biddle had written that the United States (like Britain) would have to expand its entire range of health and welfare services "as a positive and vital part of an aggressive war program." Where Biddle declared that every able-bodied citizen on the home front was expected to participate, Mrs. Roosevelt had written: "all important."[48]

Paul U. Kellogg, editor of *Survey,* indicated that once the First Lady immersed herself in the daily operations of the Division of Volunteer Participation, she perceived the possibilities it offered for serving the purposes of community revitalization, which she equated with the humanitarian social welfare policies of the New Deal. The idea was not a new one; Mrs. Roosevelt had been concerned with the preservation and extension of the New Deal's programs as early as 1940, when she had written to James Gerard of New York City, a Tammany Democrat, that "we must continue with the progressive social legislation as part

47. Eric H. Biddle, *The Mobilization of the Home Front: The British Experience and Its Significance for the United States* (Chicago, 1942), esp. intro. and ch. i.
48. *Ibid.;* McElroy, "Narrative Account of the OCD," ch. vi, 20–21, NARG 171, OCD Records.

of national defense." She now had the opportunity to translate these words into action.[49]

Whether Franklin Roosevelt believed that defense encompassed social reform as well as guns was less clear. In response to reporters' questions on September 9, 1940, the President asserted that he had to restrict assistance in the social welfare sphere to needs emanating from the expansion of industry and defense facilities. "I draw the line. I have to," he told the newsmen. But he was often ambivalent, especially when he suspected that conservatives and Republicans were out to scuttle gains recorded by the New Deal. On those occasions he could sound as determined as the First Lady, affirming that he also viewed civilian defense as "a social defense organization."[50]

Eleanor Roosevelt, in contrast, had a deep feeling for the community. Addressing a women's conference in 1936, she had declared: "All of us need deep roots. We need to feel there is one place to which we can go back, where we shall always be able to work with people whom we know as our close friends and associates, where we feel that we have done something in the way of shaping a community, of counting in making the public opinion of that community." Together each community was a link in the chain which made up the nation. This perception of the community may have been conservative, but only in the sense of wanting to preserve the best aspects of an older society. Whereas authority, tradition, and stratification had combined in the past to reinforce common values and ensure predictable patterns of behavior, to Mrs. Roosevelt the well-being of people counted for everything.[51]

The national defense program could be used to create a unity of spirit, a readiness in each community to share and sacrifice in the interests of a strengthened democracy. Mrs. Roosevelt articulated this theme in November 1941, in a speech before a

49. Paul U. Kellogg to Raymond Clapper, Feb. 9, 1942; ER to James Gerard, Nov. 9, 1940, ER Papers.
50. See FDR Press Conference Transcript, Sept. 24, 1940, microfilm copy in FDRL.
51. See Eleanor Roosevelt's speech to the Conference on the Cause and Cure of War, Jan. 21, 1936, Speech and Article File, ER Papers. Also, ER to Mrs. Raymond F. Piper, Mar. 3, 1942, in *ibid.*

Washington conference on women's activities in civilian defense. Later, in response to questions from the audience, she removed any lingering doubts that she was approaching the volunteer program as a positive instrument, extending into peacetime, for the reconstruction of America's urban and rural communities.[52]

The First Lady's words were squarely in a progressive tradition that had espoused an organic view of society—a society possessed of a unity of purpose, a cooperative and collective economy, and a purposeful, functioning government—and had given birth to such New Deal programs as Arthurdale, Greenbelt, and Houston Gardens. This tradition sought to develop a new life for urban and rural America, with community or social attitudes substituting for extreme individualism, with more emphasis put upon creative endeavor and less on social competition, with greater stability and security, and with as many as possible of the community activities organized on a cooperative rather than a competitive basis.[53] By her words and actions, Mrs. Roosevelt gradually unfurled a view of the postwar community in which voluntary, democratic cooperation replaced economic insecurity and the chaos of capitalistic individualism. Democracy encompassed freedom, economic security, and equality of opportunity. She did not repudiate urbanization or consider the process necessarily evil, but she believed that new cooperative institutions were needed to render urban society more democratic. Urban society of the future had to be controlled by the masses and democratized; it had to be rendered more efficient and responsive to the needs of all people, not just the privileged. Two urban minorities, women and blacks, had to be drawn into the volunteer program.

The chief danger to community in the United States emanated not from the central government but from the technology of a ruggedly individualistic open society. The First Lady perceived that the traditional society of nineteenth-century America owed its decline not to Franklin D. Roosevelt and the New Deal but to

52. Speech to the Conference on Women's Activities in Civilian Defense, Nov. 8, 1941, in *ibid.*
53. See Paul K. Conkin, *Toward A New World: The New Deal Community Program* (Ithaca, 1959), 3-4, 127, 150, 202.

61

Henry Ford and General Motors. The familiar pattern of inter-personal affection and shared values and goals considered more important than mere life (which sociologists referred to as *Gemeinschaft*) had been relentlessly transformed into a mecha-nistic, modern, impersonal counterpart (*Gesellschaft*). Modern-ization had involved an ineluctable process of moving from community to its negation—from emotionally satisfying rela-tions to feelings of deracination, anomie, and despair.[54]

The acceleration of the defense program in 1940–41, by luring people from smaller cities and towns to the larger urban centers of production, was subverting the standards of those leaving and those remaining behind. The growing tendency of locally elected officials to leave the solution of all problems, including non-defense-related ones, to Washington was one manifestation of an abdication of responsible decision making. In joining the OCD, Eleanor Roosevelt hoped to establish a new equilibrium by encouraging and cajoling the local defense councils to tackle community problems head-on.

One method of revitalizing older communities and giving sub-stance to the newer ones was to make neighborhoods more at-tractive *socially* as well as physically, so that people would want to live in them and put down roots. As director of the volunteer program, the First Lady believed that she would be ideally situated to build up the local councils (a policy that ran counter to the centralizing tendencies of La Guardia's administration) to meet the wartime and postwar needs of urban and rural America. Pearl Harbor strengthened rather than weakened her conviction that community revitalization was part of the na-tion's war work.[55]

In October 1941 she wrote to Lady Stella Reading, head of the Women's Voluntary Services for Civilian Defence in Britain, that the real task was not to recruit more volunteer workers (though that would continue) but to coordinate and rationalize the efforts of those whom the local councils had already re-cruited. This was also the opinion of Charles P. Taft, the assis-

54. *Ibid.*
55. ER to Jane Seaver, Nov. 10, 1941, NARG 171, OCD Records.

tant director of the Office of Defense Health and Welfare Services (ODHWS). "The plain fact," he told the National Municipal League, "is that in most of our big towns the progress in organizing these necessary home front defenses has been slow— too slow."[56]

In many communities the volunteer program was in disarray because of La Guardia's neglect, lack of resources, and uncertain lines of authority. The fault lay both in the localities and in Washington. A report of the chairman of the volunteer office in Cleveland, Ohio, to Mrs. Roosevelt was typical of the complaints received. She protested that the American Women's Volunteer Service (AWVS), a professional service organization, had been establishing offices in the city in competition with the local volunteer offices appointed by the mayor. Aware of Mrs. Roosevelt's keen interest in all aspects of community defense, she asked for clarification of the OCD's position.[57]

The First Lady was aware of the organizational difficulties of the volunteer program and already was moving to correct them. She had asked Judge Justine Wise Polier of New York City's children's court, a friend and legal adviser, for an opinion on whether the President's executive order permitted community renewal. Judge Polier assured her that it did, and shortly thereafter the First Lady was tackling the problem of tangled lines of authority from the national headquarters to the local level. The Washington office of the Volunteer Participation Division was completely reorganized to "reach down into the local communities and into our rural areas," and jurisdictional disputes were resolved in favor of the locally appointed agencies.[58] This decision had serious repercussions for the success of community renewal, but they were not immediately apparent because it tied the fortunes of the volunteer program to the willingness of local defense councils to cooperate. Such cooperation was not always forthcoming.

Nonetheless, as part of the reorganization and invigoration of

56. ER to Lady Stella Reading, Oct. 4, 1941, ER Papers; Charles P. Taft, "Home Towns Organize for Defense," *National Municipal Review* 31 (Jan. 1942), 18.
57. Maud E. Corning to ER, Oct. 24, 1941, ER Papers.
58. Lash, *Eleanor and Franklin,* 833.

the volunteer program, Mrs. Roosevelt surrounded herself with strong program specialists who shared her vision of a better America. Judge Polier took a leave of absence from the court; Paul U. Kellogg left his editorial post with the *Survey;* from the National Consumers League came Mary Dublin, who had also served as the Tolan Committee's expert on the social problems of migratory laborers; and from North Carolina came Jonathan Daniels, a recognized authority on regionalism. Together they helped clarify the First Lady's thinking about community renewal, volunteer work, and the role of women in the defense program.[59]

The philosophical thrust of the new volunteer program was best explained by the First Lady herself. OCD, she wrote in January 1942, would sponsor the creation of effective community organizations under the authority of the state and local defense councils. These organizations, in turn, would analyze the whole impact of the war effort upon the community and articulate the community's needs. The OCD would assist the community in formulating its needs. "These needs when presented to OCD shall, wherever Federal action is capable of dealing with them, be referred to the appropriate Federal agencies for action," she declared.[60]

The growing crisis in child care and the rise in delinquency among urban youth were two fertile areas in which the OCD might demonstrate the utility of the volunteer program, advance the First Lady's interest in community renewal, and demonstrate interagency cooperation. The British experience had persuaded Mrs. Roosevelt that American children should not be evacuated from the coastal industrial cities, however vulnerable to aerial bombardment they might be. This was also the viewpoint of Henrietta Gordon, an official of the Child Welfare League. Miss Gordon had called attention to the failure of the British evacuation plan and the psychological and emotional disorders it had induced in children. In response to hundreds of letters pouring into her Washington office from distraught par-

59. *Ibid.*
60. See the memorandum dated Jan. 13, 1942, NARG 171, OCD Records.

ents, Mrs. Roosevelt described as "very remote" the likelihood that children would be moved in considerable numbers from their homes and advised parents to continue their children's daily routine.[61]

Just as Eleanor Roosevelt learned from Britain's experience about the civilian side of protection, so too that beleaguered nation offered a paradigm for strengthening family and community life under wartime stress. The British approach, combining central coordination and local initiative, seemed to work well and attracted the First Lady's attention. As assistant director of the OCD and afterward, she cooperated with the Children's Bureau in the Department of Labor and the Office of Community War Services in lobbying for federal, state, and locally supported children's day-care centers for working mothers. Of necessity, the majority of the centers were to be located in the industrial cities to which migration had been heavier.[62]

The First Lady's activity on behalf of children and working mothers, while promoting community cooperation and fulfilling an immediate manpower need, also had broader implications for the quality of life in postwar America. Addressing delegates to the twenty-fifth anniversary of the Summer Play Schools Association in New York City shortly after assuming her duties at the OCD, Mrs. Roosevelt talked about the child as the protean democrat of postwar urban society. Children in a democracy should have the opportunity to build healthy bodies, enjoy recreational centers, and have "freedom from fear," she declared. Equality of educational opportunities and economic security for the family were also essential for children to grow and develop.[63]

Freedom, economic security, equality of opportunity could be realized for the child only by eliminating the waste of human life in mining camps, migrant camps, and big-city slums. Thus Eleanor Roosevelt lobbied for the continuation of the school

---

61. Henrietta L. Gordon, "The Impact of National Defense on Child Welfare," *The Family* 23 (Mar. 1942), 5; *New York Times,* Jan. 5, 1942.

62. Lady E.D. Simon, "The Working Mother in England," *The Child* 7 (Nov. 1942), 62.

63. *New York Times,* Oct. 26, 1941.

lunch program and the food stamps plan, two highly popular social programs which used products from the Federal Surplus Commodities Corporation. The school lunch program was providing nearly five million school children in 1941, the majority of whom lived in urban areas, with at least one hot meal each day. Federal and local authorities split the cost, while the PTA, Junior League, American Women's Volunteer Service, the American Legion, and other community service organizations provided labor and equipment. There was no racial discrimination in the program—to the First Lady's satisfaction—and even in the poorest rural areas and inner-city slums breakfast was often available.

In 1942, proposed cuts in the federal budget threatened to reduce by half the number of children served. From her post in the OCD, Mrs. Roosevelt argued against the cuts and also urged communities to make up any deficits with local and state funds. Otherwise, and this was her real concern, the children would receive inadequate care, which in turn would lead to "poor citizens" within a few years.[64]

Eleanor Roosevelt's uncomplicated belief that something positive for urban youth might yet be derived from the holocaust of war permeated the thinking of her colleagues in the nonmilitary side of the OCD. In a speech in January 1942 to the Women's National Emergency Committee, Eloise Davison, an assistant director, outlined a nine-point program of civilian defense participation for women. The program was intended to heighten their perception as parents and consumers but also to transform them into vibrant participants in their communities. "We must rebuild the feeling of neighborliness now more than any time in recent years, for now more than ever we need our neighbors," she observed. The tenor of Miss Davison's remarks exhibited all the earmarks of Mrs. Roosevelt's inspirational influence.[65]

In other spheres related to urban youth and young adults, the

64. See Mrs. Roosevelt's radio address, Mar. 1, 1942, copy in Speech and Article File, ER Papers.

65. *New York Times,* Jan. 5, 1942; Eleanor Roosevelt, "American Women in the War," *Reader's Digest* 45 (Jan. 1944), 43–44.

First Lady employed her position in the OCD to further her aim of community renewal. Speaking to a radio symposium on the topic of "College Students and Civilian Defense," she emphasized that youth must be entrusted with civilian defense tasks that were both meaningful and responsible. Matching words with deeds, she dispatched instructions to OCD regional directors for the appointment of youth members to state and local defense boards and encouraged their registration with local volunteer offices.[66]

Without belittling their participation in scrap collection drives, the planting of victory gardens, and the like, the First Lady hoped to steer urban youth toward useful community projects that would endure beyond the war to enhance the quality of city living. She told a youth conference in October 1941 that the largest contribution they could make to civilian defense would be to insist on increased recreational facilities in their home communities, particularly in the larger defense cities. The volunteer program, she observed, was already having the effect of strengthening communities, especially as it influenced long-range planning for the postwar period.[67]

Even after she was no longer formally associated with the OCD, Mrs. Roosevelt's interest in community action was unflagging. At a special meeting of the Children's Bureau in the White House in February 1943, convened to explore the problem of juvenile delinquency and the community's responsibility for providing services, she offered practical suggestions from her observations of provisions for youth in Great Britain. Once again she noted that youth needed the satisfaction that could come only with participation in the community's war effort, and she urged that they be given the opportunity to fill service jobs previously held by adults, to plan and administer recreational projects, and to perform other tasks that enhanced community life.[68]

66. See "Active Role for Youth in OCD," *OCD Newsletter* 2 (Oct. 11, 1941), 1-2, copy in ER Papers.
67. *New York Times*, Oct. 24, 1941.
68. Howard W. Hopkirk, "A Critical Year for American Youth," *Child Welfare Bulletin* 22 (Feb. 1943), 8.

Besides assigning a vigorous, positive role in the community action program to the federal government, women, youth, and blacks, Mrs. Roosevelt adhered to the maxim that success breeds success. For her purposes, the District of Columbia was ideally situated to demonstrate the volunteer program in action: it was accessible, the seat of OCD's national headquarters, and because of its anomalous status as a federal city the usual inter-governmental disputes might be kept to a minimum. The opportunity to renew a community wracked by overcrowding, poor housing, slums, and racism was irresistible.

OCD initiated the community war program in the District on December 16, 1941. The Central Planning Committee, which reviewed local requests for Lanham Act construction funds, made a concerted and largely successful effort to mobilize all segments of the civilian population. Below the coordinating level, volunteer workers did the legwork, establishing committees for almost every purpose imaginable. Their record of accomplishment was truly impressive considering the years of federal neglect. The Child Care and Protection Committee investigated the need for day-care facilities for children of working mothers and submitted budgets to the Children's Bureau and Office of Community War Services of the Federal Security Agency (FSA) for the operation of two racially segregated centers for pre-school children. The Family Security Committee developed a program to meet welfare needs aggravated by wartime dislocations. The Health Committee conducted campaigns to eradicate venereal disease and prostitution and, with the cooperation of local physicians and public health officers, drafted plans to protect milk and food supplies in the event of enemy attack. The Nutrition Committee pursued its educational activities in keeping with the motto "U.S. Needs U.S. Strong."[69]

Similarly, the Consumer Interest and Recreation committees were busily engaged in their own work. The former had been established to educate consumers to stretch their dollars, conserve supplies and equipment, and fight inflation. To protect the consumer from profiteering and wartime exploitation, the members

69. For details see "Community War Programs," May 27, 1942, ER Papers.

kept a record of Washington's food prices since the start of the defense program in 1939, testified before Congress on rent controls, and scheduled lectures on consumer issues. The Recreation Committee approached the FSA for Lanham funds to construct recreational facilities, developed neighborhood recreation programs, and promoted community sings. In a city marked by stringent racial attitudes and swollen by a transient military and civilian population, the committee did well to persuade the Police Boys' Club to extend overnight sleeping facilities to black soldiers.[70]

In other equally effective ways, with results both tangible and psychological, the Division of Volunteer Participation reached out into this community to persuade residents that their participation was vital to the final defeat of the aggressor nations.[71] At the request of Cornelia (Leila) Pinchot, who was in charge of the OCD's morale-building program, the First Lady spoke to the members of the District's Emergency Food and Housing Corps, an organization that had set up billet posts throughout the city to take care of Washingtonians temporarily made homeless as a result of air raid or enemy action. While Mrs. Roosevelt did not seriously believe the city would be bombed, she nevertheless appreciated the value of publicity to the OCD's community volunteer program. Whenever her busy schedule permitted, she lent visible encouragement to such activities in the federal city.[72]

The results in the District demonstrated to the First Lady's satisfaction the value of democratic, civilian participation despite the nagging persistence of racial segregation, a problem that would take more time and energy to eradicate. But the experiment also revealed deficiencies in the operation of the community volunteer program which might limit its potential and endanger the New Deal's social programs in the postwar period. Enlisting the aid of Paul Kellogg, she lost no time in reorganizing the program to maximize efficiency.

The Division of Volunteer Participation was replaced by a

70. *Ibid.*
71. *Ibid.*
72. ER to Mrs. Gifford Pinchot, Oct. 19, 1942, in *ibid.*

69

Community Planning and Organization Division, a title that described the functions and permanent character of the agency most aptly. The new bureau functioned as a central clearinghouse for data concerning each community's problems and as a resource bank to which the community could turn for programs to meet specific needs. Below it was a new Program Making and Community Counseling Division to render practical assistance to each locality.[73] The members of this division were not intended to be specialists on any one urban problem but generalists who went into the communities, lived among the people, helped them to identify and frame solutions to their problems, and reported back to Washington gaps in federal services. No mere conductors of surveys, their presence in the community on a continuing basis hopefully would give the entire program sorely needed flexibility.[74]

Despite La Guardia's studied indifference to the volunteer program, Mrs. Roosevelt's efforts received a sympathetic reception from liberals and intellectuals. One OCD consultant, discussing the impact of the war on community life and organization, declared: "In communities—almost 14,000 communities—. . . we have seen painstaking efforts to develop an efficient machinery for community war service. . . . These are functions which will be equally important to community life in the afterwar years."[75] It remained, however, for the sociologist Louis Wirth to sum up the importance of the community volunteer program for America's cities. Addressing a group of social scientists at the University of Chicago in 1943, he declared: "If we are able to salvage even a part of the war-born capacity for concerted community action for the peace to come, the cities may thereby find the strength and the means whereby to deal with

73. Paul U. Kellogg to Francis Biddle, Jan. 13, 1942, and Kellogg to Judge Justine Wise Polier, Feb. 20, 1942, in *ibid.* See also McElroy, "Narrative Account of the OCD," ch. vi, 45, NARG 171, OCD Records.

74. Paul U. Kellogg to ER, Feb. 8, 1942, ER Papers.

75. David Cushman Coyle, " 'Belonging': To Revive the Old American Heritage of Community Spirit," *American City* 56 (Aug. 1941), 71–73; Kenneth L. Heaton, "The Impact of War on Community Life and Organization," July 12, 1943, NARG 171, OCD Records.

some of their most serious problems which have hitherto defied solution."[76]

The effort to use the OCD as a vehicle for establishing viable community action agencies throughout the United States fore-shadowed in some respects the VISTA program of a later Democratic administration. Unhappily for urban and rural dwellers alike, official indifference at the local and national levels, congressional conservatism, and politics permitted Eleanor Roosevelt neither the time nor the opportunity to organize such community services. Immediately after Pearl Harbor, for example, she flew to the West Coast, stopping from time to time to inspect the emergency preparations of local defense councils. She discovered to her dismay that practically nothing had been done about civilian defense in most cities. The mayor of Los Angeles had "to practically be beaten over the head to make him acknowledge that there is any danger," she confided to Joseph P. Lash.[77]

The volunteer program was in even worse shape. La Guardia's persistently casual treatment of it fostered apathy on the part of many local defense officials which precipitated a state of continuous tension in the relationship between himself and Mrs. Roosevelt. After her tour of Tacoma on December 13, 1941, she complained that La Guardia had managed to see all the protection people—police and fire department heads—in Portland, Tacoma, Seattle, and other communities but completely ignored the volunteer bureaus.[78]

Apart from bureaucratic apathy, the "politics-as-usual" attitude of the politicians made it impossible for the First Lady to bring her program to fruition in the form she envisioned. Ironically, she may have contributed to her own undoing when, shortly after assuming the directorship of volunteer activities,

76. Louis Wirth, "The Urban Community," in William F. Ogburn, ed., *American Society in Wartime* (Chicago, 1943), 75.

77. ER to Alice Huntington, Dec. 16, 1941; ER to Joseph P. Lash, Dec. 11, 13, 1941; "Mrs. Roosevelt's Report of Trip Through December 10th" [1941], ER Papers.

78. "Memorandum of Trip: Tacoma, Washington, Saturday, December 13, 1941"; ER to La Guardia, Feb. 18, 1942, in *ibid.*

she appointed Mayris Chaney, a rhythmic dancer and close personal friend, to teach dancing to children as a device to keep up their morale. She compounded this error by asking Melvyn Douglas, the motion picture star and advocate of liberal causes, to organize community entertainment programs. For their services, Miss Chaney was to have received a salary of $4,500, and Douglas, $8,000. The appointments were relatively insignificant matters in themselves, but congressional conservatives seized upon them as pegs on which to hang general criticism of La Guardia's administration and, in particular, Mrs. Roosevelt's community services activities, whose political potential they feared. The very persistence of the attacks long after all the principals had resigned from the OCD indicates that the critics' real target was not the agency per se but the President and past New Deal social programs.[79]

Conservatives were also haunted by the fear that the First Lady, by invoking the community ethos to bestir the less fortunate classes to action, would disturb the racial issue. In some respects community action and race relations were intertwined, especially in the larger metropolitan centers. A city like Atlanta, for example, did not want blacks participating in its civilian protection program or otherwise organizing in their communities, but Mrs. Roosevelt was equally bent on using the war emergency as a vehicle for advancing the cause of civil rights.[80] James M. Landis, the director of OCD after La Guardia, a man who held no brief for the First Lady's community activities, attested to her civil rights motive: "Now, Mrs. Roosevelt tackled that in her usual manner and naturally there were outcries against that, and a lot of people rallied to that banner," he recalled.[81]

As charges of communism, socialism, and fiscal irresponsibility clouded the air, several friends and political allies took up

79. ER to John B. Kelly, Oct. 27, 1941, *ibid.; Reduction of Non-Essential Federal Expenditures,* Hearings before the Joint Committee on Reduction of Non-Essential Expenditures, U.S. Congress, House and Senate, 77th Cong., 2d sess., pt. 3 (1942), 1062ff.; *First Supplemental National Defense Appropriation Bill for 1943,* Hearings before the Subcommittee of the Committee on Appropriations, U.S. House of Representatives, 77th Cong., 2d sess., pt. 1 (1943), 822–23, 851–54.

80. *Congressional Record,* 77th Cong., 2d sess., 88 (Jan. 9, 1942), 1147.

81. "The Reminiscences of James M. Landis," IV, 610, OHRO.

the cudgels on Mrs. Roosevelt's behalf. Lieutenant Governor Charles Poletti of New York wrote on February 26, 1942: "We realize that the majority of the persons attacking the work of the OCD which isn't directly related to civilian protection are fundamentally interested in curtailing, and if possible, destroying the many social advances made during recent years." But it was to no avail. Congressional hostility had terminated Mrs. Roosevelt's effectiveness as director of the volunteer program. La Guardia had already tendered his resignation as director, and on February 20, 1942, she followed suit. Her letter of resignation evinced a keen appreciation of political reality.[82]

Unhappily, the First Lady also succumbed to her emotions and allowed strong moral indignation to overwhelm her political sense, for she chose to prolong the controversy in her weekly radio broadcast two evenings later. She wanted the American people to know that the attacks upon the community volunteer program were part of the general opposition to the social measures of the New Deal that she deemed essential to the future vitality of urban and rural America. Her address of February 22, 1942, was intended to bring the conflict sharply into focus; but if she was expecting or hoping for a mass outpouring of public support, she was disappointed. Few citizens saw social, economic, or political issues from her highly moralistic perspective. Her error lay in a failure to understand that public indignation was directed toward expenditures that did not seem vital and toward a conception of wartime morale that, however appropriate to Britain, seemed highly unrealistic for America. To insist upon the involvement of every citizen, as Mrs. Roosevelt did, was expecting a nation removed from the terror of bombing and the horror of war to respond as if the enemy stood ready at the gate.[83]

James M. Landis, the new director of the OCD, proved to be unsympathetic to the community renewal program. Until his resignation in 1943, Landis focused his energies on rebuilding

82. Charles Poletti to ER, Feb. 26, 1942; ER to Charles H. Seaver, Mar. 4, 1942; James M. Landis to ER, Feb. 19, 1942, ER Papers.
83. For a copy of the address dated Feb. 22, 1942, see the Speech and Article File in *ibid.*

the agency's shattered prestige with Congress by turning back many of its civilian protection functions to the local community, perhaps more than were justified in the opinion of the socially activist Office of Community War Services. He purged the volunteer program of its community-social work orientation and fired its head, Jonathan Daniels. He also renamed the Community Planning and Organizational Division the Civilian War Services (CWS) bureau and tied it more closely to protective services. CWS, of course, could not ignore totally the spirit of community participation and civilian morale that the First Lady had encouraged, but these qualities were channeled into more narrow "passive defense" programs. The rehabilitative aspects of the community action plan were discouraged.[84]

By the end of 1943 CWS had established nearly 4,300 volunteer offices and also maintained files on five million volunteer workers. On the surface, it appeared that Landis was demonstrably more successful in running the OCD than his predecessor, but this interpretation is misleading. In June 1943, for example, Landis testified that huge gaps still persisted in the OCD's program, the worst deficiencies occurring in the large metropolitan centers. The difficulty there was not in securing personnel or funds, nor was it lack of patriotism; it was an organizational problem deriving from the urban condition—the same condition which Mrs. Roosevelt had perceived and which underlay her determination to reinculcate the spirit of community. "Persons in a big city by and large are not usually as active in government as persons in a smaller city; they do not have quite the same experience in community organization; they do not know their neighbors as well and they are not as anxious to work together in organized groups," Landis admitted.[85]

Moreover, an ill-conceived attempt in the fall of 1942 to exer-

84. "The Reminiscences of James M. Landis," IV, 315–16, OHRO; ER to Joseph P. Lash, July 26, 1942, and Landis to ER, Aug. 24, 1942, ER Papers; Dean Snyder to Charles P. Taft, Mar. 8, 1943, NARG 215, Records of the Office of Community War Services (OCWS), Reading File of Dean Snyder, Corr. for Mar.-Apr. 1943; Landis to FDR, Feb. 10, 1942, OF 161, FDR Papers.
85. *First Supplemental National Defense Appropriation Bill for 1943*, pt. 1, 803–4.

cise tighter central control over local defense councils ran afoul of municipal authorities. It also rekindled the fears of hostile congressmen who believed that the block leader program (wherein neighborhoods were divided into blocks, each having a leader responsible for that block's participation in civilian defense activities) was a cover for partisan politics or worse.[86] Representative J. William Ditter, Republican of Pennsylvania, likened the program to the Nazi party system, and recalled Mark Hanna's infamous boast that if he had a block system with a captain for every twenty people "he could elect anybody he wanted to." Even civil libertarians feared it might function as an information or spy network for the administration. Despite Landis's conciliatory stance, he never succeeded in erasing lingering doubts that the block leader program was another "social experiment."[87]

A Bureau of the Budget study in December 1943 further confirmed the agency's difficulties. The bureau reported that the effectiveness of local volunteer offices in recruiting and placing workers in civilian defense programs had deteriorated to a point where their discontinuance should be considered a definite possibility.[88] In only a few states and cities had the local councils demonstrated sufficiently broad interest, social awareness, or organizational capacity to institute the community renewal programs Eleanor Roosevelt had in mind. Chicagoans were among the leaders whose high aspirations were spelled out in ambitious plans for the postwar period. In April 1945 a select committee of local citizens and officials presented a report on the future of the OCD in the Chicago metropolitan area. Historically, the document is less important for the number of proposals that were actually brought to fruition than for its statement of philosophy. Its "tone" represented the most articulate enunciation

86. McElroy, "Narrative Account of the OCD," ch. vii, 6–8, NARG 215, OCD Records.

87. *National War Agencies Appropriation Bill for 1943,* Hearings before the Subcommittee of the Committee on Appropriations, 78th Cong., 1st sess., pt. 1 (1943), 359–68.

88. See Walter Lawes, "Confidential Memorandum Concerning OCD," Dec. 1943, 24 typewritten pages, Bureau of the Budget Library.

of the new community synthesis that Mrs. Roosevelt had been trying to achieve.[89]

The report was anchored in four assumptions that had come to dominate the thinking of reformers about the postwar city: (1) that a need for organized community cooperation would continue into the period of reconstruction and rehabilitation; (2) that the services of thousands of OCD volunteers offered both personal satisfaction and values to the community that should be perpetuated; (3) that an effective plan of community organization had to be based upon voluntary cooperation; and (4) that cooperation required decentralization and specialization of functions at the division, community, zone, and block levels.[90]

For all practical purposes, however, the community services program that Eleanor Roosevelt intended to serve the social outsiders, the "little people" as well as the prestigious, perished. Of course, discussion of it occurred from time to time after Mrs. Roosevelt departed the OCD, but the grand vision of building grass-roots organizations in each urban and rural community to carry on the progressive social welfare programs no longer had the moral urgency she brought to it.[91]

In December 1943, while Bernard Baruch was drafting his reconversion plan, John Martin, the OCD's interim director after Landis, presented the case for continuing Civilian War Services' activities. Martin argued that the need for imaginative community planning was urgent because the social and physical problems of postwar urban localities were certain to be acute, and remedial action would have to emanate from within the community. OCD's volunteer offices could serve as the nucleus of such community leadership. Whether Baruch gave this plea any consideration is uncertain, but in his report to the director

---

89. "Report of Steering Committee to Study the Future of OCD," Apr. 30, 1945. Mimeographed report of the Council of Social Agencies of Chicago and the Chicago Recreation Commission, NARG 215, OCWS Records. The War Area Reports file contains hundreds of similar reports from other cities throughout the nation.

90. *Ibid.*

91. See *National Defense Migration Hearings,* pt. 25, 9766–67.

of the Office of War Mobilization he made no mention of the community services program of CWS.[92]

OCD officials broached the subject once more in late November 1944, when Thomas Devine, chief of the Division of State and Local Cooperation, met personally with the President. During the conference, Devine argued for a continued federal presence in community service programs and noted that the wartime cooperation between the community councils and the OCD had proved to be "a major factor in improving the relationship between Federal, State and local governments."[93]

Rather than give Devine an affirmative commitment, Roosevelt resorted to evasive tactics. He passed Devine's memorandum to Budget Director Harold Smith for review, knowing full well that Smith was campaigning for a sharp cutback in the agency's functions and staff. Not unexpectedly, the Budget Bureau turned thumbs down on the OCD proposal, arguing that the gains the nation had achieved were the fruit of wartime patriotism rather than of the OCD's community action program. It also cited the considerable opposition to federal activity in this sphere emanating from the states and localities and concluded that the OCD did not offer "a solid foundation for a long-range program to improve Federal-State-local relations."[94]

Roosevelt fundamentally agreed with this assessment, although he was reluctant just then to liquidate the OCD's programs for fear the public would conclude prematurely that the war was over. He also hesitated to commit his administration to social experimentation and the onerous, long-term financing that continuation of the community action program necessarily entailed. Roosevelt's attitude undoubtedly was influenced by rising congressional pressures, spearheaded by Democratic Senator Harry F. Byrd of Virginia, to reduce nonessential fed-

92. Harold D. Smith to FDR, Sept. 28, 1943, Harold D. Smith Papers; McElroy, "Narrative Account of the OCD," ch. ix, 18–19, NARG 171, OCD Records.

93. Thomas Devine to FDR, Nov. 24, 1944, and FDR to ER, Jan. 8, 1945, OF 4422, FDR Papers.

94. Harold D. Smith to FDR, Dec. 9, 1944, *ibid.*

eral expenditures. In the end he supported the continuance of protective measures and effectively vetoed the community services program.[95]

This action reflected the President's perception of the political facts of life in 1944 wherever Congress and domestic spending were concerned. Roosevelt appreciated, perhaps far more than the First Lady, just how difficult it would be to sustain the spirit of sacrifice and cooperation after the crisis had passed. The decision was not arrived at lightly or precipitately but was the bitter fruit of long and hard deliberation. A letter written on February 28, 1944, to Lieutenant General (Ret.) William N. Haskill, the new head of the OCD, indicates that Roosevelt reaffirmed both the valuable contribution of the civilian protection program to the total war effort and his desire to continue it. Then he addressed himself to the future of the community services program. "The great task of aiding the States and people to organize in the greatest free, popular war enterprise has largely been accomplished," he concluded. "State and local governments are aware of their continuing tasks. More and more now we can depend upon State and local knowledge and initiative in doing the war job in which a whole nation has had to be trained. The Federal Government can now reduce its direction and expenditures."[96]

In retrospect, the experiment in civilian defense conditioned the war's impact on the cities and the cities' response to the war. The OCD and the state defense councils brought the machinery of government into the daily lives of urban dwellers on a scale previously unmatched.[97] The belief, nurtured by the civilian defense agencies, that urban dwellers had to do their share to bring about victory strengthened each civilian's sense of his own worth. The activities undertaken by urban dwellers often called for a high level of community cooperation and served an integrative function. But it is doubtful whether the values of sacri-

95. FDR to Herbert A. Olson, Oct. 23, 1944, OF 4929, *ibid.;* Harold D. Smith to FDR, Oct. 30, 1944, Harold D. Smith Papers.
96. McElroy, "Narrative Account of the OCD," ch. ix, 23, NARG 171, OCD Records.
97. A good brief discussion of the war's impact on society is contained in Polenberg, *War and Society,* ch. 5.

fice, self-denial, and cooperation that urban liberals such as Eleanor Roosevelt sought to inculcate as part of their goal of community rejuvenation ever gained full acceptance.

The difficulty of encouraging new forms of cooperative behavior in a country that had always put a premium on individualism should not be underestimated. Some urban dwellers never accepted either the wartime mores or the liberals' emphasis on community renewal, others accepted them as long as they imposed only slight inconveniences, and still others accepted them at first but reverted to more traditional ways of behaving as the war progressed. As the threat of invasion diminished, urban dwellers became more likely to look out for themselves and to lose interest in useful community projects. The more the balance shifted from public and collective to private and personal concerns, the less likely it became that the OCD would serve as the nucleus of postwar community revitalization.

III. Defense Housing: Future Slums or Planned Communities?

Decent and inexpensive housing for urban workers was as much a part of the defense establishment of the nation as were cantonments for the armed forces or factory buildings for crafting the tools of war. Nonetheless, housing reformer Charles Abrams was forced to admonish the *New York Times* in June 1940 for omitting housing in a series of editorials devoted to national defense preparations. He reminded the readers of the experience of World War I, when a housing shortage in the urban-industrial centers nearly threatened to disrupt labor efficiency and production schedules.[1] In spite of such warnings and the plain lessons of the earlier conflict, the Roosevelt administration floundered for nearly eighteen months before it was at last able to coordinate a national housing program with industrial production.[2]

The first steps in formulating a defense housing policy were taken in the spring of 1940, when the President assigned the task to the newly formed National Defense Advisory Commission (NDAC). The commission turned for assistance to the Central Housing Committee, an intergovernmental body which submitted on June 14, 1940, a lengthy analysis of probable wartime housing needs. The committee concluded its report with a recommendation that the President appoint a "coordinator" to expedite implementation of the policy; accordingly, Roosevelt appointed Charles Forest Palmer to the post on July 18, 1940.[3]

A native of Grand Rapids, Michigan, Palmer had attended

1. *New York Times,* June 5, 1940.
2. "Report of the Committee on Defense Housing, Central Housing Committee," June 14, 1940, National Archives (NA), Record Group (RG) 207, Records of the Division of Defense Housing Coordination (DDHC).
3. Central Housing Committee to U.S. Council of National Defense, Advisory Commission, June 14, 1940, Franklin D. Roosevelt Papers, Franklin D. Roosevelt Library (FDRL), Hyde Park, N.Y.

Dartmouth College and served as a cavalry officer in World War I. After returning to civilian life, he founded his own real estate company in Atlanta. During the depression of the 1930s, when most realtors strenuously opposed federal entry into the housing field, Palmer gained a reputation as one of the leading proponents of federal intervention to reclaim slums. Unlike other realtors, he and his associates assembled parcels of land in downtown Atlanta, tore down the dilapidated structures, and erected a federally financed project for two thousand tenants. Techwood Village was one of the first public housing projects in the nation to receive federal assistance. It demonstrated that government and private enterprise could cooperate to provide decent and inexpensive housing.[4]

Although many individuals and agencies had a hand in drafting the housing policy of World War II, perhaps none was as influential as Miles L. Colean, a former assistant administrator in the Federal Housing Agency (FHA).[5] Colean's report entitled *Housing an Industrial Army,* a confidential statement of defense housing policy produced for the Twentieth Century Fund, identified the essential objectives of a well-integrated housing policy as being (1) to assure an adequate supply of dwelling units conveniently located near the points of industrial production, and (2) to protect against the future social costs that a rapidly accelerating demand for housing might impose upon cities so affected. The first objective was predicated on the belief that limiting nonessential migration during the period of mobilization and war would create fewer special housing requirements and necessitate fewer readjustments afterward. The second objective flowed from the first and was not really separable in Colean's report: the greater utilization of resources at hand would result in less delay and expenditure in meeting wartime needs and minimize future loss and waste.[6] Such a policy would guide federal activity primarily toward the facilitation of private

4. See Palmer's obituary in the *New York Times,* May 17, 1973.
5. Miles L. Colean, *Housing an Industrial Army,* unpub. report, July 20, 1940, NARG 69, Records of the Public Works Reserve (PWR).
6. *Ibid.* Colean, however, recognized that government-sponsored public housing would still be needed for low-income defense workers.

housing operations, avoiding wherever possible the need for direct governmental intervention. In this way, the war would neither weaken nor destroy the institutions of private enterprise.[7]

Colean's recommendations served as the basis of Palmer's actions, although from the outset the latter became the focal point of controversy arising from bureaucratic jealousies and his own single-minded determination to accelerate construction without regard to the future cost it exacted from the New Deal's housing program.[8] The bureaucratic infighting that engulfed defense housing was encouraged both by its organization and its daily operation, and this in turn weakened the position of housing reformers in the immediate postwar period.

As outlined by the President, Palmer's assignment was to determine the housing requirements of congested defense centers and to mesh the daily operations of nine or more federal agencies having an interest in the program.[9] The difficulty was that the President's executive order had separated responsibility from authority. According to the procedure agreed upon, participating federal agencies would conduct the initial locality surveys to ascertain employment requirements, current rates of construction, vacancies, and rentals. They would submit the raw data to the Analysis Division of the Division of Defense Housing Coordination (DDHC), which would use them as the basis for writing up its own tentative Locality Program Report (LPR). The LPRs confirmed the existence of a housing shortage and ascertained the permanency of the need in relation to defense activity and in-migration; they also suggested the type and cost range of additional dwelling units and a formula for providing them. The LPRs were then resubmitted to the agencies for revision. Only then did Palmer transmit the final recommendations to the President, who exercised final approval of all new defense housing. The financial allotments for construction were controlled not by Palmer but by the administrator of the Federal Works Agency (FWA), John Carmody, a tired veteran of the New

7. *Ibid.*
8. See "Housing Impasse: Coordinator Palmer Feeling Pinch of Federal Agency Rivalries," *Business Week* (Feb. 15, 1941), 30–32.
9. *Ibid.*

Deal wars. The letting of contracts for construction was handled through any one of the quasi-independent federal agencies.[10]

On paper, the organization of the program was very logical: the Chief Executive at the apex of the administrative hierarchy, beneath him the Defense Advisory Commission, and then the FWA with its Division of Defense Housing Coordination, from which the lines of control and responsibility radiated out to the nine great bureaucratic workshops along Pennsylvania Avenue. In practice, however, the system had a delicate balance wheel requiring all the parts to mesh smoothly in order to keep it functioning. This was the element missing during the period of mobilization and preparation for war. Palmer was something less than a "housing czar," but it was not altogether clear whether he was more than a traffic cop. Roosevelt's reluctance to define more exactly the extent of the coordinator's authority, his penchant for secrecy within the administration, and his deliberate assignment of overlapping jurisdiction to competing bureaucracies indicated not only his own ambivalence toward the administrative canons of unification, coordination, and integration but also his determination to keep control of all important aspects of mobilization.[11]

The price the nation paid for both the disregard of customary administrative procedures and the bureaucratic infighting that resulted from it was high. Planning and construction of defense housing lagged until well after American entry into the war. The need for good inexpensive housing—which might have served hundreds of thousands of families from the slums, as well as returning veterans—went largely unfilled.[12]

The bureaucratic clashes that kept New Deal liberals, realtors, builders and mortgage bankers, and congressional friends and foes in a continual state of turmoil took on a larger importance.[13] The coordinator's eagerness to carve out a dis-

10. Jacob Crane, "Defense Housing Coordination," Nov. 6, 1941, NARG 207, DDHC Records.

11. "Whose Fault?" *Time* 38 (Oct. 13, 1941), 88–91.

12. Charles Abrams, *The Future of Housing* (New York, 1946), 301.

13. "Informal Notes of the Executive Session of the Commission," Jan. 14, 1941, Records of the National Defense Advisory Commission (NDAC), FDRL; "Minutes of the

tinctive role for the DDHC collided with the vested interests of the U.S. Housing Authority (USHA) and the public housing lobby. For, unlike Eleanor Roosevelt and the public service bureaucrats in the Office of Community War Services, Palmer had declared that sociology was no part of his job.[14] He refused to concede that the federal government still needed to build inexpensive housing for low-income defense workers—housing which would not cut into the private builders' market but would serve in the postwar period as the nucleus of new neighborhoods and communities.[15] This insensitivity made it inevitable that defense housing would be transformed into a political problem involving fundamental issues of New Deal policy.

To the dedicated housing reformers of the thirties and early forties, public housing was a humanitarian program to alleviate the socially pathological behavior associated with slums and urban poverty.[16] They maintained that public housing would elevate the aspirations of the residents, transform them into industrious and useful citizens, and inculcate in them the basic ideals of democracy. It would also serve to cushion the shock of postwar unemployment.[17]

The importance of public housing to urban liberals both as an instrument of national economic stabilization and as a strategy for slum clearance is vital to an understanding of the opposition to Palmer on the part of USHA administrator Nathan Straus and the public housing lobby. For they recognized that the decision to move to a war economy, involving as it did industrial mobilization, migration, and full employment, had rendered public housing no longer vital as an antidepression tool. Indeed, the growing scarcity of building materials and labor in 1940 had virtually halted the slum clearance and public housing programs.

Regional Coordinators' Meeting," Apr. 28–29, 1941, NARG 215, Records of the Office of Community War Services (OCWS).

14. *New York Times,* Nov. 8, 1940.

15. Abrams, *The Future of Housing,* 301.

16. See Robert Moore Fisher, *Twenty Years of Public Housing* (New York, 1959), and Timothy L. McDonnell, S.J., *The Wagner Housing Act* (Chicago, 1957), esp. ch. 3.

17. Report of the President's Committee on Urban Housing, *A Decent Home* (Washington, D.C., 1968), 54; National Resources Planning Board, *Housing, the Continuing Problem* (Washington, D.C., 1940), *passim.*

Yet Straus and his supporters were convinced that an unfulfilled need still existed for housing low-income workers, a need which would intensify after the war. They also were afraid that Palmer's decision to rely upon the private builders while ignoring the USHA would deliver the New Deal's housing program into the hands of its enemies. Congressional conservatives and their allies—the builders' and realtors' associations—might well use the war as an excuse to scuttle all programs for postwar public housing.[18]

Thus the issue was joined. The only way to sustain the New Deal's low-income housing program into the postwar period, when community revitalization through slum clearance and the provision of decent inexpensive housing could go forward, was to give it fresh impetus by expanding public housing's role in the defense emergency beyond what the DDHC or the congressional conservatives seemed willing to allow.[19]

The combination of hardheaded realism and idealism brought the reformers into open conflict with Palmer, who was determined to abide by the President's instructions to build and locate defense housing as expeditiously as possible. An urgent meeting of the Central Housing Committee on August 28, 1940, illustrated the tensions and conflicting goals that threatened to strangle the defense housing program in its infancy. Besides Palmer and USHA Administrator Nathan Straus, others present at the meeting included presidential assistant Lowell Mellett, Ormond E. Loomis of the Federal Home Loan Bank Board (FHLBB), M. Max Dunning of PBA, Abner Ferguson of FHA, and George B. Williams representing the Reconstruction Finance Corporation. After some preliminary remarks, Mellett called upon Palmer to review the steps the administration had taken to date to flesh out the housing program. One by one, Palmer ticked off the things that had been done.[20] He reminded his col-

18. Charles Abrams, "Must Defense Wreck Housing?" *The Nation* 151 (Oct. 19, 1940), 359–61; *New York Times,* Aug. 17, 18, 1940.
19. *New York Times,* Feb. 8, Mar. 24, Apr. 24, Sept. 15, 16, 27, Nov. 14, 20, Dec. 6, 1940.
20. "Transcript of the Meeting of Aug. 28, 1940," NARG 207, Records of the Housing and Home Finance Corporation (HHFC).

leagues that the President himself had affirmed the decision to rely upon private builders to supply the bulk of defense housing, noting that Roosevelt had been quite emphatic that the federal agencies should supplement and not displace private enterprise. This was the principle which dictated that the USHA should receive funds only for projects in communities where low-rent housing would be needed after the emergency; the PBA's funds were for homes, trailers, quonset huts, and the like that would be torn down after the crisis.[21]

But as *Time* accurately observed afterward, "The question of whether some of the defense housing can be 'salvaged' after the emergency to provide permanent low-rent housing" was at the heart of the controversy.[22] The USHA, with its experienced staff and proven record of building good housing units quickly, was fighting for the integrity of its slum clearance program in the postwar world.[23] This was the basis of Straus's protest against the decision to allocate the lion's share of funds to the PBA for shelters that could afterward be converted to public housing.[24] It also explained his other grievances against Palmer, such as employing the DDHC to manage housing projects in disregard of the existing management unit within the USHA and instructing the staff to plan projects with local housing authorities in Pittsburgh and other cities without reference to the USHA.

These actions over a period of months formed in Straus's judgment a pattern of conduct designed to eliminate the USHA and gut the national low-rent housing program.[25] Not surprisingly, then, the meeting of the Central Housing Committee degenerated into an acrimonious exchange between the public housing administrator and the coordinator. What distressed Straus particularly was Palmer's unwillingness to clarify public housing's role in the defense program, a sure sign that he was

21. *Ibid.*

22. "Gothic Gazebo," *Time* 29 (Jan. 5, 1942), 29.

23. Nathan Straus, "Proposal for a Program of Defense Housing Which Will Produce Results," Dec. 26, 1940, FDR Papers, Office File (OF) 4240–a, FDRL.

24. "Whose Fault?" 88–91.

25. *New York Times,* Dec. 4, 1941.

bending to conservative pressure.[26] Straus warned his colleagues that USHA would not surrender without a fight and that he personally would seek out congressional and liberal friends of the public housing program.[27]

Confronted with an impasse that threatened further to delay new construction and bring down the wrath of Congress and the President, Lowell Mellett and one or two others interrupted in a desperate effort to work out a compromise between the two adversaries. Ormond Loomis reassured Straus that the coordinator's mandate was narrowly limited to defense housing and did not encompass the sphere of postwar public and private housing. There would be room enough for both to operate then, Loomis observed. He added that the FHLBB had given moral support to the USHA's service to slum dwellers in the past, but he cautioned: "The Defense Housing Coordinator's task is a complicated one and will be more difficult if the public housing opposition, due to misunderstandings, blocks his program in any city or areas and if it makes it difficult for the private organizations and the Government to cooperate with the USHA."[28]

Despite this warning, compromise was out of the question, but in any event the pendulum of support within the administration was swinging away from Straus and the USHA. Bureaucrats like Mellett and Loomis wanted to avoid another donnybrook between public housing advocates and the builders' associations and were reacting to newspaper and congressional criticism of the housing program. They refused to confront the fundamental question that Straus's protests had raised: What would be the impact of their actions upon the postwar future of the New Deal's slum clearance program and, in essence, the whole movement for community revitalization?

However reluctantly, administration officials were willing to write off the USHA and the slum clearance program in exchange for votes on other legislation. In Congress, fiscal conservatives

26. "Transcript of the Meeting of Aug. 28, 1940," NARG 207, HHFC Records.
27. *Ibid.*
28. *Ibid.*

like Senator Harry F. Byrd of Virginia, anti-New Deal Democrats, and Republicans from rural constituencies were tight-fisted over appropriations for defense housing. They did not want the money channeled to the USHA and the big cities for "socialistic experiments," and they intended to make certain that public housing would not emerge after the war to compete with private enterprise.[29] Congressman Fritz G. Lanham, Democrat of Texas, the chairman of the House Committee on Public Buildings and Grounds, introduced legislation which stipulated that defense housing units had to be of a temporary nature and demolished or sold at auction as soon as the war was over.

Meanwhile, the program in virtually every state was on the verge of paralysis and collapse. This was the somber conclusion of Addison G. Foster, a staff member of the DDHC, and it was confirmed by innumerable press accounts.[30] In Ohio and Texas, housing officials criticized the DDHC for being remote, insensitive to local problems, and unwilling to consult with local housing agencies. In Virginia, the federal bureaucracies were bidding against one another for sites and construction contracts.[31] At Willow Run, the much publicized "Bomber City" located twenty-eight miles from the center of Detroit, local builders and realtors protested that federal financing would bring centralized control of the housing industry, while townspeople feared that newcomers would upset the political status quo. In Detroit, estimates of housing need were closely tied to automobile production. Although the housing authority reported vacancies of 2 percent and 0 percent in key industrial areas, the local CIO organizer reported that private builders were "not going to build any further than the actual purchase market goes."[32] The story was repeated elsewhere with local variations.

The threatened collapse of the vital shipbuilding industry in Newport News, Virginia, highlighted the particular plight of black

29. Entries of Sept. 14, Oct. 25, 1940, John Ihlder Diaries, John Ihlder Papers, FDRL; "Congress in Defense Housing Snarl," *Business Week* (Sept. 14, 1940), 20.

30. Addison G. Foster to Charles F. Palmer, June 13, 1941, NARG 207, DDHC Records.

31. *Ibid.*

32. *Ibid.*

defense workers. The largest employer in this Tidewater city, located on the lower James-York peninsula, was the Newport News Shipbuilding and Dry Dock Company, which in 1940–41 held naval defense contracts worth half a billion dollars. Defense officials were alarmed because the company's employment policy was to maintain a ratio of two-thirds white workers to one-third black, roughly corresponding to the demographic composition of the region. With the coming of mobilization, the company added 3,000 blacks to the payroll in all categories of employment, thereby raising the total to 5,000 out of an overall work force of 17,000. Because the local labor supply was exhausted, the company anticipated hiring an additional 1,000 black in-migrants, the only obstacle being the shortage of housing.[33]

The situation with regard to decent living quarters for black workers within the city limits could only be described as calamitous. The director of the Newport News housing authority told Robert R. Taylor, Palmer's assistant in charge of housing black workers, that "overcrowding and doubling up have reached an appalling stage." Statistics attested to the plight of black workers and the failure of the DDHC to move promptly to rectify their distress: there were no longer any vacant dwellings of minimally acceptable standards to house blacks; black rentals in the six months ending June 1941 had advanced 25 percent; in the same period, only two segregated public housing projects containing 400 units had opened; between 1939 and 1941, private enterprise had constructed only 150 homes for sale to blacks, and practically none for rental. The chairman of the Hampton Roads Defense Council emphasized to Taylor the urgency of making available additional (segregated) housing units. And like USHA administrator Nathan Straus, he too preferred homes of a permanent nature "so as to be used for a lasting improvement of housing conditions in the city."[34]

Racism, greed, indolence, bureaucratic confusion, and the fear of federal usurpation of local authority were the barriers to

33. For the situation of Negroes in Newport News see Robert R. Taylor to Charles W. Farrier, July 9, 1941, and "Travel Report of Interviews of Robert R. Taylor," July 9, 1941, in *ibid.*
34. Ben Amidon, "Negroes and Defense," *Survey Graphic* 30 (June 1941), 320.

an integrated program coordinating housing with war production. A large number of Americans, as late as the summer of 1941, were unwilling to make the individual sacrifices that a total commitment to national defense implied. Perhaps this was because Roosevelt still did not ask it, and the people wanted to believe his 1940 campaign pledge to keep the nation out of war. Perhaps, also, the Commander-in-Chief had failed in his efforts to educate Americans to the true dimensions of the fascist threat to national security. Wherever the explanation lay, by refusing to erect a strong organization for defense housing from the instant he ordered an acceleration in the production of military hardware, Roosevelt ensured that the DDHC would not maximize the output of defense housing during the critical one-and-a-half years prior to Pearl Harbor.[35]

By the end of 1940, the White House could no longer afford to ignore the delays in construction without risking a major revolt in Congress. On January 7, 1941, the President, acting by administrative fiat, terminated the Defense Advisory Commission and transferred its functions to the newly established Office of Emergency Management (OEM). Four days later Roosevelt made what appeared to be a decisive move to resolve the housing crisis when he issued Executive Order 8632 establishing the DDHC as an independent entity within the umbrella of the OEM.[36]

The reorganization order provoked a stormy reaction within the bureaucracy. Nathan Straus was predictably furious because the executive order had omitted any mention of the USHA. After cataloguing the USHA's accomplishments for Samuel I. Rosenman, the President's close political adviser, he sighed: "Of what use is this—and a hundred other achievements of the USHA— if all of the carefully built up edifice is to be ignored at the time when it could be of the greatest service?"[37] Others, whose prestige was only tangentially affected by the bureaucratic re-

---

35. See James M. Burns, *Roosevelt: The Soldier of Freedom* (New York, 1970), 54, 355, 466.
36. Harold D. Smith to FDR, Jan. 11, 1941, FDR Papers, OF 4240–a, FDRL.
37. "Informal Notes of Executive Session of the Commission," Jan. 14, 1941, NDAC Records; Nathan Straus to FDR, Jan. 14, 1941, FDR Papers, OF 4240–a; Straus to Samuel I. Rosenman, Feb. 7, 1941, Samuel I. Rosenman Papers, FDRL.

shuffling, recalled the experience of World War I to justify support of the President's action. "It was a necessary step if we are to get anywhere, but it calls for a strong man," observed John Ihlder, the director of the District of Columbia's Alley Dwelling Authority.[38]

The reorganization order had not really clarified the situation. The President still was unwilling to relinquish control over mobilization to a housing "czar"; he had merely shifted the DDHC from one bureaucratic domain to another, giving Palmer the illusion but not the substance of independence. In fact, although it was not immediately apparent, the coordinator was actually more vulnerable as a result of the reorganization.[39]

Palmer recognized that his effectiveness depended upon his ability to overcome bureaucratic sniping and enlist the cooperation of both the public housing lobby and private builders' associations. For this reason, he had instructed his two most trusted aides, Jacob Crane and Herbert S. Colton, to conduct a thorough review of past actions as a guide to a new, more workable policy. The report, largely written by Colton, concluded that existing legislative tools were inadequate to meet present and future defense housing needs and that in the circumstances the best the coordinator could expect was to ameliorate rather than to resolve the housing shortage. Anticipating the worst, Colton advised Palmer to protect his flanks by alerting Congress and the administration. He urged the coordinator to request complete jurisdiction over all phases of the housing program, especially priorities over building materials and labor. If Palmer failed to receive the necessary authority, Colton reasoned, he could hardly be held accountable for any deficiencies that persisted.[40]

The housing program had reached a critical juncture. Colton had doubts that the Lanham Act and other emergency legislation could produce the volume of defense housing that was required.[41] He therefore proposed a solution that ran directly

38. Entry of Jan. 13, 1941, John Ihlder Diaries, John Ihlder Papers, FDRL.
39. Jacob Crane, "Defense Housing Coordination," Nov. 6, 1941, NARG 207, DDHC Records.
40. Herbert S. Colton to Charles F. Palmer, Apr. 18, 28, 1941, in *ibid.*
41. *Ibid.*

91

counter to the philosophy and program advocated by the USHA and the public housing lobby.

Colton's solution was predicated on two assumptions: (1) that there existed a very tenuous connection between defense housing and the New Deal's construction of permanent low-cost public housing as embodied in the Wagner Act of 1937, and (2) that congressional hostility to public housing was so intense that the coordinator could not afford to rely upon the USHA. The kind of carefully planned and executed housing advocated by the USHA was expensive and time consuming and required quantities of raw materials in short supply, an argument not wholly borne out by the facts in 1940 and 1941, as housing reformers noted. In lieu of public housing, Colton recommended a huge expansion of the mobile emergency shelter program utilizing prefabrication and other technical advances as the quickest and cheapest methods of bringing shelter to defense workers. He coupled this with a policy of more lucrative financial incentives to private enterprise to build in congested production areas, along with closer control over the FWA's financial allotments. The last recommendation, so essential to the centralization of the program, eventually precipitated a bitter fight between Palmer and Carmody, culminating in the latter's resignation.[42]

While his staff was recommending centralization and tighter control over the program, forces outside government were pulling Palmer in other directions, proposing solutions to the crisis that were in some cases farfetched and in others designed to advance the special interests of their sponsors. Perhaps the best-known and most articulate group was the National Committee on the Housing Emergency, Inc. (NCHE), which had very strong ties to the public housing movement. The NCHE was organized in early 1941 under the chairmanship of Dorothy Rosenman, the wife of presidential adviser Samuel I. Rosenman, to serve as a bridge between the wartime and postwar periods of housing, a nucleus around which those interested in community revitaliza-

42. Abrams, *The Future of Housing,* 301; Robert H. Jackson to John Carmody, Sept. 27, 1941, and FDR to Carmody, Oct. 1, 8, 1941, John Carmody Papers, FDRL; Carmody to FDR, Oct. 7, 1941, FDR Papers, OF 4240-a, FDRL.

tion could rally. The NCHE presented and appraised new methods in planning, financing, land assessment, and construction as part of its goal of rehousing America.[43]

It was in anticipation of these activities that the NCHE had addressed itself in June 1941 to the specific problem of sheltering low-income migrant defense workers. Its report, *A Program for Action on Housing for Defense Workers and Families of Low Income,* came down hard on the failure of federal officials under Palmer to work more closely with local housing authorities. It conceded that Washington must have the ultimate responsibility for determining the existence and extent of the housing need but asserted that truly cooperative federalism involved local public and private participation at each stage. Critical of the DDHC's centralizing tendencies, the NCHE also asserted that the local authorities were in the most favorable position to fit defense housing into the physical pattern of the community because they possessed "the requisite knowledge of the community; it is they who have the continuing responsibilities of the local administration."[44]

The report also sought to formulate a modus vivendi between the public and private housing interests that would continue into the postwar era. It asserted that the Wagner Act of 1937 had already delineated their respective spheres of operation. Public housing authorities were only permitted to furnish shelter to low-income families for whom private enterprise could not provide economically profitable rentals. There was no reason why the same general principle should not apply to defense housing.[45]

Running fuguelike throughout the report was the reformers' classic argument: that wartime housing need not create an intolerable community burden but might even become a valuable asset for neighborhood and community revitalization. Before this could occur, however, federal and local housing officials and

43. "National Conference on Postwar Housing," Mar. 8–10, 1944, Dorothy Rosenman Papers, Columbia Univ., New York.

44. National Committee on the Housing Emergency, Inc., *A Program for Action on Housing for Defense Workers and Families of Low Income* (New York, 1941), 2, 8.

45. *Ibid.,* 6.

public and private enterprise would have to cooperate with one another. Only then could the program serve as the cornerstone of a new community synthesis.[46]

While acknowledging the difficulty of transforming wartime shelters into quasipermanent residences, the report nonetheless recommended that the National Resources Planning Board (NRPB) conduct a full investigation into the postwar disposition of defense housing. The NCHE recorded its opposition to wholesale demolition of the structures, as conservatives demanded, preferring to employ some of the housing for neighborhood and community renewal. This, of course, was the viewpoint espoused by the public housing lobby; it was also the view to which the builders' associations had strenuously objected, fearing that government competition would drive them out of business.[47]

Where the choice was between centralization and greater reliance on local housing authorities, between near total dependence on the private builders and an enlarged role for public housing, between immediate short-term and long-range national housing goals, Palmer in every instance selected the former option.[48] He read the past difficulties of the DDHC as stemming from his own indecisiveness rather than, as critics charged, his efforts to control every aspect of the housing program. Hence he decided to act more firmly and with greater authority, which meant that the DDHC would exercise greater jurisdiction over constituent federal agencies—centralizing the flow of housing data and securing priority control over building materials from the OPM. The DDHC would also "tell" the local housing authorities where it intended to build and would forge cooperative links between government and private enterprise by removing the public housing threat. Discouraging migration to the industrial cities, relying instead upon local labor (single and married women with children, blacks, and Chicanos), and as-

46. *Ibid.,* 1.
47. *Ibid.,* 7.
48. Dean Snyder to Mrs. Samuel I. Rosenman, Nov. 3, 1942, NARG 215, OCWS Records.

94

signing housing priorities only to defense workers were part and parcel of the coordinator's new approach.[49]

Responding to the plight of black workers, Palmer issued a policy statement on January 28, 1941, which declared unequivocally that "equitable provision [must] be made for Negro defense workers." He appointed Robert R. Taylor, manager of Chicago's Rosenwald Negro Housing Project, to oversee their housing. Taylor was instructed to promote friendly contacts among enlightened and responsible white community leaders and organizations in anticipation of the time when the DDHC would have to locate interracial defense housing in formerly all-white neighborhoods.[50]

Palmer's decision to buck the traditional development of the federal housing program on the racial question was a matter of conviction and expediency. If production could be stepped up by providing more and better shelter for black workers, then the DDHC had an obligation to make such housing available. It would also quiet urban liberals who were pressuring the administration to open both jobs and defense housing to blacks. Demands in the one area fueled demands in the other. Thus Robert Weaver, a member of the so-called "black cabinet," reminded Taylor of the President's executive order of June 1941, which outlawed discrimination in defense employment. He urged the DDHC to pursue an interracial housing policy even more flexible than the one Palmer had initiated.[51]

Congressional pressure to break the logjam of construction also facilitated Palmer's decision to exercise tighter control over all aspects of the housing program. Not only did the legislature move unusually quickly in the first quarter of 1941 to strengthen financing of new construction, but it also went to considerable lengths to manifest displeasure toward the USHA and the public

49. Crane, "Policy on Defense Housing for Fiscal 1942," Nov. 25, 1941, NARG 207, DDHC Records.

50. Charles F. Palmer to Staff, Jan. 28, 1941, Ira Reid to Collis Stocking, Apr. 28, 1941, and Robert R. Taylor to Roy Wilkins, June 4, 1941, in *ibid.* See also Palmer to FDR, Feb. 1, 1941, FDR Papers, OF 4240–a, FDRL.

51. Robert Weaver to Robert Taylor, Sept. 24, 1941, NARG 207, DDHC Records.

housing lobby.[52] Palmer took his cue from Congress and assumed that private enterprise would shoulder the burden of the new defense construction and work with the administration to avert a postwar economic slump.[53]

Altogether, in the nineteen months of industrial mobilization, more housing had come into being than the total production before coordination. Congress voted $1,302.5 million outright in appropriations for defense housing and authorized an additional $300 million for special FHA insurance. Translated into human terms, the coordinator's office used the public funds to accommodate over 3,000 families and close to 8,300 single workers. In the month of December 1941, housing completions reached a peak of 10,000, well above the monthly rate of 6,000 homes for the fourteen-month period from January 1941 to February 1942. The USHA, which had converted its slum clearance projects to war worker use, supplied over 45,363 units.[54] More important than the number of public housing units was the stimulus which the DDHC had given to private enterprise. Using federal monies, the builders' associations produced a greater volume of privately constructed defense housing than for any comparable period since 1928. Half the privately built homes were selling for $6,000 or less, which indicated to Palmer that private enterprise was indeed capable of building within the price range of the working class, and that "the National Defense Program was not (being) impeded by lack of housing."[55]

Besides the numbers of new houses, the DDHC also nurtured important advances in urban building technology. The most

52. See Colton to Palmer, Apr. 18, 1941, in *ibid.;* "Stop-gap Housing," *Business Week* (Mar. 22, 1941), 32.

53. Crane, "Defense Housing Coordination," Nov. 6, 1941, NARG 207, DDHC Records.

54. "Report to the President Re: Defense Housing Coordination, July 21, 1940–February 24, 1942," FDR Papers, OF 4240–a, FDRL; United States Congress, House of Representatives, *Building the American City: Report of the National Commission on Urban Problems to the Congress and President of the United States,* House Doc. 91, 91st Cong., 1st sess. (1968), 130.

55. "Report to the President Re: Defense Housing Coordination," FDRL; and "Role of Federal Housing Administration and Federal Home Loan Bank Board in Defense Housing Program," Jan. 2, 1941, and Palmer to Staff, Dec. 4, 1941, NARG 207, DDHC Records.

highly publicized was the prefabrication of practical demountable homes. Less spectacularly, the need to conserve strategic materials such as copper impelled the DDHC to collaborate with other agencies in drafting a new plumbing code that soon became standard throughout the home-building industry. Technology was being conscripted to fulfill Palmer's pledge that war production would not be hampered by a shortage of housing.[56]

Others, however, were less sanguine. They questioned both the DDHC's use of statistics and Palmer's belief that private enterprise would be able to shoulder the burden over the long haul. Herman B. Byer, a housing expert for the Bureau of Labor Statistics, cautioned against overconfidence in relying upon private enterprise to satisfy housing demand. Analyzing construction statistics for 1941, he told an emergency gathering of the National Public Housing Conference that the provision of a large volume of new housing did not itself solve the problem of sheltering war workers. "The supply must be made available at prices and on terms within the reach of war workers." In December 1941 fully half of the 5.6 million wage earners in the six major groups of manufacturing industries most closely tied to defense production earned less than $37 per week, *including* overtime and bonuses! This group was hard put to afford the $6,000 homes. Byer predicted a shortage of two million homes in urban defense areas unless public housing took up the slack.[57]

Moreover, housing accommodations for black defense workers continued to deteriorate as the volume of their migration increased. The chances of their being integrated into the federal public housing program, which was the hope of Robert Weaver, Ira Reid, Floyd Reeves, and other members of the "black cabinet," diminished. Indeed, the coordinator's efforts to open up white ethnic neighborhoods (predominantly Polish Catholic) to black in-migrants both in Buffalo and Detroit were precipitating racial violence.[58] The opposition in several instances was organized or led by the local parish priest, prompt-

56. "Report to the President Re: Defense Housing Coordination," FDRL.
57. "Shortage of 2,000,000 Homes for War Effort is Foreseen," *Public Housing Progress* 8 (Mar. 1942), 1-2.
58. Robert Weaver to Robert Taylor, Sept. 24, 1941, NARG 207, DDHC Records.

ing Lester B. Granger of the National Urban League to write to the bishop of the Buffalo diocese to intervene.[59]

A local housing official reported that a similar situation existed in Detroit.[60] A letter to Palmer from one pastor, whose church was located in the city's "Seven-Mile-Fenelon" district, shows how the fear of locating an interracial defense housing project in a neighborhood could precipitate community-wide panic: "This, my dear Mr. Palmer, would mean utter ruin for many people who have mortgaged their homes to the F.H.A., and not only that, but it would jeopardize the safety of many of our white girls, as no colored people live closely by. Lastly, it would ruin the neighborhood, one that could be built up into a fine residential section. It is the sentiment of all people residing within the vicinity to object against this project in order to stop race riots in the future."[61] To defuse this potentially explosive situation, the DDHC turned for assistance to the executive director of the Catholic Conference on Family Life. His solution was to obtain information about the proposed sites of black housing in advance so that he might ask the bishop of the diocese in question "to tip off the local pastor so that there would be no more of this organized opposition on the part of the Church."[62]

Social prejudice ingrained over many years proved intractable to Christian charity and the policies of the DDHC. Much of the interracial animosity was concentrated in Detroit, the one Northern city that more than any other symbolized the promise of a decent life to transplanted rural Southern blacks. Detroit was the "arsenal of democracy," but the in-migration of 50,000 black defense workers between 1940 and 1943 put an unbearable strain on the community's facilities, especially housing. Neither Washington nor the local housing authorities were able to keep up with the demand for housing. Where competition was keen with other ethnic groups for employment, shelter, and the other amenities of urban living, serious friction developed. In Febru-

59. Lester B. Granger to Bishop John A. Duffy, Oct. 22, 1941, in *ibid.*
60. Frank A. Vanderlip to Jacob Crane, Oct. 22, 1941, in *ibid.*
61. Quoted in Charles S. Johnson et al., *To Stem This Tide: A Survey of Racial Tension Areas in the United States* (Boston, 1943), 168.
62. Frank A. Vanderlip to Jacob Crane, Oct. 22, 1941, NARG 207, DDHC Records.

ary 1942, 2,000 National Guardsmen had been called out to protect fourteen black families who were moving into an all-white housing project. A more serious riot occurred in 1943, during which 38 people were killed, 500 injured, and 1,000 left homeless. Although Palmer resigned in January 1942 and thus was relieved of direct responsibility for the first riot, it was his and the local authorities' failure to cope with the housing shortage in the months before that brought on the disturbance.[63]

By contrast to the vigorous but ultimately futile policies in the North, the DDHC beat a retreat in Southern cities. There the agency followed "local custom" in selecting housing sites for black defense workers.[64] Invariably, this meant that they were crammed into already congested quarters in the ghettos or, as vacant land in the center of the city became scarce, were pushed to the periphery. Whatever Palmer's original intent in his policy statement of January 1941, the DDHC (and its successor, the National Housing Agency) tolerated the continuance of a prewar housing policy that imposed upon black defense workers a pattern of residential segregation. When wedded to a discriminatory racial occupation pattern, this policy resulted in the spread of slum conditions into new sections of the postwar cities of the South and North. In some instances, the DDHC actually created black ghettos where none had existed before; for example, segregated housing was built in Ann Arbor, Michigan, a university city in which segregation had been virtually unknown before the war.[65]

To make matters worse, the DDHC's underestimating of both the volume and destination of black migration in its formulas for allocating materials specifically for black housing

---

63. Robert Shogan and Tom Craig, *The Detroit Race Riot* (Philadelphia, 1964), 25–110.

64. Robert R. Taylor to Charles W. Farrier, July 9, 1941, NARG 207, DDHC Records; Herbert Emmerich to Marvin McIntyre, Feb. 16, 1943; McIntyre to Paul V. McNutt, Mar. 14, 1943, and McIntyre to John B. Blandford, Jr., Mar. 29, 1943, FDR Papers, OF 63, FDRL.

65. Robert R. Taylor to Roy Wilkins, June 14, 1941, NARG 207, DDHC Records; Rose Helper, *Racial Policies and Practices of Real Estate Brokers* (Minneapolis, 1969), 230–31; Herman H. Long and Charles S. Johnson, *People v. Property: Race Restrictive Covenants in Housing* (Nashville, 1947), 61–62.

precipitated a dispute with the USHA. With support from the public housing lobby, that agency had, at the start of mobilization, committed itself as part of its urban renewal program to building new units for low-income defense workers in the ghetto. Palmer, however, preferred to build black housing on new open spaces outside the ghetto where vacant land was available. Hence he blocked USHA petitions to build a 156-unit project in Hartford, 50 units in Bakersfield, 82 in Long Branch, New Jersey, 120 in Providence, 270 in Shreveport, 70 in Champaign, Illinois, and 30 in Tucson.[66]

The real losers in the on-going bureaucratic conflict, of course, were blacks. Mobilization and war presented unique opportunities to invoke national unity, patriotism, and the martial virtues to break down old patterns of segregated living in the urban centers of war production, but the bureaucrats and administrators shrank back from social experimentation. Compared with what might have been accomplished, the results were meager. Not only were private and public enterprise building an inadequate number of housing units to shelter black defense workers and their families, but the federal government was doing very little to break down the pattern of segregation in public housing. Before the war, two-thirds of black-occupied public housing was totally segregated, a figure which declined only to 42 percent during the war years. More significantly, the segregated projects composed 53.7 percent of all dwellings inhabited by blacks. Eleanor Roosevelt was correct when she observed that unless racially restrictive covenants, zoning laws, and other forms of housing discrimination were abandoned, Negroes "will live under conditions which are a menace to the entire population."[67]

There was other evidence to indicate that Palmer needed to temper his belief that the corner had been turned. Centralization was producing the inevitable clashes with communities predicted by the housing reformers. In its haste to provide shelter

66. "Statement Concerning the Effect of Priorities on USHA-Aided Projects for Negro Occupancy," 1941, NARG 207, DDHC Records; Bernard Baruch to Dorothy Rosenman, Oct. 16, 1942, Dorothy Rosenman Papers, Columbia Univ.

67. *New York Times*, Jan. 18, Mar. 26, 1944.

for defense workers, the DDHC had been little concerned about a city's overall plan, its tax structure, or its ability to absorb the new houses or supply sufficient schools, water, and sewage. Its agents had told local officials where they would build, whether they liked it or not. Their inexperience in site selection and management, coupled with inefficiency, produced a number of absurdities: projects built in the wrong place, rent schedules set too high, vacancies in one neighborhood and overcrowding in another. The PBA's buildings, ill-planned, flimsy, and ugly, turned out to be constructed at much higher costs than the well-built dwellings erected by the USHA. When confronted with the evidence, Palmer's reply was that the imposition of uniform standards would discourage builders; he and the FHA were satisfied as long as the workers were willing to live in the houses.[68]

The consequences of this laissez-faire attitude, as housing reformers were quick to point out, were devastating to community revitalization. The FHA's Title VI, which authorized loan insurance on homes in defense areas, had been enacted only after testimony that such homes would be rented, not sold. Probably not more than one out of four such homes was being rented, while workers were saddled with the others by means of forced sales. With nearly two million defense migrants seeking shelter, the DDHC's lax standards were a godsend to speculators and home-ownership hawkers, who turned a quick profit without regard for the long-term welfare of the community. But even low-income workers, unable to rent, were being pressured into ownership, usually with a $100 down payment and the balance of the equity in eighteen monthly installments. With monthly charges of $56, only a few defense workers could afford to pay them. The National Association of Real Estate Boards spoke wisely when it observed in its confidential weekly letter: "An attractive feature of Title VI is that it hasn't a great many restrictions . . . a builder has no strings as to who should rent or buy his homes."[69]

The pattern emerging from various pieces of evidence could

68. Charles F. Palmer to Staff, Dec. 4, 1941, NARG 207, DDHC Records.
69. *Ibid.*

not be mistaken: the presidential reorganization of January 1941 had made some improvement, but not nearly enough to placate those critics who wanted to use the war housing program to further the creation of a new community synthesis.[70] The rekindling of the dispute between housing reformers and the coordinator before the Truman committee investigating the national defense program in 1941 threw into sharp relief the conflicting goals of public service bureaucrats and liberals, who viewed defense housing as the fulcrum of a broader program of federally assisted community renewal. USHA Administrator Straus accused both Palmer and the FWA of relegating public housing to an inferior position in the defense program and predicted "the most desperate housing conditions in defense centers this winter, [and] dangerous congestion," which could have been avoided "if there had been an early enough recognition of the real housing need and if the tested machinery of established housing agencies had been used to meet that need." Two weeks later, testifying before the Public Buildings Committee of the House of Representatives, Straus renewed his attack, accusing Palmer of heeding the "siren song of the speculator" and of accepting uncritically the "erroneous notion" that private industry could provide a large part of the defense housing. He reiterated that Congress should entrust the program to the USHA, arguing that because it functioned through the local public housing authorities it was actually a *local* agency and could best serve the interests of cooperative federalism.[71]

By stressing both the local nature of USHA and its tangible accomplishments, Straus rather ingeniously hoped to disarm the

70. Entries of June 22 and July 24, 1941, John Ihlder Diary, John Ihlder Papers; Dorothy Rosenman to FDR, July 3, 1941, and FDR to Dorothy Rosenman, July 21, 1941, FDR Papers, OF 4501; Walter Reuther, *Memorandum on Housing and Defense in Detroit, Michigan,* Sept. 26, 1941, John Carmody Papers, FDRL, and United States Congress, Senate, *Investigation of the National Defense Program,* Hearings before a Special Committee Investigating the National Defense Program pursuant to S. Res. 71, 77th Cong., 1st sess. (1941), pt. 8, 2332–33, 2341–50, 2376, 2385–2401, 2683, 2877.

71. *New York Times,* Oct. 30, 1941; United States Congress, House of Representatives, *To Transfer from the District of Columbia Departments, or Bureaus Thereof, and Independent Agencies to Other Localities,* Hearings before the Subcommittees of the Committee on Public Buildings and Grounds pursuant to H. Res. 209, 77th Cong., 1st sess. (1942), pt. 8, 138–41.

committee, whose members made no effort to disguise their hostility to public housing. The hearing enabled him to couple his attack upon Palmer with the now familiar argument that the cities could utilize the defense housing, built by local authorities under USHA auspices, in their postwar slum clearance plans. By contrast, the temporary shelters of the DDHC would constitute the slums of the future, perpetuating and spreading blight, an obstacle in the path of orderly and planned development of urban areas.[72]

Straus's performance was a tour de force, but there is little evidence that the members of the Public Buildings Committee were persuaded by his arguments beyond the fact that the war housing program was fouled up and was threatening to choke defense production. Meanwhile, demands for Palmer's dismissal were heard with distressing frequency. Only a handful of municipal officials and private builders rallied to his defense.[73]

Ironically, the gravest challenge to the coordinator originated with the same private entrepreneurs on whose support the success of the housing program depended. It was the criticism of these men, whom Palmer had cultivated so assiduously, that left him vulnerable. The letter of Morton Bodfish, executive vice president of the United States Savings and Loan League (the nation's largest private mortgage lender) and one of the most influential lobbyists in Washington, was a case in point. Written on December 19, 1941, the letter was a ringing defense of private enterprise and an impassioned tirade against the New Deal's housing program. It was also a plea to the coordinator to withdraw government from defense housing in toto or, failing that, further to restrict its activity.[74]

The USHA was the primary target of the author's strongest language, but his critique also encompassed the DDHC's rental poli-

---

72. *To Transfer from the District of Columbia . . .*, pt. 8, 143, 150–51; *New York Times*, Nov. 13, 1941.
73. "Housing As Usual," *Business Week* (Mar. 28, 1942), 24–29; "Gothic Gazebo," *Time* 39 (June 5, 1942), 29; John Griffith to Palmer, Oct. 4, 1941; N.H. Dosker to Palmer, Oct. 30, 1941, and John W. Cramer to Palmer, Dec. 19, 1941, NARG 207, DDHC Records.
74. Morton Bodfish to Palmer, Dec. 19, 1941, NARG 207, DDHC Records.

cies and postwar disposition of Lanham Act projects. Bodfish repudiated Straus's contention that projects converted to public low-rent housing would not affect the postwar private housing market. He did not understand why workers, fully employed in defense industries, could not afford an economic rent. If this were so, it must be attributable to the extravagant costs of Lanham Act projects. His solution was to slash construction costs to the bone. He also endorsed a House proposal that would have tied rentals to the value of the dwellings.[75]

As the war progressed, private realtors and builders were to employ rhetoric identical to Bodfish's as they hounded and sniped relentlessly at the public housing program. The National Association of Home Builders, the spearhead of private enterprise, took credit for putting public housing on the defensive. Its front men skillfully manipulated the mass media to cast aspersions on the benefits of public housing. The NAHB adhered closely to a sophisticated scenario that went as follows: (1) the realtor deplored slums as much as urban liberals and was constantly seeking new ways to eliminate them; (2) private enterprise still awaited concrete evidence to support the assertion that public housing effected slum clearance and that, given identical conditions, such housing was less expensive than private-enterprise housing; (3) public housing was a political threat to our form of government because it perpetuated one-party (Democratic) tenure by establishing a dependent class of voters; and (4) public housing was alien and un-American.[76]

After procrastinating for nearly a year and six months, the administration had to confront both the antipathy of the home builders and the unimpeachable evidence of numerous eyewitnesses—friend and foe alike—that defense housing was on the verge of collapse. The President was stung by the criticism and feared a congressional revolt; in February 1942 he asked his friend and political adviser, Samuel I. Rosenman, to recommend changes in the defense housing program.

75. *Ibid.*
76. "Nation's Home Builders Lash Out Against Public Housing in Fiery Sessions," *National Real Estate Journal* 44 (Dec. 1943), 18; "Stop Public Housing," *ibid.*, 45 (Mar. 1944), 11.

After consulting with Leon Keyserling, deputy administrator for the USHA, Senators Robert R. Wagner and James Byrnes, and representatives of several federal agencies, Rosenman concluded that both personality differences and bureaucratic jealousies (arising from the original failure to delineate precisely the extent of the coordinator's jurisdiction) had undermined the program. Although he shared the opinion of his wife Dorothy, a proponent of the USHA's slum clearance program, that the homes constructed by the PBA were jerry-built "architectural monstrosities," he had to balance this against Roosevelt's diminishing confidence in the USHA, especially as conservative criticism of the agency increased.[77] As an exchange of correspondence between Roosevelt and Straus makes abundantly clear, the President was not anxious to force a confrontation with congressional conservatives when so much of the defense program depended upon their cooperation.[78]

At first Rosenman attempted to clarify the coordinator's role, but once he fully realized the extent of the animosity toward Palmer from local housing authorities and public housing supporters and the hostility to the USHA from conservatives and real estate interests, he abandoned this strategy. He concluded that only a drastic reorganization could salvage the defense housing program at a minimum cost to the New Deal's broader social goals.

In the House, conservatives had threatened to take matters into their own hands, to amend the Lanham Act so as to destroy forever the public housing program. Straus had seen the handwriting on the wall: housing built with public money would not be used to serve public needs, "but shall instead be sold at bargain prices to real estate speculators, to become the slums that will blight our nation for generations to come." The foes of

---

77. Samuel I. Rosenman to Leon Keyserling, Jan. 24, Feb. 24, 1942; John Ihlder to Rosenman, Jan. 28, Feb. 3, 7, 1942; Carl Bradt to Rosenman, Feb. 21, 1942, Samuel I. Rosenman Papers, FDRL; Dorothy Rosenman, "Defense Housing: Are We Building Future Slums or Planned Communities," *Architectural Record,* 90 (Nov. 1941), 56–58.

78. FDR to Nathan Straus, Oct. 28, 1941; Straus to FDR, Jan. 5, 1942; "Summary of Telephone Conversation with Mrs. Roosevelt," Jan. 8, 1942, Nathan Straus Papers, FDRL.

slum clearance (a reference to the National Association of Real Estate Boards) would block every public housing proposal as long as he was USHA administrator, so he resigned as of January 5, 1942.[79]

Shocked and stunned, liberals decried both the House's threatened emasculation of public housing and Straus's resignation. But when the sound and fury subsided, this much also was clear: Straus's resignation had not simplified matters for Rosenman. Congressional liberals were not going to accept the attack on public housing impassively. They retaliated by blocking an amendment to the Lanham Act which would have brought a windfall profit to private builders. The liberals substituted a new amendment requiring every contract to be let on the basis of competitive bids—exactly the procedure followed by the USHA![80] This kind of politicking simply reinforced Rosenman's belief that a thoroughgoing reorganization was necessary. On February 24, 1942, the President acted upon Rosenman's recommmendations by issuing Executive Order 9070 which consolidated all sixteen federal housing agencies into one superbody, the National Housing Agency (NHA). The agency was to be composed of three major divisions: the Federal Public Housing Authority, an amalgam of the several governmental agencies building with public monies, headed initially by Herbert Emmerich and, after his resignation, by Phillip Klutznick; the Federal Home Loan Bank Administration; and the Federal Housing Administration. Roosevelt also announced that John D. Blandford, Jr., who had the respect of both urban liberals and private builders, would serve as administrator of the NHA.

The legal basis for the reorganization was the World War I Overman Act which, Roosevelt explained, was intended to facilitate the "swifter and more efficient prosecution of the war." The effect, however, was to phase out the position of Defense Housing Coordinator. The President had acted in a typical manner: despite a progressive loss of confidence in Palmer,

79. *New York Times*, Feb. 18, 24, 1942.
80. "Here in Washington," *Survey* 78 (Jan. 1942), 15.

Roosevelt was unwilling to fire him. Instead, he eased Palmer out of the position by requesting that he undertake "as soon as possible" a study of Britain's war housing program. The coordinator's job was thereafter left vacant.[81]

However belated, the President's action gained the support of liberals, whose patience was strung out after months of bureaucratic skirmishing. Mary K. Simkhovitch, president of the Public Housing Conference, was particularly gratified to see that "a sharp-cut distinction has been shown with regard to the different purposes served by public and private housing agencies." She agreed that Blandford was the right man for the job. But one housing reformer, alert to the long-term implications of the changes for postwar public housing, added a caveat: "Reorganization is an excellent thing, but we must not be too optimistic and let down our guard . . . . While consolidation has advantages, it will have disadvantages, too. It would not take an act of Congress to shift FPHA around the corner to FHA. More than ever, [public] housers must not think that the road is clear."[82]

The private realtors also applauded the President's order as long overdue, mainly because they interpreted it as the death knell for public housing and urban renewal. In this reading of the President's action, they appeared to have the support of a substantial segment of the press. Arthur Krock, the distinguished *New York Times* columnist, observed that if the NHA confined its duties to war housing, treating the task "not [as] a socio-economic experiment, with an eye always fixed ahead on post-war political philosophies," the reorganization would turn into a successful marriage of business and government and would produce homes for defense workers. But, he cautioned, if the NHA was going to be "guided toward State socialization of

81. Press release, Feb. 24, 1942, NARG 207, DDHC Records; FDR to Palmer, Feb. 24, 1942, and Mar. 1, 1943; John D. Blandford, Jr., to FDR, Oct. 9, 1942, FDR Papers, OF 4844, FDRL.
82. Herbert Emmerich to Samuel I. Rosenman, Feb. 26, 1942; Mary K. Simkhovitch to Rosenman, Feb. 25, 1942, Samuel I. Rosenman Papers, FDRL; "U.S. Reorganization Gets Approval, But—" *Public Housing Progress* 8 (Feb. 1942), 2.

realty after the war,'' then ''the battle of philosophies will be resumed with much greater intensity.''[83]

The only discordant notes emanated from bureaucrats whose bailiwicks were threatened by a diminution of status or authority. They ignored the one central consideration underlying the President's action: the machinery to service the nation's wartime housing needs had not been able to cope with the problem. The DDHC was really a presidential creature designed to keep control over the housing aspects of mobilization in the executive branch. As an ad hoc institution with no legally defined status, neither it nor the other sixteen housing agencies had fully exhibited a grasp or command of the strategic concepts inherent in making housing policy. Palmer, who was good at running out reports, was woefully remiss in mobilizing the cooperation of constituent housing agencies. His own rigid personality and some questionable appointments made it unlikely that he could ever persuade the housing agencies and public and private enterprise to transcend their narrower interests and work as one team, one unit, in building defense housing.[84]

In the end, the bureaucracy of defense housing had grown so large and cumbersome that it stumbled over itself and allowed substantive considerations to be lost amid personal and interdepartmental infighting. Executive Order 9070 was intended to rectify this situation. Blandford was given the mandate to ride herd over the program because of his ''amazing administrational ability,'' and not because of any attachment to a particular social philosophy or experience with housing problems.[85]

A mechanical engineer by profession, Blandford was a New Yorker by birth but educated in New Jersey and Chicago. Before joining the federal bureaucracy, he had acquired familiarity with urban problems, serving in Cincinnati in the 1920s as head of the Bureau of Governmental Research and Director of

---

83. *New York Times,* Feb. 22, 26, 1942; ''Housing As Usual,'' *Business Week* (Mar. 28, 1942), 24–29.

84. Baird Snyder to Leon Keyserling, Jan. 28, 1942; Keyserling to Snyder, Jan. 28, 1942; Jesse Jones to Samuel I. Rosenman, Feb. 14, 1942; Abner Ferguson to Rosenman, Feb. 11, 1942, Samuel I. Rosenman Papers, FDRL.

85. ''Meet Blandford of NHA,'' *Pencil Points* 23 (Apr. 1942), 186.

Public Safety. He entered federal service as general manager of the Tennessee Valley Authority and in 1939 was appointed assistant director of the Bureau of the Budget. As administrator of the NHA, he was being asked to take in tow the enormous federal housing bureaucracy and coordinate its activities into a war housing program that was at once cohesive and comprehensive. This required a higher degree of cooperation from local city agencies, realtors, and private citizens than Palmer had been able to achieve.[86]

With the creation of the NHA and subsequent demise in 1943 of the National Resources Planning Board (NRPB), a fundamental shift in the federal government's perspective on urban rehabilitation also occurred. The NRPB had believed that comprehensive replanning was the foundation of sound urban redevelopment. NHA executives had a more limited goal: their chief interest was to increase the nation's supply of decent housing in good neighborhoods and to destroy slums. Hence, the NHA promoted a national housing policy, not a national urban policy. Urban renewal, in the hands of the most influential city-oriented federal agency, became a device "to make cities out of housing programs"—much to the dismay of many urban liberals.[87]

The task was particularly challenging because Blandford agreed in principle that housing was fundamentally a community responsibility. Without doing violence to the spirit of cooperative federalism, he also recognized that the war had made it necessary to modify temporarily the local obligation in order to ensure that housing production was integrated into the total defense effort. Thus Blandford used his considerable powers of persuasion to reorient urban redevelopment thinking among his heterogeneous staff. He also kept a close ear to congressional cloakrooms to avoid giving the impression that he was a social reformer.[88]

Despite the persistence of problems, the NHA formulated its

86. "National Housing Agency Established," *Public Administration Review* 2 (Spring 1942), 177–78.

87. Mark I. Gelfand, *A Nation of Cities: The Federal Government and Urban America, 1933–1965* (New York, 1975), 104, 126.

88. John B. Blandford, Jr., "The Role of the City in Full Housing Development,"

own guidelines to direct building activity. At the head of the list was the H-1 program, giving construction priority to the sheltering of essential civilian workers in congested production areas. The agency also decided that, wherever possible, communities should fill their housing needs by making more efficient use of existing structures. Since it affected rent control policies, this decision required close coordination with the Office of Price Administration. Further, the NHA would continue to permit private financing to underwrite all other housing requirements, which included the conversion and remodeling of existing structures and the building of new ones. This policy decision kept the home-building industry alive during the war years. Ultimately, private enterprise constructed nearly one million units. The sheltering of low-income workers, however, remained a source of difficulty with the public housing lobby.

The NHA decided, where private builders and financiers were unable to accommodate the needs of these workers, to channel public funds into the construction of temporary structures. Since nearly all construction after 1942 was for defense housing, this decision conserved men, money, and material but rendered it difficult to use many of these structures in postwar slum clearance programs.[89]

The NHA was also conscious that any well-conceived endeavor to increase postwar housing production had to be based upon a solid understanding of the urban environment. Blandford therefore formed a Division of Urban Studies within his office to assist in relating the total programs of the NHA to the other elements of city building and rebuilding and to urban life as a whole. The division's influence began to be felt in 1944 when it helped shape NHA policy on the crucial issue of urban redevelopment. In that year, the division initiated a study of postwar

reprinted in American Municipal Association, *Proceedings of the Twenty-second Annual Conference* (Chicago, 1945), 18.

89. Herbert S. Colton to John B. Blandford, Jr., Mar. 20, 1942; Coleman Woodbury to Blandford, Nov. 14, 1945, NARG 207, WHP National Housing Agency (NHA) Records; United States Congress, Senate, *Post-War Economic Policy and Planning,* Hearings before the Subcommittee on Housing and Urban Development of the Special Committee on Post-War Economic Policy and Planning, 79th Cong., 1st sess. (1944-45), pt. 4, 1017-18.

housing needs on the basis of a ten-year program (i.e., between 1946 and 1955). Its analysis was predicated upon three factors: (1) American housing needs in terms of capacity to pay; (2) housing volume required to contribute toward "investment opportunities, jobs and prosperity"; and (3) the elimination in ten years of half the substandard housing now existing. The division concluded that the nation would need 12,600,000 units over the ten-year period, or an average of 1,260,000 a year. About half this need for new construction was based on the estimated increase in the number of families. The other half was based on the goal of replacing a number equaling half the nonfarm units substandard in 1940, plus those becoming substandard after 1940.[90]

This data-collecting enterprise became a double-edged program in the hands of the NHA officials. Gathering facts about urban life assisted municipalities in planning for their own postwar needs, but it might also result in the formulation of a national urban policy. Thereby, the federal government would become a positive force in shaping a better urban environment. Although their hopes did not materialize immediately, the NHA's estimates did serve as the basis of congressional discussion of postwar housing needs for both the Wagner-Ellender-Taft bill of 1945 and the National Housing Act of 1949.[91]

Extrapolating from Palmer's experience, Blandford ought to have anticipated that, short of coercion, some realtors and citizens would not cooperate with the administration's housing policies. And, indeed, the opposition was most overt in communities where the housing shortage was greatest and the potential for federal intervention strongest. But it was the intensity and broad base of the resistance more than the fact that surprised Blandford, especially because he had gone to great lengths to allay fears that the NHA would encroach upon the private housing market. Nonetheless, as early as July 1943, the NHA conceded that the policy to convert private domiciles into rental apartments for civilian war workers was a failure. The Willow

90. United States Congress, Senate, *General Housing Act of 1945,* Hearings before the Committee on Banking and Currency, 79th Cong., 1st sess. (1946), 34–128.
91. Gelfand, *A Nation of Cities,* 103.

Run housing project located near the Detroit Ford factory was also in trouble. Whether it was because of Henry Ford's implacable opposition to the United Auto Workers or because he wanted to exclude large numbers of industrial workers from Washtenaw County (who might vote to unseat his friend, Congressman Earl Michener) is uncertain, but Ford proved to be a real thorn in the side of the NHA.[92]

The home builders of America showed little inclination to meet the NHA half way. They considered any federal effort to oversee their operations as the entering wedge of public housing socialism. This attitude even extended to housing for the poorest segments of the population, whom private enterprise could not possibly afford to accommodate. The *National Real Estate Journal* accused the NHA of misleading the public by implying that "private enterprise had failed to house Americans of all classes." Beneath the rhetoric the fear persisted that government would continue to meddle in the affairs of the homebuilding industry after the war was over.[93]

How the NHA met the challenge of wartime housing—despite persistent opposition from the private sector, the lingering distrust of public housing supporters, shortages of material and labor, and some policy miscalculations—is one of the wonders of the time. By the close of 1944 more than 3,970,000 housing units had been targeted; 3,828,000 were available for use, 82,000 were under construction, and 60,000 were on the drawing boards. Of the total housing need, 53 percent was satisfied by the more efficient use of existing structures; 5 percent by private conversion; 21 percent by private new construction; 1 percent by public conversion; 15 percent by publicly financed temporary housing (e.g., trailers and demountables); and 5 percent by new, publicly financed permanent construction. The funds for publicly financed building were made available under the Lanham Act and the Federal Public Housing Authority. Blandford could truthfully tell a special Senate committee in

92. "Housing Jam," *Business Week* (Jan. 23, 1943), 16; Helen Fuller, "Ford Fights War Housing," *New Republic* 107 (July 20, 1942), 77.

93. "Stop Public Housing," *National Real Estate Journal* 45 (Mar. 1944), 11; "Let Us Know Where We Stand," *ibid.*, 46 (Mar. 1945), 13.

1944–45 that wartime industrial production was not being impeded for want of an adequate supply of housing. Roosevelt could feel justified that his decisions to create the NHA and appoint Blandford had been correct ones.[94]

This is not to say that the NHA always functioned smoothly or could not have improved upon its performance. In a remarkably lucid critique of the war housing program, assistant administrator Coleman Woodbury enumerated several weaknesses that had reduced its efficiency. Woodbury disclosed that in the first year-and-a-half of the NHA's existence, the central office in Washington, D.C., which was charged with reviewing the quantity and quality of the program, was often at odds with the regional representatives, who made the initial housing recommendations, despite a number of personnel and policy changes.[95]

Looking at the substance of the program rather than its administration, Woodbury concluded that the greatest weakness had been the absence of effective instruments for controlling the sales prices of existing housing. The NHA consistently miscalculated or underestimated the slow but insidious toll inflation took upon housing prices and the consequent squeeze upon consumers at war's end. Nor did the agency enforce the priority conditions governing sales, price, and occupancy for private housing (over which it had total control) as fully as it might have. Finally, the NHA had erred in not acting more vigorously to inform war workers of their housing rights. This failure had put the prospective buyer or tenant at a disadvantage in negotiations with landlords and builders.[96]

As the defeat of the Axis powers loomed closer, Blandford's energies were redirected to the problem that had earlier plagued Palmer: the ultimate disposition of the war-generated housing. How the matter was resolved was important not only to the future of the NHA but to the private builders as well. The spokesmen of private enterprise were far from united in their thinking,

94. *Post-War Economic Policy and Planning,* pt. 6, 1197, 1200–2; John B. Blandford, Jr., to FDR, Mar. 25, 1943, and FDR to Blandford, Mar. 26, 1943, FDR Papers, OF 4806, FDRL.

95. Coleman Woodbury to Blandford, Nov. 14, 1945, NARG 207, WHP, NHA Records.

96. *Ibid.*

knowing that the hundreds of thousands of GIs would be seeking decent and inexpensive homes on their return.[97] Herbert U. Nelson, vice president of the NAREB, was spokesman for those realtors who were prepared to accept limited federal intervention in the private housing market. The United States Chamber of Commerce, by contrast, adamantly hewed to a laissez-faire position, asserting that the federal government should "not undertake any activities in the field of housing which will compete with private builders or interfere with the community's responsibility for enforcement of minimum housing standards and the relief of needy families."[98]

Public housing lobbyists and their congressional supporters were quick to remind Blandford that Roosevelt had included housing in his pithy statement of social distress when he saw a third of the population ill fed, ill clothed, and ill housed. Although the Lanham Act could not result in low-income public housing, it had demonstrated to reformers the vast potentialities of a program of similar size, aimed at the elimination of slum housing. In their concern, some reformers also saw creative possibilities for urban redevelopment, and talk about the one frequently included the other. Blandford's sensitivity to the public interest in housing provided encouragement. Roosevelt added his voice to the growing demand in the country for decent housing in his 1944 State of the Union message, the controversial "Economic Bill of Rights." This speech gave presidential sanction to the movement for public housing and urban rehabilitation, something that had been absent before.[99]

To Sydney Maslen, chairman of the National Committee of

97. See "Demobilization and Post-War Adjustment Problems of the National Housing Agency," Nov. 23, 1943; Blandford to Bernard Baruch, Nov. 26, 1943; "Changes in War Housing Program in Pre-Victory Period," Mar. 20, 1944; Coleman Woodbury to NHA Regional Representatives, Sept. 22, 1944, in NARG 207, WHP-Housing and Home Finance Authority (-HHFA), NHA Records.

98. "Private Builders Can Do Whole Job—Nelson," *Public Housing Progress* 10 (Feb. 1944), 2; "Postwar Planners Ignore Slum Issue," *ibid.,* 10 (Feb. 1944), 4.

99. John B. Blandford, Jr., "Speech to the National Association of Housing Officials," *American City* 58 (June 1943), 58; Samuel I. Rosenman, comp., *The Public Papers and Addresses of Franklin D. Roosevelt,* 13 vols. (New York, 1938–50), XIII, 41.

Housing Associations, wiping out the slums of the central city was a prerequisite to reversing the process of metropolitan dispersal and to the building of a new spirit of community in the inner city. Maslen's hopes rested on the Wagner Housing Act of 1937. Under the law, each unit of slum housing demolished had to be replaced by one unit of public housing. Besides providing housing, a federal urban redevelopment program might also generate funds for cities to purchase and clear slum areas. Maslen thought that local redevelopment authorities should have the option of building public housing, erecting municipal buildings and parks, or reselling the land to private investors who could use it as they wished, subject to the approval of the city planning commission and the local authority.[100]

Thus were the lines drawing tighter as the end of the war came near. Each side eyed the other suspiciously, which made a clash over the future course of postwar housing policy unavoidable. Public housing enthusiasts were pressuring the administration to reinvigorate the federal housing program as a cushion against postwar depression.[101] They also were lobbying Congress to suspend Section 4 of the Lanham Act, which stipulated that all of the units had to be either sold or demolished immediately after the war.[102]

In this clash over future housing policy, ideological consistency was sometimes thrown to the winds and party lines breached. By a strange anomaly, the proponents of public housing were now arguing in favor of the traditional approach of capitalism: they were anxious to give private enterprise the opportunity to provide decent housing for the poor. For the builders' failure would clear away the last remaining obstacles to federally subsidized public housing. The real estate establish-

100. Sydney Maslen, "U.S. Must Speed Post-War Plans," *Public Housing Progress* 8 (Oct. 1942), 2. Also see the report of the National Committee on the Housing Emergency, Inc., *Recommendations for the Disposition of Federal War Housing* (New York, 1943) and Richard O. Davies, *Housing Reform During the Truman Administration* (Columbia, Mo., 1966), 12–13.

101. *Post-War Economic Policy and Planning*, pt. 8, 1708.

102. Allen J. Ellender, "What Congress Thinks," *Public Housing Progress* 10 (Apr. 1944), 12–13.

ment, by the same token, did *not* want the government to withdraw from the field but rather to expand its activities further than even starry-eyed reformers ever dreamed. The realtors talked openly of the federal government serving *their* needs as opposed to the needs of the poor. They wanted the administration to acquire slum properties valued at a total of $30 billion, which it would sell to developers at nominal cost; they advocated rent doles for tenants running into billions of dollars annually which would also be siphoned into the hands of slum owners; they sought special tax immunities which they claimed would automatically make real estate investments profitable.[103]

Small wonder that the average citizen did not know what to make of the situation! In the perspective of history, the reversal of attitudes was not half as strange as it appeared. Large enterprises that become unprofitable have often urged the government to bail out the unhappy investor. The process, "socializing the losses," appeared frequently in the record of the housing economy. Thus the lines separating true private and true public housing became blurred, and the fight by Washington lobbyists degenerated into a struggle for control of the federal purse strings. Charles Abrams, director of the National Public Housing Conference, warned that if the real estate lobby triumphed public housing and urban redevelopment would have suffered an irrevocable blow, and "one of the most dramatic opportunities for rebuilding our cities may be lost forever."[104]

Fearful that the dispute might imperil home construction and disrupt plans for an orderly transition to a peacetime economy, the administration made several—and in the long run futile—gestures to reconcile the belligerent factions. On the issue of whether free competition or government control was to predominate in the postemergency period, Roosevelt, in a letter to Dorothy Rosenman, affirmed himself on the side of private enterprise, subject only to its ability to live up to its responsibilities. The government would facilitate land assemblage by developers and make available mortgage money for middle-class

103. Charles Abrams, "Real Estate's Radicals," *ibid.,* 10 (Apr. 1944), 6–7.
104. *Ibid.,* 7.

116

housing, but it would also assist low-income families for whom private enterprise could not build profitably.[105]

NHA Administrator Blandford agreed that the administration's basic task in housing was to achieve a cooperative federalism that would strike the proper balance between community responsibility and local initiative and the social welfare concern of the federal government. The acute housing shortage, the inflationary pressures on housing prices, and the difficulties in reviving home construction after wartime curtailments made it imperative that the NHA bring together the warring factions.[106]

As Blandford wrote in the *American City* in September 1945, housing was the primary responsibility of communities and local governments. Within the community, the full resources of competitive enterprise should be stimulated to make a maximum contribution to quality and quantity. The role of government normally was to supplement through research and financial assistance the amenities which a community needed but could not provide from its own limited resources. The times were not normal, however. Drawing upon the Urban Studies Division's estimates, Blandford told a Senate subcommittee on housing that the country would need 12.6 million units in the first decade following the end of the war. This need vested housing with a public-interest character.[107]

Too optimistically, perhaps, Blandford and the President had hoped to gloss over the enmity that divided public and private housing interests into warring camps. When Roosevelt died in April 1945, Blandford followed the example of the new head of state, Harry S. Truman, and tried to walk the narrow line separating the two adversaries.[108]

It was in this politically charged atmosphere that the Wagner-

105. *New York Times,* Mar. 9, 1944. See also National Committee on the Housing Emergency, Inc., *A Program for Action on Housing for Defense Workers and Families of Low Income* (New York, 1941), 11.

106. Blandford, "The Role of the City in Full Housing Development," 18.

107. John B. Blandford, Jr., "Setting and Meeting Housing Goals," *American City* 60 (Sept. 1945), 94. See also "John B. Blandford Proposes Housing Principles for America," *Architectural Forum* 80 (Apr. 1944), 66, and *Post-War Economic Policy and Planning,* pt. 8, 1325.

108. Harry S Truman, *Memoirs,* 2 vols. (New York, 1955–56), I, 512–15.

Taft-Ellender housing bill emerged from the subcommittee on housing and urban redevelopment of the Senate's Special Committee on Postwar Economic Policy and Planning. The bill was a godsend to Blandford, embodying just the sort of compromises he had advocated. Not only did it propose to continue and improve the prewar federal programs in aid of housing and home finance that could be expected to appeal to the private building industry, but it also offered something to the proponents of public housing. To this extent, it appeared to create a national consensus on housing reform. Basically, the bill provided authorization (1) to stimulate and assist technical and economic housing research in industry, the communities, and the federal government; (2) for a variety of new financial aids to stimulate greater production of good private housing at lower costs than hitherto possible; (3) for a system of federal financial assistance to acquire slums and blighted areas for redevelopment at economical land costs; and (4) for assurance of unified and coordinated federal policies in housing. For public and private housing advocates alike, the bill authorized renewal of the low-rent public housing program, but on a basis that was noncompetitive with private enterprise and grounded in local initiative and control.[109]

The value of the Wagner-Taft-Ellender bill lay chiefly in the housing authorizations for low-income families and in the fact that the urban renewal provisions were the first efforts to establish a practical formula for reclamation of substandard neighborhoods. The public housing authorization was no more than enough to continue public housing as an experiment; even the urban renewal provision was in the nature of a demonstration rather than a full-scale effort to clear out substandard neighborhoods. As housing reformer Charles Abrams noted, responsibility for a comprehensive program to clear urban and rural slums within a definite period of time had not yet been accepted.[110]

To the degree that the Wagner-Taft-Ellender bill was a com-

109. Blandford, "The Role of the City in Full Housing Development," 18–20.
110. Abrams, *The Future of Housing,* 310.

promise, it mirrored the turbulent political atmosphere of the times. Roosevelt was dead, the New Deal coalition was in disarray, congressional conservatives were flexing their newfound political muscle, and thousands of returning veterans were demanding shelter. For all its shortcomings, the bill was a small step in the right direction, but the real estate associations and mortgage builders opposed it with all their resources. Though the legislation passed the Senate with administration and bipartisan support, it failed to emerge from the House Banking and Currency Committee for a vote on the floor. Pressure from the private builders and lenders also worked its way into the White House, and President Truman, who read the 1946 election returns as a popular mandate for a return to the old days, was reluctant to come to the bill's rescue. Wilson W. Wyatt, the dynamic former mayor of Louisville who had succeeded Blandford in January 1946, had worked long and hard for the measure's passage. Disappointed with Truman's lack of action, he quit as NHA administrator shortly thereafter.[111] The following year congressional conservatives killed legislation that would have established the NHA as a permanent agency.

111. *Ibid.,* 307–11. See also Davies, *Housing Reform During the Truman Administration,* 47–49.

119

IV. Citizens of Tomorrow: The Wartime Challenge to Community Action

Long before the fall of France in the summer of 1940 federal officials anticipated that industrial expansion, the movement of population to centers of defense activity, and the general dislocation attending the growth of boom-towns would create new social problems and intensify old ones. "There is no question that the expansion of industry now underway is bringing new life-blood to countless communities," noted Frank Bane, head of the Division of State and Local Cooperation of the National Defense Advisory Commission (NDAC), "but it also brings problems and raises questions that vitally affect every aspect of community life." The defense program, he declared, "will necessitate readjustment and extensions in our community housekeeping and public service."[1]

The Organization of Community Services

On November 28, 1940, the NDAC, with presidential approval, designated Paul V. McNutt, administrator of the Federal Security Agency (FSA), as coordinator of health, medical welfare, nutrition, recreation, and other civilian activities affecting the national defense.[2] For administrative purposes, Roosevelt established on September 3, 1941, the Office of Defense Health

1. Frank Bane, "National Defense: A Cooperative Job," *Public Welfare News* 8 (Nov. 1940), 4.
2. For convenience's sake, I am using the title Office of Community War Services (OCWS) throughout, recognizing that the precise reference from November 28, 1940, to September 3, 1941, should be to the Office of the Coordinator of Health, Welfare, and Related Defense Activities, and the reference from 1941 to 1943 to the Office of Defense Health and Welfare Services. See "Health, Welfare and Related Aspects of Community War Services," unpub. memorandum, June 1942, and "Regional Offices, Defense

120

and Welfare Services (ODHWS) in the Office of Emergency Management. Then, in April 1943, to ensure greater efficiency after the country had converted to war, the President renamed the ODHWS the Office of Community War Services (OCWS) and transferred its operations back to the Federal Security Agency.[3]

The designation of the Federal Security Agency to house the community war services program was logical in two respects. Among its constituent social service agencies were the U.S. Public Health Service, the Social Security Board, the Office of Education, the National Youth Administration and Civilian Conservation Corps (before their demise in 1943), and the Food and Drug Administration. The U.S. Children's Bureau, though technically part of the Department of Labor, had formed a close working relationship with the FSA. Also, the FSA had the reputation of being an advocate of cooperative federalism. This was a factor of considerable importance because the President had earlier instructed the NDAC to involve the states and localities in every step of the defense of the home front. Within the parent organization, the OCWS public service bureaucrats adhered to this principle. Except in cases of unusual emergency, the existing relationship of federal social service agencies with their cooperating state and local counterparts, and the existing division of responsibility among the various levels of government, was recognized and maintained.[4]

At its first meeting in 1941, McNutt outlined the tasks that the President and the Defense Advisory Commission had set for the community war services agency. These were (1) to afford protection to individuals and communities suffering disproportionate economic, social, or health burdens as a result of military or industrial defense activity; (2) to assist civilian agencies

Health and Welfare Services: Statement of Function," unpub. memorandum, Apr. 1942, National Archives (NA) Record Group (RG) 215, Records of the Office of Community War Services (OCWS).

3. McNutt's continuous presence throughout the early months of administrative reshuffling afforded the community war services program a greater degree of continuity and stability than was apparent from the government's organizational chart.

4. See "Health, Welfare and Related Aspects of Community War Services," June 1942, and "Regional Offices, Defense Health and Welfare Services: Statement of Function," NARG 215, OCWS Records.

and individuals in making an effective contribution to the health, welfare, and morale of men engaged in military service; and (3) to promote the health, security, and morale of the civilian population. The first two mandates were straightforward, and studies of the war's impact on the home front have usually focused upon them.[5]

The third mandate, vague and ambiguous, was like an empty vessel waiting to be filled. From the outset it attracted ambitious public service bureaucrats, liberals, and reformers whose thoughts were directed beyond the immediate crisis to the configuration of postwar cities. The community services program presented them with a unique opportunity to satisfy the immediate demands of war-affected communities while advancing further the humanitarian achievements of the New Deal pertaining to the urban condition.[6]

OCWS bureaucrats and urban liberals alike were disturbed by the growing loss of *communitas* in American cities, a condition intensified by the long-term physical deterioration of the urban environment and wartime disruption of family and individual life.[7] The war services program offered the opportunity to re-create the spirit of the older, consensual community[8] in which the individual's relationship to the larger society still had meaning. One liberal New Dealer articulated this sentiment when he explained: "The main task of the War, and the task of the peace, in broadest terms is to achieve a better world, in which men can live and work together peacefully and fruitfully. This achievement is an individual and a world task. Only a community is both large enough and small enough to assert a pattern of fruitful living which influences the individual citizen and to

5. See, for example, two recent works: Richard J. Polenberg, *War and Society: The United States, 1941–1945* (Philadelphia, 1972), and Geoffrey Perrett, *Days of Sadness, Years of Triumph: The American People, 1939–1945* (New York, 1973).

6. Wayne McMillan, "Social Work and National Defense," *Social Service Review* 15 (June 1941), 284.

7. For the concept of community see Roland Warren, *The Community in America* (Chicago, 1972), 9–13.

8. For a good description of this older idea of community in the Progressive Era see Clarence A. Perry, *Ten Years of the Community Center Movement* (New York, 1921), and Jean B. Quandt, *From the Small Town to the Great Community* (New Brunswick, 1970).

forge the common will to have the kind of world we want." Then, in a perceptive observation, he added: "But so often in this century the community has been impotent to do these things because the community itself has been shattered. Mass production industry has built great populations but deprived the people of the communal and creative life which human beings need. The dispersive influence of the automobile, the telephone, and the radio have all hastened the disintegration of community life. People have been separated from responsibilities for the general welfare and left untouched by any community purpose."[9]

The community was an extension of the city's neighborhoods—those parts of a populated area where citizens found it practicable to come together face to face in a personal, lasting, and actively humanitarian process to decide for themselves matters of community import. As a starting point for the restoration of *communitas,* these neighborhoods needed to rejuvenate the human and social fabric within them. They needed symbols, some visible expressions of community life, whether they took the form of child-care facilities, recreation centers, or school hot lunch programs.

An organized community was one that possessed the machinery not only for experimentation but also for becoming an intelligent, coordinated, wise-acting civic unit. It was an agency of educational effort and general culture, the focus of social life and the best interests of the people, as well as a rallying point for civic patriotism. The Committee on Community Organization of the OCWS expounded this view in June 1942 when it urged the local organization of the civilian front to sustain the battlefront. It then added: "We must likewise organize to deal with the human problems which must be met if the Home Front is to be kept secure and if we as a people are to make the all-out effort which we must make. We must organize our efforts and our resources to deal with new and intensified problems of health, nutrition, consumer services, housing, education, welfare and child care, and recreation for industrial workers and members of

9. Porter Butts, "To Serve the Community Purpose," *Recreation* 39 (Sept. 1945), 315, 328.

the armed forces. The planning and coordination of these community war services is an important task in each community."[10]

The larger purposes of the public service bureaucracy may be discerned from analysis of four of the most important community war services programs: nutrition, child and juvenile care, social protection, and recreation. The origins and evolution of these federal programs reveal that they were to have a deeper import than simply funneling money to cities temporarily overburdened. The OCWS programs, administered locally by like -minded state and city officials, were to serve as the foundation stones for a new community synthesis.

Nutrition and National Defense

Good nutrition became an issue of transcendent importance in 1941 with the shocking revelation that nearly 400,000 of the first million draftees had failed their physical examinations. The consensus of medical opinion was that one-third of the conscripts had been rejected because of malnutrition. Even granted that the physical fitness standards of 1941 were more rigorous than those of 1917, if the nation was not worse off a quarter century later, it was certainly no better. General Lewis B. Hershey, the director of the Selective Service System, branded the situation "a national disgrace."[11]

Immediately thereafter, statistical information in other areas confirmed the national dimensions of malnutrition, wrought largely by the Depression of the thirties. Milo Perkins, president of the Federal Surplus Commodities Corporation, called public attention to the findings of his agency's survey of incomes for 1935–36, the most recent years for which data were available. The study covered 29.4 million families and 10,000 unmarried people, representing a total of 126 million individuals. Two -thirds of the families surveyed had annual incomes of less than

10. Quoted in "Health, Welfare and Related Aspects of Community War Services," NARG 215, OCWS Records.

11. Quoted in "Food Is Also Power: Nutrition Becomes National Policy for War and Peace," *Fortune* 24 (Aug. 1941), 105.

$1,500, with the average being $826 per annum, or $69 per month for an entire family. The figures portrayed a striking paradox, as Perkins noted: In a land of plenty, low incomes had required American families to make do with inadequate amounts and insufficient variety of good nutritious food, while surplus crops rotted in the fields.[12]

The sting of malnutrition was felt most acutely in the cities and towns, as Paul McNutt reminded citizens in speeches before national and local nutrition conferences throughout 1941 and 1942. He never discounted the reality of pellagra and other diseases attributable to vitamin deficiencies in poor rural counties, particularly in the South, but he insisted to the Nutrition Committee of Greater New York that "among country families, fully half have been found to have good diets, one-fourth fair and one-fourth poor." By contrast, "only a fifth of the families living in towns and cities have good diets, nearly half rate just fair, and more than a third are classed as definitely poor." In July 1941 the *Milbank Memorial Fund Quarterly,* the highly respected journal of population research, published the results of a careful study of subclinical malnutrition among urban youth of New York City's Lower East Side that seemingly confirmed McNutt's observations.[13]

The *Milbank* findings were cause for alarm not only for what they revealed about the health situation of America's youth, but also for what they implied about the well-being of thousands of young industrial workers flocking to the urban war centers. If the latter's nutritional state also was poor, the entire war effort could suffer, observed Professor John D. Black of Harvard University, a member of the Food and Nutrition Board of the National Research Council. Paul McNutt declared that indus-

---

12. *New York Times,* Jan. 22, 1941. But see also Hazel K. Stiebling, "How Well Fed Is the American Family?" in Federal Security Agency (FSA), ODHWS, *The Food Front: A Series of Eleven Lectures, March 11–April 15, 1942* (Washington, D.C., 1942), 18–19.

13. *New York Times,* Jan. 19, 22, 1941; Dorothy Wiehl and H.D. Kruse, "Medical Evaluation of Nutritional Status," *Milbank Memorial Fund Quarterly* 19 (July 1941), 241–51.

trial productivity was contingent upon good civilian morale and healthy workers.[14]

Gradually, from governmental and private sources, a definite philosophy emerged concerning nutrition and its relation to the national defense program. This new doctrine affirmed that good nutrition was no less a citizen's right than clothing, shelter, or education. Many observers, such as the editors of *Fortune* magazine, commented that the nutrition policy was challenging one of our oldest and most deeply entrenched social attitudes, feeding of the poor. A home economist, writing specifically about the urban poor, declared: "To neglect these people is to menace the health and morale of all of us. . . . These people must be given proper diets if we are to win both the war and the peace." FSA Administrator McNutt asserted, "If any real improvement is to be made in this situation [malnutrition], we will have to assume a far larger social responsibility for the physical well-being of every single person in the nation than we have ever done before."[15]

Because too many state and municipal officials were uninformed or reacted passively to the need to organize and structure their health care systems, the civilian population's nutritional deficiencies were in danger of being neglected or accorded low priority in the total mobilization program. It was to crystallize interest in nutrition and give it guidance that President Roosevelt called a National Nutrition Conference for Defense to convene in Washington, D.C., during May 26–28, 1941. This meeting, the first of its kind ever held in the United States, brought together 900 delegates, including physicians and other scientists, educators, home economists, social workers, and representatives of agriculture, labor, the food industry, consumers, and government. Vice President Henry A. Wallace left no doubt in anyone's mind that the social gains of the New Deal were going to be preserved and extended despite the war. Dis-

14. John D. Black, "Food: War and Postwar," *Annals of the American Academy of Political and Social Science* 224 (Jan. 1943), 2; *New York Times,* May 19, 1941.
15. See FSA, ODHWS, *Proceedings of the National Nutrition Conference for Defense, May 26–28, 1941* (Washington, D.C., 1942), v–vi (cited hereafter as *NNCD Proceedings*); *New York Times,* Jan. 19, 1941.

cussing good nutrition, Wallace declared: "This conference is firing the opening gun in a real new order; not a new order based on fear, compulsion and slavery, but a new order based on physical well-being, equal opportunity, and freedom of the 'soul.'"[16]

Indeed it was. As the working session of the conference revealed, the delegates quickly decided to make temporary wartime nutrition programs more enduring. A physically fit citizenry, regardless of economic class or social position, became their overall objective, a decision that accorded nicely with the OCWS bureaucrats' desire to revitalize the communal bonds of our postwar cities. Harriet Elliott, assistant administrator for consumer protection in the Office of Price Administration, spoke of national defense nutrition in this broader context of the humanitarian goals of the New Deal. "We cannot set the defense program on one side and our 'social gains' on the other side and ask how many of our social gains we must sacrifice for the sake of defense. Our social gains, those instruments of social protection which we have forged, are an essential part of our national defense," she declared. The fear of a postwar slump was no excuse for backsliding. A sound nutrition program that would continue after the war required intergovernmental cooperation and the coordination of public and private voluntary efforts.[17]

The subcommittee on urban affairs, which was examining community nutrition planning, had also come to the conclusion that good health and nutrition were a birthright and therefore too important to be identified solely with national defense. The delegates opted instead to promote community nutrition programs as a permanent long-range goal, recognizing that their success was contingent upon reaching into every neighborhood with their message and making every segment of the population conscious of good nutrition. Anthropologist Margaret Mead advised home economists to make nutrition education part of

16. Cf. "Minutes of the Regional Coordinators' Meeting," Apr. 28–29, 1941, NARG 215, OCWS Records, War Area Reports and Correspondence; *NNCD Proceedings,* 40; *New York Times,* May 27, 1941.

17. *NNCD Proceedings,* 61–62.

their regular routine, "as plans mature for national models for block—and neighborhood—leader organizations, and as city after city and county after county begin to select leaders from each small segment of their population."[18]

Chaired by Howard Y. McCluskey, associate director of the American Youth Commission, the urban subcommittee's recommendations to the conference reflected the belief that a national nutrition program was useful for inculcating in urban dwellers the earlier shared experiences of the neighborhood in ways supportive of the larger community and democratic ideals. This put the subcommittee squarely in the mainstream of progressive thinking with respect to nutrition's importance in reconstructing the social fabric of cities. It was a view also shared by others who saw in good nutrition the opportunity to lay the foundations of a better America in urban neighborhoods. People would become more fit, have greater strength and vigor, and be blessed with greater longevity as well as better mental and physical competence. The editors of *Fortune* had written: "A child of war . . . [O]ur national nutrition program looks beyond victory and lays the foundation for a better world." Paul Cornell, a nutrition consultant to the ocws, agreed. He told a Department of Agriculture symposium in 1942, "The nutrition program is going to succeed . . . because there is [*sic*] in this Nation enough people who care about the American dream." Once local neighborhoods and the larger community of city, state, and nation were reconstructed, the next step logically was the world community.[19]

Following the conference, and mainly because no extant federal agency had specific responsibility for promoting good nutrition, President Roosevelt issued an executive order on September 3, 1941, establishing within the ocws a new Nutrition Division. Until March 1943, when its functions were transferred to the Food Distribution Administration in the Department of

18. *Ibid.,* 186–96, 215; Margaret Mead, "Reaching the Last Woman Down the Road," *Journal of Home Economics* 34 (Dec. 1942), 710.

19. "Food Is Also Power," 108; Paul Cornell, "Factors Affecting Public Acceptance of the Nutrition Program," *The Food Front,* 17.

Agriculture, the staff of the ocws–Nutrition Division served as liaison to the states and cities, providing professional and technical counsel and operating as a secretarial and administrative center for the national nutrition program. It encouraged state nutrition committees and local defense councils to spearhead the campaign for good nutritional habits that would serve the population in war and in the peace to follow. Thanks to the joint efforts of schools and colleges, business and civic organizations, and dedicated individuals, together with advertising space, radio time, and motion pictures contributed by the communications media, the educational campaign stimulated active participation by millions of average citizens.[20]

The Nutrition Division capitalized on a wave of popular sentiment to underwrite the cost of ten urban demonstration projects having national potential as models to be emulated in peacetime as well as in war. In South Bend, Indiana, for example, the division financed a survey to show that few city families were regularly eating all the protective foods essential to good health and strength. This knowledge was crucial to the future planning of diets. In other large and small cities around the country—such as Seattle, Terre Haute, and Blacksburg, Virginia—the division organized workshops to instruct teachers how to devise imaginative methods of presenting nutrition instruction to youths. This was part of the process of instilling good eating habits in the younger generation. In Syracuse, New York, the division encouraged city officials to employ the block leader system for disseminating information on nutrition to neighborhood residents. In Austin, Texas, the Nutrition Division supported a project to develop successful techniques for teaching low-income, minority blacks and Chicanos how to achieve nutritionally balanced diets, even on meager budgets. This was important in the urban ghettos, where healthy citizens were the indispensable ingredient in any program for postwar reconstruction.[21]

20. The literature is abundant, but see FSA, OCWS, *Teamwork in Community Services 1941–1946: A Demonstration in Federal, State and Local Cooperation* (Washington, D.C., 1946), 63–64, and Vera Hills Day, "Denver's Nutrition Program," *Journal of Home Economics* 34 (Oct. 1942), 515–17.

21. *Teamwork in Community Services,* 64–65.

Toward a Federal Child Care Program

Though rationing and the food shortages of the latter war years were necessarily reflected in a changing emphasis, this early educational program had far-reaching effects. It not only prepared people and governments for the wartime task of making the best possible use of available funds but also highlighted the necessity of proper nutrition for health. This, in turn, focused governmental and popular attention on the wartime plight of children, especially the children of working mothers. Their well-being was vital to the larger interests of the city, state, and nation. Children, as the Advisory Commission on Children in Wartime stated in 1940, were the hope of mankind, the mortar that held together American family life, and thus communities, against the disruptive effects of war.[22]

This long-cherished progressive belief was one to which Franklin D. Roosevelt wholeheartedly subscribed. Along with specialists in the field of child welfare and education, the President saw in the conservation of family life, with all its traditions and values, the preservation of social solidarity in our postwar cities. This concern was frequently expressed and incorporated in the broader aspirations of the Atlantic Charter—hopes of fostering democratic ideals locally in the neighborhoods, nationally in cities, towns, and villages, and across the globe. Thus sociologist Israel A. Laster, writing in the *American City,* asserted that "we must cherish the children because, unless they are healthy in mind and body and spirit, we shall have no national greatness." They were the investment that, as a nation, we made in the future. "An all-embracing program of child care," he wrote, "will contribute toward this survival and extension of democracy."[23]

Perhaps no two individuals put the welfare of children into

22. *New York Times,* Apr. 16, 1942; Sidonie M. Gruenberg, ed., *The Family in a World at War* (New York, 1942), 295.
23. See Henrietta L. Gordon, "The Impact of National Defense on Child Welfare," *The Family* 23 (Mar. 1942), 3, and Israel A. Laster, "Child Care in Wartime: What Responsibilities Ought Municipal Governments to Assume?" *American City* 59 (Mar. 1944), 50.

the context of community renewal and extension of the New Deal more explicitly than Katherine F. Lenroot, head of the Children's Bureau, and Eleanor Roosevelt. Addressing the Children's Association of Westchester County, New York, in May 1942, Miss Lenroot asserted that citizens and voluntary groups must "equip [urban] youngsters of every race to take their places in a democracy." The necessity for progressive social engineering, even as the holocaust of war consumed the nation's energies, was immediately taken up by Mrs. Roosevelt.[24] Earlier that spring she had urged delegates attending a Children's Bureau conference to form pressure groups and lobby for congressional recognition of the symbiotic relationship between child welfare programs and the nation's war work. "We must get home to our communities, and through them to Congress, that to win the war is not enough. Because the war, to be worth fighting, has to win something for the people who are going to live afterward all over the world."[25]

Until the spring of 1942, however, the War Manpower Commission, social workers, and educators generally believed that mothers should remain in the home. But as more and more communities housing industrial plants exhausted available sources of male labor, their attitude changed. Once employers overcame their initial reluctance to hire women for assembly-line work, it was relatively easy for them to pass from hiring single women to hiring working mothers. At first, because employment in defense industries paid well, employers adopted the position that working mothers should make their own child-care arrangements, going so far in some instances as to dock wages or threaten them with discharge for requesting leave to care for ill children. The result of this early laissez-faire attitude on the part of employers, and the absence of any positive governmental child-care policies in the congested production centers, was

24. *New York Times,* May 8, 1942. See also *Wartime Care and Protection of Children of Employed Mothers,* Hearings before the Committee on Education and Labor, United States Senate, 78th Cong., 1st sess. on S. 876 and S. 1130, June 8, 1943 (1943), 53–55.
25. *New York Times,* Mar. 18, 1942, and "Children's Charter in Wartime," *Survey* 78 (Apr. 1942), 108–10.

often counterproductive in worker efficiency. Employee absenteeism rose, contagious childhood diseases went unreported, pregnancies were concealed, prenatal care neglected, and additional strains put on family life.[26]

Evidence of child neglect mounted as working mothers resorted to makeshift arrangements. The press commented daily on the phenomenon of "latch-key" children—urchins with door keys strung around their necks who were left to play outside while waiting for their mothers' shifts to end, but who more often roamed the streets creating mischief. Other children had been told to report after school to a neighbor's apartment, or else were locked in their homes all day, sometimes with tragic results.[27] With private day-care facilities in short supply, some mothers turned to institutional and foster home placement for their children, a practice that evoked a storm of criticism from Civilian Defense Director Fiorello La Guardia, who contended that the worst home environment and working mother was superior to institutional care.

Yet another hardship was the provision of medical care for sick children, aggravated where a community had been stripped of its physicians for the war effort. Besides physical care, the children of working mothers needed love, affection, and recognition, declared Dr. Martha W. MacDonald, psychiatric adviser to the Children's Bureau. They also needed assurance that the killing and violence were wrong and would eventually cease, that their fathers would come home again, and that their communities would once more be safe and happy places.[28]

To call official attention to the impending crisis and its consequences for full worker productivity, the Children's Bureau lobbied for an American equivalent of the British child-care

26. "Policies Regarding the Employment of Mothers of Young Children in Occupations Essential to the National Defense," *Child Welfare* 21 (Mar. 1942), 7; Grace Reeder, "Community Planning for the Care of Children of Employed Mothers," *ibid.*, 21 (Sept. 1942), 10–11.

27. *New York Times,* Dec. 5, 1941.

28. "Door Key Children," *Journal of Home Economics* 33 (Dec. 1941), 736–38; Howard Hopkirk, "Children Bear the Promise of a Better World," *Child Welfare* 20 (Dec. 1941), 9; Martha W. MacDonald, "The Impact of the War on Children and Youth," *The Child* 7 (Mar. 1943), 135.

program. On July 31 and August 1, 1941, the bureau sponsored a conference in Washington, D.C., from which emerged a Joint Planning Board on the Day Care of Children. After careful analysis of the problem, the board agreed that the most effective child-care program was one that combined the best features of local initiative with central coordination and supportive services. By March 1942 the bureau's conference on "Children in Wartime" had drafted a blueprint for the organization of day-care facilities by the states and also a model state ordinance for regulating commercial child-care centers.[29]

The realization that mothers not only *would* work but in a growing number of industrial centers *must* work to maximize output persuaded McNutt, who was also chairman of the WMC (War Manpower Commission), that a reassessment of the existing policy was overdue. On July 8, 1942, he held a meeting of the nine federal agencies having an interest in child care. After the conference McNutt disclosed that the WMC was prepared to relax its opposition to working mothers, a decision which should not imply any diminished concern for family and community stability. Further, the WMC reaffirmed the principle of working through the existing network of state and local welfare agencies, asserting that the child-care programs must evolve from community-wide participation.[30]

The interaction of ordinary citizens, voluntary associations, and local government would strengthen the child-care program and pull together the disparate elements of the community. To facilitate this McNutt authorized the establishment of a Day Care Division as a new section within the OCWS and issued Directive IX ordering all federal agencies "to develop, integrate, and coordinate federal programs for the day care of working

---

29. See the testimony of Charles P. Taft, OCWS director, in *Wartime Care and Protection of Children*, 10. Also, Lady E.D. Simon, "The Working Mother in England," *The Child* 7 (Nov. 1942), 62, and "For Our Children in Wartime," *ibid.,* 7 (Oct. 1942), 6.

30. See *Wartime Health and Education,* Hearings before a Subcommittee of the Committee on Education and Labor, United States Senate, pursuant to S. Res. 74, 78th Cong., 1st sess., pt. 1, *Juvenile Delinquency* (Washington, D.C., 1944), 157, and "Policy of the War Manpower Commission on Employment in Industry of Women with Young Children," *The Child* 7 (Oct. 1942), 51.

mothers' [children]." This action theoretically turned the ocws-Day Care Division into the federal clearinghouse for all data and action relevant to child-care services, except for facilities built with Lanham Act funds, which remained securely in the hands of the more conservative Federal Works Agency (FWA).[31]

This was not immediately apparent, however, for procedures under the Lanham Act were unbearably slow. The law was first interpreted as applicable to day-care centers in February 1942, but not a single community saw a cent of the money until October. By then the cities' efforts to provide and expand such facilities from their own resources were faltering.[32] Cleveland, for example, had established an emergency child-care commission as early as 1941. Two years later, it had been able to provide only ten centers—for a population of 878,000. It was not until May 1943 that Lanham Act funds began to pour in and the commission was able to open seventeen additional centers. The pattern was repeated in urban communities as diverse as St. Louis, Baltimore, Oak Park (an affluent suburb of Chicago), and Washington, D.C.[33]

The states, meanwhile, had confined their assistance to hiring qualified staff, planning day-care activities, and stimulating local programs. Most states stopped short of committing funds for the actual construction of facilities. There were some exceptions, of course: Connecticut and Washington, where conditions were particularly serious, dipped into their own coffers; New York appropriated $2.5 million, but only for communities that were not eligible for Lanham funds; Pennsylvania appropriated $187,000 to purchase nursery school equipment. But these were usually short-term or stopgap measures, forcing ur-

31. See *Wartime Care and Protection of Children,* 10; Alice T. Dashiell, "Day Care: A Review of Organization and Administration," *Child Welfare* 23 (Apr. 1944), 1-3.

32. For evidence see *Wartime Care and Protection of Children,* 73-74, 81-82, and *Teamwork in Community Services,* 63.

33. Cf. Henry L. Zucker, "Cleveland's Program of Community Service for the Care of Children of Working Mothers," *The Child* 8 (Nov. 1943), 168; Callman Rawley, "Case Work and Day Care—Beginnings of a Municipal Program," *The Family* 24 (Mar. 1943), 22; Susan M. Lee, "Meeting the Normal Recreational Needs of Children in Wartime," *Child Welfare* 21 (Dec. 1942), 12.

ban officials to put greater pressure on the federal government to eliminate the delays.[34]

Considerable jubilation therefore attended the announcement that the President on August 22, 1942, had addressed identical letters to the chairmen of the Committee on Ways and Means of the House and the Committee on Finance of the Senate recommending an amendment to Title v of the Social Security Act. The amendment authorized the ocws-Day Care Division to make grants amounting to $7.5 million to states for maternal and child health and welfare services. Bills incorporating the President's suggestion were immediately introduced in both houses. In letters to the congressional managers of the bills, Roosevelt reiterated more sharply than before his fear that the war was having an adverse impact upon community stability through the erosion of the family bonds. The funds, he wrote, would go a long way toward shoring up families and neighborhoods. Six days later, on August 28, 1942, Roosevelt gave tangible evidence of his concern by releasing $400,000 from the President's emergency fund to ocws for grants-in-aid to the states.[35]

As it turned out, the $400,000 had some heavy strings attached that prevented it from being used for operating purposes, but the money did prove useful on both state and local levels in the planning and coordinating of day-care programs.[36] A congested production area such as New Jersey was able to secure funds from the ocws-Day Care Division for the appointment of highly trained staff to the state's Department of Institutions and Agencies and Department of Public Instruction, who labored to overcome community inertia. By mid-1943 150 child-care committees were functioning in New Jersey, 20 had well-

34. Kathryn Close, "After Lanham Funds—What?" *Survey* 81 (May 1945), 131.

35. *Congressional Record,* 77th Cong., 2d sess., 88 (Aug. 25, 1942), 6950. Also see the address of Katherine F. Lenroot, "State and Community Action for Children in Wartime," Nov. 10, 1942, in NARG 171, Records of the United States Office of Civilian Defense (OCD).

36. James Brunot to Leonard Logan, Oct. 14, 1942, in NARG 215, ocws Records, and "Policies for Grants to States for Promotion and Coordination of Programs for Services to Children of Working Mothers," unpub. memorandum, Aug. 28, 1942, in *ibid.*

developed programs, and 10 had submitted applications for Lanham Act funds. More importantly, the competition from OCWS provided an impetus to the FWA to oil its machinery so that Lanham money for construction would flow more speedily into the hard-pressed urban-industrial centers. The challenge proved partially effective. Between October 1942 and the summer of 1943, FWA approved funds for 464 programs, including 3,700 day-care units. In some instances the process had so accelerated that neither state agencies nor the Children's Bureau and Office of Education, acting for the OCWS in the field, knew anything about it until the community had received the award.[37]

The Adolescent in a World at War

If concern for the well-being of young children stemmed from the belief that they were urban America's citizens of tomorrow, the same interest in family preservation as the keystone of community rejuvenation kindled federal and local awareness of the troubled adolescent, the juvenile delinquent. Virtually every expert agreed that the incidence of teenage delinquency had increased during the war, although the exact dimension of the problem was less certain. In 1943, Mayor Fletcher Bowron of Los Angeles told Senator Claude W. Pepper's subcommittee, which was investigating juvenile delinquency and its relation to the future stability of the country, that "conditions directly attributable to the war, including great influx of new population, inability of the city to assimilate them rapidly, inadequate housing, employment of mothers, enlistment of youth leaders in armed services, have resulted in youthful depredations, gang tendencies and juvenile delinquency which are giving this city much concern."[38]

The OCWS, too, was troubled by the rise in delinquent child

---

37. By June 1, 1943, the OCWS-Day Care Division had made 68 grants through the Children's Bureau and Office of Education to 42 states and the District of Columbia; 38 grants to departments of education; 30 awards to welfare departments. See *Wartime Care and Protection of Children*, 11–12. For data on New Jersey see Kathryn Close, "Day Care Up to Now," *Survey* 79 (July 1943), 194, 197.

38. *Wartime Health and Education*, pt. 1, 56, 304.

behavior and attributed it to the disruption of the usual community norms of behavior. In a widely circulated pamphlet, *Citizens of Tomorrow,* ocws had written: "The sense of upheaval, of tremendous activity in which they have little or no part, the glamour of war adventure just beyond their grasp—these pressures weigh heavily on all boys and girls. Even the best adjusted, with stable, sympathetic homes, may feel shut out. It is no wonder those with no anchor to windward—in themselves, in their homes, in their communities—think a war-dizzy world gives license to grab whatever excitement they can find, without counting cost or danger."[39]

Not surprisingly, child welfare authorities, municipal officials, and the news media perceived deviant adolescent behavior as an urban phenomenon. In overcrowded cities the problem was more concentrated and more visible, and the consequences more readily understood. The city environment seemed to impose fewer constraints on youthful activities than a rural setting.[40] But was juvenile delinquency exclusively or even predominantly a scourge of the crowded war-industry centers? The most comprehensive statistical profile of deviant adolescent behavior was provided by Charles L. Chute, executive secretary of the National Probation Association, in testimony before the Pepper subcommittee. During February and March 1943 Chute had sent out a questionnaire to the chief probation officers in juvenile courts in all cities or urban counties of 50,000 population and over, asking for the total number of boys and girls dealt with officially and unofficially by courts for each of the three years 1940, 1941, 1942—the period of industrial mobilization and the first full year of war. Chute received returns from 153 jurisdictions: 55 urban counties of more than 200,000 population, 42 from counties of 100,000–200,000 population, and 56 returns from localities under 100,000 population. All but seven

39. FSA, OCWS, *Citizens of Tomorrow: A Wartime Challenge to Community Action* (Washington, D.C., 1943), 5.
40. This was the opinion of Senator Kenneth S. Wherry, Republican of Nebraska and member of the Pepper subcommittee, who attributed the rise in delinquency to the breakdown of traditional institutions in the urban centers. See *Wartime Health and Education,* pt. 1, 99.

counties in the nation containing cities of 200,000 population and more were included, and more than half the cities in the 100,000–200,000 bracket.[41]

The returns from the 153 jurisdictions were both revealing and disturbing. Juvenile courts in 1940 reported a total of 103,571 cases of delinquent child behavior; 111,311 cases in 1941; and 120,811 cases in 1942. The 1941 increase, occurring in a year of rapid industrial expansion for defense, over 1940, a normal year wherein delinquency in many cities such as New York was reported to have dropped to an all-time low, was 7.5 percent. The increase in the war year 1942 over 1941 was 8.5 percent. Comparison of 1940's "normal, basic" figures with those for 1942 disclosed an increase of 16.6 percent. Insofar as the court figures were accurate, the incidence of delinquency had risen in 1941 and 1942 compared with each previous year. What was most alarming, however, was the very rapid incidence of delinquent behavior among adolescent girls. Extrapolating from these trends, Chute predicted that juvenile delinquency would become more serious each year the war was prolonged.[42]

The association's findings clearly supported the contention that delinquency was an urban blight, but a concurrent survey undertaken by the Children's Bureau disclosed that deviant adolescent behavior had increased by 44 percent in the same period in rural areas of declining population. Hence the problem was national in scope, affecting nearly every community to a greater or lesser degree, regardless of location, size, or extent of urbanization. Moreover, contrary to popular impression and press reports, the Probation Association was not prepared to concede that the greatest incidence of delinquency was occurring in war-industry centers. A large number of cities, undoubtedly centers of war production, reported no increase whatever in 1942. Chute cited Newark, Trenton, Buffalo, Rochester,

---

41. Charles L. Chute, "Juvenile Delinquency in Wartime," in *ibid.*, pt. 1, 236–40.

42. The association's survey disclosed that while boys' cases in all juvenile courts had increased in 1941–42 by 4,325 (52 percent), girls' cases had increased by 4,787 (23.4 percent). However, the association concluded that "girls' cases are increasing much faster than boys'; in fact, in many courts the chief problem developed by war conditions appears to be the increase in girls' cases." See *ibid.*, pt. 1, 237–38.

Syracuse, Cincinnati, Memphis, Milwaukee, and Atlanta, attributing their stability to strong neighborhood and community action programs.[43]

Although the picture changed rapidly and dramatically in 1943, the caveat is worth noting because of the tendency to believe that delinquency was primarily a problem of the war-industry centers.[44] Judge Justine Wise Polier of New York City alerted the subcommittee to delinquency in noncongested production areas as well and pointed out the need for federal and state assistance there. In large communities like New York which did not have a great influx of new workers or war plants, unskilled and welfare mothers were going into employment of various kinds, often jobs with the longest hours and poorest pay, which released other men and women to go into defense factories or the armed services. "I think that unless we are going to be willing to include their children in any program we are going to face a very small proportion of the problem, and not really meet the problems of the 'children of Mars,'" Judge Polier declared.[45]

An appropriate response required the coordination of governmental resources, recognizing in the words of the Children's Bureau that there was "no quick, sudden, or dramatic method of dealing with the problem of juvenile delinquency." Primary responsibility for protecting youth was still the parents', but the community also had an obligation to assist, chiefly by making available outside the home services that promoted wholesome growth and development. Why was this also a community, an intergovernmental, responsibility? Because, to quote from the

43. "Juvenile Court Statistics," *The Child* 9 suppl. (June 1945), 20–22; Alice S. Nutt, "Wartime Influences on Juvenile Delinquency," *Child Welfare Bulletin* 21 (Nov. 1942), 1.

44. The Children's Bureau reported a 31 percent increase in juvenile delinquency from 145 juvenile courts in 1943 over 1942. The percentage increase in the urban centers of war production was particularly notable: Multnomah County (Portland), 125 percent; Tulsa, 114 percent; Spokane County, 112 percent; Norfolk, 69 percent; San Francisco County, 60 percent; Dallas County, 55 percent; Cuyahoga County (Cleveland), 48 percent; Los Angeles County, 24 percent; Wayne County (Detroit), 15 percent; Alleghany County (Pittsburgh), 15 percent; Milwaukee County, 13 percent; Washington, D.C., 12 percent. See *New York Times,* Apr. 12, 1944.

45. *Wartime Health and Education,* pt. 1, 406.

ocws's pamphlet, *Citizens of Tomorrow:* "After the family, the community is the most important influence on young people's lives."[46]

A concerted program of new and improved educational opportunities, constructive recreational activities, and meaningful participation in protection of the home front would serve as deterrents to wartime delinquency. But the collective involvement of parents and teachers, social workers and policemen, federal and local government, and young people themselves was also the catalyst for community renewal. It was in this context that public service bureaucrats and liberal Democrats perceived the juvenile delinquency program: they anticipated that it would continue beyond the immediate wartime emergency and advance the social welfare aims of the New Deal. Eleanor T. Glueck, a noted research criminologist at the Harvard Law School, wrote in the *Survey* of February 1942: "First of all, it is vitally important to preserve the welfare services that have been built up over many years." Recreation, health and essential hygiene services, vocational guidance, counseling for disintegrating and broken families, decent housing, and adequate relief were the forward line of defense against delinquency. But it was not enough merely to preserve these welfare services, she concluded. "They must be strengthened and enlarged, particularly in those considerable areas of our country where they are now extremely meager."[47]

Encouraged by the ocws, the Children's Bureau assumed leadership in stimulating new programs and reinforcing existing ones for ameliorating delinquent behavior. It published in 1943 a handbook, *Controlling Juvenile Delinquency,* that outlined a complete community action program for local officials to whom the problem was relatively unfamiliar. Among other things, the manual recommended (1) individual guidance for maladjusted youth, developed in cooperation with police, courts, schools,

46. *Ibid.,* pt. 1, 107; *Citizens of Tomorrow,* 6; "Report of the Advisory Committee on Community Child Welfare Services," *The Child* 25 (Jan. 1941), 177.
47. [Katherine F. Lenroot], "American Childhood Challenges American Democracy," *The Child* 5 (July 1940), 8; Eleanor T. Glueck, "Juvenile Delinquency in Wartime," *Survey* 78 (Feb. 1942), 71.

and other community agencies; (2) assistance to state and local defense councils, planning and coordinating bodies; (3) advisory service in relating recreational and leisure-time programs to individual needs; (4) cooperation with state labor departments and local agencies in the supervision and protection of employed youth, particularly in the amusement and refreshment industries; (5) operation of facilities for temporary care of children in localities where they were not available currently; (6) cooperation with state and local training schools and other institutions in rehabilitating delinquent minors; and (7) assistance in developing resources to train personnel for child welfare work and for children's services in police departments.[48]

The guidelines set forth in the manual evolved from a project worked out jointly by OCWS, the Children's Bureau, and the Social Security Bureau in cooperation with the state department of public welfare of Virginia and the city of Newport News, one of the most heavily affected military-industrial-urban complexes of World War II.[49] The objective of the pilot program, initiated in 1942, had been to demonstrate how a community could mobilize its resources to prevent and control juvenile delinquency. On a deeper level, this was an experiment in intergovernmental relations to find ways by which all levels of government might work together to solve a given problem. Although sponsored and financed by federal agencies, the project was carried on by local leadership and citizen participation, which was enlisted through a broadly representative committee with members drawn not only from the traditional white power structure but also from among blacks and organized labor, "the second minority."[50]

48. U.S. Children's Bureau, *Controlling Juvenile Delinquency: A Community Program* (Washington, D.C., 1943), *passim*. See also Dean Snyder to OCWS Regional Directors, Aug. 7, 1943, and Charles P. Taft, "Juvenile Delinquency," unpub. memorandum, July 5, 1943, in NARG 215, OCWS Records.

49. For an analysis of this interesting experiment, which paired one urban community (Newport News) with one rural community (Pulaski County) in southwest Virginia, see Charles F. Marsh, ed., *The Hampton Roads Communities in World War II* (Chapel Hill, 1951), 22–23, 261.

50. For details see U.S. Children's Bureau, "A Community Program for Prevention and Control of Juvenile Delinquency in Wartime," Sept. 1943, in NARG 215, OCWS Records.

Evaluating the general results of this joint undertaking three years after the war, Herbert G. Ross, superintendent of the city's social service bureau, observed that the project developed important information and statistics for the social agencies which they had not had access to before, stimulated closer coordination and cooperation between the social agencies and the city, brought together public officials and citizens who received a good grounding in the principles of community organization and social welfare, and initiated a number of worthwhile movements in the city for new welfare facilities.[51]

Other communities adopted the manual but modified its recommendations to fit their own particular needs. The result was a wide-ranging and creative response from city and state governmental as well as neighborhood associational bodies. In Kansas City, the welfare department organized a new division of community councils which sponsored teenage clubs and community centers and provided additional playgrounds. In Chicago, the South Side Community Committee sponsored four neighborhood centers with full recreation and leisure-time programs, in an area where ten years earlier twenty out of every hundred boys under twenty-one years of age were going before the juvenile court. In a section of Los Angeles populated by 100,000 blacks and 140,000 Mexicans, Mexican-Americans, and others of Latin stock, ten private recreation agencies combined under one coordinator, who used a $234,000 grant from the local defense council to expand recreational services. In Gary, Indiana, the defense council enlisted youth in the "All-Out-America" program, which conducted drives for scrap metal, used clothing, and war bonds.[52]

Careful scrutiny of these and other programs suggests that OCWS officials were using the war, like the Depression, to foster intergovernmental cooperation, coordination among the agen-

---

51. The question remains, however, of how successful this experiment was in curbing the incidence of delinquency—apparently not very. The number of delinquents appearing before the Juvenile and Domestic Relations Court in Newport News rose from 383 in 1940 to 647 in 1942, and to 919 in 1944. See Marsh, *The Hampton Roads Communities,* 123, 263–64.

52. "Good Ideas at Work," *Survey* 80 (Mar. 1944), 84–85.

cies of local government, and closer ties between public and private social welfare agencies. The Children's Bureau took the initiative in lobbying for continuation of these programs beyond the present emergency and as part of the broader movement to rejuvenate the social fabric of postwar urban communities.[53] Katherine F. Lenroot wrote that "the awakened interest in children on the part of legislators, government officials, and the public generally, must not be allowed to die out as the nation faces the 'change over.'" Child neglect in the period of reconversion would have disastrous consequences for family and community stability, she predicted, adding that "we must take steps now to see to it that for children and youth peace will ring in both protection and opportunity." This required all segments of the neighborhood and community to pull together, function as a unit, and never lose sight of the broader social objective.[54]

The public service bureaucrats of OCWS bestowed their blessing on the bureau's efforts and cooperated at every opportunity. Mark McCloskey, director of the OCWS-Recreation Division, asserted in May 1941, in an address to the National Probation Association meeting in Cleveland, that the war had taught citizens the value of the community approach to social pathologies, and he insisted that there was a direct link between the amelioration of delinquent child behavior and the task of rendering postwar cities more humane and responsive to individual needs. The problem of delinquency in the cities would be aggravated by the migration of families back to their places of origin and by returning veterans, many of them disabled, more of them emotionally torn. "The problems of veterans will be hard," he noted, "the plight of kids may be harder. Whatever strength and judgment they can build for themselves now, with our help, will stand them in good stead for the roaring forties to come."[55]

53. See "Goals for Children and Youth As We Move from War to Peace: Children's Bureau Conference on Children in Wartime," *The Child* 8 (Apr. 1944), 147–49; Katherine F. Lenroot, "Federal and State Action," *Survey* 80 (Mar. 1944), 94.

54. *Wartime Health and Education,* pt. 1, 157–60; Lenroot, "Federal and State Action," 106. See also Elsa Castendyck, "Preventing Juvenile Delinquency," *Public Management* 25 (June 1943), 168–73.

55. Mark A. McCloskey, "Wartime Delinquency and the Job Ahead," in Marjorie

The War Against VD

Another special area of community concern arising from the interest in youth was social protection, the wartime euphemism for the national program to suppress commercialized prostitution and curb the spread of venereal disease (VD). Dr. Howard Ennes, a public health service physician attached to the U.S. Navy Bureau of Medicine and Surgery, described the rising incidence of venereal infections as symptomatic of a "social disorganization of tremendous depth," and not simply the result of casual sexual relationships or ignorance of prophylactic measures.[56]

Statistics, particularly from urban areas of industrial production and localities adjacent to military encampments, gave credence to Ennes's portrayal of communities in disarray in these areas: defense migration, selective service, and the war had clearly loosened the bonds of kinship, family, church, and school. In 1943 nearly 600,000 cases of *civilians* contracting syphilis were reported to public health authorities, 100,000 more than had ever been reported in one year during the history of the national control program, which dated from 1938.[57] Venereal disease was not equally prevalent over the country, or within a state or community during the war, but most military, medical, and legal authorities agreed that the rates were higher in the urban South than in the North, and far higher in some urbanized Northern states than in others.[58]

Bell, ed., *Cooperation in Crime Control: Annual Yearbook of the National Probation and Parole Association for 1944* (New York, 1944), 135–42.

56. Quoted in Helen V. Tooker, "Venereal Disease—Far from Beaten," *Harper's Magazine* 189 (Nov. 1944), 549.

57. Selective service examinations in 1941 established the fact that more than 3.2 million Americans had syphilis, or one out of every forty-two. The wartime incidence of gonorrhea, a disease more difficult to diagnose, is unknown because no official agency kept accurate records. See *ibid.* and FSA, OCWS, *Challenge to Community Action* (Washington, D.C., 1945), 9.

58. Venereal disease was especially prevalent among Negroes. Expert opinion was unanimous on this point, even when conceding the difficulty of getting reliable statistical data on the black population. In 1945, the OCWS–Social Protection Division estimated that blacks accounted for 50 percent of all reported cases, although they constituted only 10 percent of the total population. See FSA, OCWS, *Challenge to Community Action,* 13, 27.

At first the experts were inclined to attribute the epidemic spread of VD almost exclusively to commercialized prostitution, which they saw as a threat to the welfare of every American community. The call girl undermined the defense effort by sidelining infected soldiers and industrial workers and by promoting big-time crime. The American Social Hygiene Association encouraged municipal officials to view prostitution in this light by delineating the call girl as a threat to family stability and community values. Prostitution was invariably accompanied by parasites—madams, pimps, pandering taxi drivers, corrupt police and municipal officials, porno dealers, racketeers, and shady amusement promoters. "This unholy union between respectable citizens and commercialized vice makes police honesty impossible. The end result is the disfranchisement of every honest man or woman who has the temerity to attack the system," declared L.D. Morrison, chief police inspector of Houston.[59]

Only after a time did these same experts come to recognize that the chief source of infections, particularly the more-difficult-to-diagnose gonorrhea, was not the professional prostitute but the "victory girl," the casual, the juvenile delinquent who willingly gave herself to the boy in uniform and factory worker in coveralls. This was the informed judgment of Elliott Ness, director of the OCWS-Social Protection Division, Katherine Lenroot, Boston physician Dr. Augusta F. Bronner, and the president of the International Association of Police Chiefs. Police statistics from several cities—Seattle, San Antonio, Little Rock—indicated that one- to two-thirds of the girls arrested for sex-related offenses were under twenty-one years old. Not even smaller urban communities were immune: in Fall River, Massachusetts, for example, more than 20 percent of the girls arrested for sex offenses were under eighteen.[60]

New York City, a magnet for servicemen on leave, industrial workers seeking relief from stepped-up production schedules, and unattached females of all ages, graphically illustrated this

---

59. *Ibid.,* 8–9.
60. See *Wartime Health and Education,* pt. 1, 6–7, 79–85, and *Challenge to Community Action,* 2.

new problem. Juvenile court records dating from 1903 disclosed a steady decline in all categories of juvenile delinquency until the war. Then, in the ten-month period ending in December 1944, the incidence of syphilitic infection among young girls aged fifteen to nineteen was 204 percent greater than in the same period of 1941. Admittedly this figure reflected a cumulative increase over three crisis-ridden years; but even when the incidence from January to October 1944 was compared with the corresponding months of 1943 the increase still amounted to 31 percent! The seriousness of juvenile sexual delinquency can be gauged from the often bitter exchanges among federal and state officials and indignant congressmen, who demanded to know why "our boys" were not "safe" in Times Square, and a besieged Mayor La Guardia. Paradoxically, New York City had long been in the forefront of progressive action in all areas of juvenile delinquency, but nothing the Little Flower said or did was able to shake the image of "Sin City."[61]

Until March 1941 social protection had not fallen within the purview of any single federal agency. Then, alarmed by reports of rising venereal infections around the country, the Council of National Defense authorized creation of a Social Protection Division within the OCWS. The division's function, as outlined by Director Elliott Ness in a staff memorandum dated September 10, 1941, was "to safeguard the health and morale of the armed forces and of the workers in war industries . . . by the reduction of venereal disease." This involved attacking the problem from several directions but mostly by suppressing prostitution, protecting youth and children from unwholesome situations, and providing medical care and rehabilitation for delinquent girls. Nationally, the division was to coordinate its operations with the VD control program of the military and the U.S. Public Health Service, following up their contact investigative reports by sending agents into affected communities to assist local officials to set up social protection programs. Locally, this required community organization down to the neigh-

61. *New York Times,* Jan. 13, 1945.

borhood level, coordinating the activities of police, health officers, welfare agencies, and local leaders.[62]

As in the areas of child care and delinquent behavior, the public service bureaucrats staffing the Social Protection Division interpreted their mandate generously. The first director, Elliott Ness, and Raymond F. Clapp, his assistant, approached social protection not as an ad hoc program of the wartime emergency but as a permanent, long-range one requiring the cooperation of municipal officials and citizens alike to embed its principles into community consciousness.[63] They too believed that the physical and mental well-being of the urban (and rural) population was a prerequisite for re-creating the spirit of purposive cooperation that would become the essence of the postwar city. Thomas Devine, Ness's successor, offered the best and most explicit correlation between the physical reconstruction of American cities and the rejuvenation of their social fabric through programs similar to social protection. After carefully scrutinizing the progress made in the war against VD, he observed in 1945: "One of the outstanding city planners in the country, Mr. Walter Blucher, Director of the American Society of Planning Officials, has frequently made the statement that the main cause of failure in city planning projects is that of not including citizen participation from the beginning of the planning to the actual carrying-out of the projects under consideration." Then he added: "This is one principle of community action which should be stressed to safeguard communities during the postwar period against the expected letdown in measures to repress prostitution and control venereal disease."[64]

In suppressing commercialized prostitution, the OCWS-Social Protection Division drew from a battery of legal weapons, espe-

62. Elliott Ness, "Program of Social Protection Section," unpub. memorandum, June 1942, in NARG 215, OCWS Records. See also "Repression of Prostitution in Social Protection Program," unpub. memorandum, June 30, 1942, in *ibid.*
63. Ness, "Program of Social Protection Section," Sept. 10, 1941, and Raymond F. Clapp, "The Repression of Prostitution," n.d., unpub. memorandum, in *ibid.*
64. Thomas Devine, "Our Strength Is in United Action," *Journal of Social Hygiene* 31 (Nov. 1945), 511.

cially the 1938 VD Control Act and the May Act of July 11, 1938, which enabled localities to close down brothels located near military installations. These complemented the 1939 "Eight-Point Agreement," wherein the Federal Security Agency, the American Social Hygiene Association, and the military agreed to coordinate their campaigns against venereal infections.[65] The legitimacy of the policy of suppression seemed to be confirmed when American military authorities discovered that the Nazis had failed to reduce the incidence of VD in Paris by a policy of "controlled prostitution." By contrast, the U.S. Army VD rates in the period 1941–43 had fallen from forty-one infections per thousand to twenty-six, while the Navy's rates had dropped from forty to twenty-five per thousand.[66]

Below the federal level, each state turned to its antiprostitution laws, half of which the American Public Welfare Association deemed inadequate. Then, in July 1942, the cities secured their own potent instrument for eradicating vice. The Arkansas Supreme Court ruled that the city of Little Rock had the right to enforce a local ordinance that provided for both the apprehension and medical examination of persons suspected of having a venereal disease and their quarantine in hospitals or other facilities designated by the city's health officer. The decision had repercussions extending far beyond Little Rock or the state's boundaries. The *American City,* considering this a landmark ruling because it affirmed the right of a municipality to invoke the constitutional police power to protect citizens of the neighborhood and larger community, called the decision to the attention of other municipalities.[67]

Underpinning the crusade against VD was a calculated awareness that suppression was more likely to be tolerated during a national emergency—a time of sacrifice—than after the end of

---

65. See *Challenge to Community Action,* 14, and Exhibit 15: "Venereal Disease Control," in *Wartime Health and Education,* pt. 1, 595–96.

66. See Tooker, "Venereal Disease—Far from Beaten," 552, and *Challenge to Community Action,* 5, 8.

67. The case was *City of Little Rock* v. *Smith,* 163 S.W. 2d, 703. See also "The War Program and Prostitution," *American City* 57 (Sept. 1942), 109, 111.

hostilities. The psychology, timing, and contact investigating made possible by Army and Navy reports were all-important, but as one physician noted, "venereal disease control is essentially a local affair."[68] What success the policy of suppression ultimately enjoyed was the result of local officials' willingness to cooperate. Thus the stringent penalties of the May Act were invoked in a dramatic counterthrust that shuttered the red-light districts of nearly seven hundred cities by 1944. The percentage of municipalities rated "bad" by the American Social Hygiene Association was greatly diminished. Besides blitzing the brothels, authorities instituted serological tests, distributed sulfanilamide tablets, and situated "pro stations" in strategic locations in every city and town. These measures enabled the OCWS, state, and local governments to keep the incidence of syphilitic infections below World War I levels.[69]

Tacoma, Washington, provides a good example of a city in which the policy of suppression worked reasonably effectively. Social Protection Division personnel cooperated with the health and police departments there to set up committees on education, detention and law enforcement, and prosecution. Factories distributed nearly 85,000 pamphlets explaining VD and the community's protection program, while the local utility company tucked 25,000 leaflets into its customers' bills. Contact investigative reporting enabled the military to identify professional prostitutes and brothels for local authorities. Steadily, commercialized prostitution was suppressed, jail facilities were improved, detention facilities were provided for younger uninfected girls, and a medical social worker was hired to assist in rehabilitation. Within a year the number of infections of syphilis from prostitutes fell by 47 percent and of gonorrhea by 25 percent. Encouraged, the city fathers turned their attention to the amateur prostitutes by working on stricter tavern supervision,

68. Thomas B. Turner, "Immediate Wartime Outlook and Indicated Post-War Conditions with Respect to the Control of Venereal Diseases," *American Journal of Public Health* 33 (Nov. 1943), 1313.

69. "The War Against Prostitution Must Go On," *Journal of Social Hygiene* 31 (Nov. 1945), 500–7; Polenberg, *War and Society,* 150–51.

an ordinance prohibiting unaccompanied women in night spots, and a long-term program of better housing to ease the conditions that encouraged vice and promiscuity.[70]

In contrast to their no-nonsense attitude toward the professional prostitute, the OCWS and local governments adopted a more enlightened and humane approach to the delinquent adolescent and the casual sex seeker who had contracted VD. This usually took the form of establishing community clinics and, in some instances, going beyond the purely routine prophylactic treatment. When the war ended in 1945, OCWS had helped to set up 3,800 VD clinics, a major improvement over the 1,122 that existed in 1938. Not only did this figure represent a threefold increase, it also meant a doubling of the number of patients treated. Every state and most large cities boasted Divisions of Venereal Disease Control, though the coverage was far from complete since nearly half the counties in the nation still lacked a full-time health department. As to the best urban clinics, such as San Francisco's, Little Rock's, and Denver's, their involvement in the entire physical and mental health of their patients, who were usually ordinary citizens, made them focal points of community interaction.[71]

The successful application of federal and local resources to a serious sociomedical problem in turn strengthened the belief that rehabilitation of communities (1) was a feasible goal and (2) must accompany plans for the cities' physical renaissance. Colonel Thomas B. Turner, on the staff of the Surgeon General's Office, put the social protection program into this broader context. "We are witnessing in many communities the successful control of disease through close integration of health, law enforcement, welfare, and other civic agencies," he declared. *"This is dynamic social action, which can be just as effective in peace as in war."*[72]

---

70. *Challenge to Community Action,* 12, 20, 26–27, 52–54.
71. *Ibid.,* 20.
72. Turner, "Immediate Wartime Outlook . . . with Respect to the Control of Venereal Diseases," 1313. Emphasis mine.

Community Recreation and National Defense

In keeping with the other social programs, the impetus for a national defense recreation program originated in the need to maintain full worker productivity and to combat the disruptive effects of transient populations upon cities and towns. Before long, however, the OCWS-Division of Recreation, which came into being in 1941, was establishing a foundation whereby its program, organized around the nucleus of community clubhouses and centers, might continue to offer service long after the war's end. The clubhouse forged social bonds that OCWS officials believed helped to integrate the multiplicity of citizens and groups living together in the neighborhoods, tying each neighborhood to the larger community of state and nation.[73]

Unlike the federal officials of World War I, who had permitted defense recreation to lapse, the public service bureaucrats of the New Deal viewed recreation as more than a wartime imperative. Mark A. McCloskey, head of the Division of Recreation, told Senator Pepper's subcommittee in 1943, "We make no claim that recreation is a cure for delinquency, but we do know . . . that it is a powerful preventive." He added: "And we are firmly convinced that wholesome recreation, under good citizenship, is one of the soundest investments that a community can make in its citizens of tomorrow."[74]

In McCloskey's hands the recreation program outgrew its original narrow function. Community recreation became a dynamic instrument for rejuvenating social life and values in much the same way as architects and planners intended to reconstruct the physical form of postwar cities. The transformation began in December 1941 when McCloskey first instructed his field staff to begin the arduous process of educating local officials, industrial and labor leaders, and ordinary citizens to the impor-

---

73. *National Defense Migration Hearings,* pt. 11, 4239, and pt. 17, 6719–20. See also "What They Say About Recreation," *Recreation* 37 (Dec. 1943), 508.

74. *Wartime Health and Education,* pt. 1, 36, 55. See also Mark A. McCloskey, "Recreation in Defense Communities," *Recreation,* 35 (Aug. 1941), 323–24, and "Community Recreational Programs a Post-War Must," *American City* 60 (Mar. 1945), 97.

tance of comprehensive recreation planning for national defense.[75] This was no mean task, because twelve months into mobilization local officials either were dragging their heels in providing recreational facilities or, if they had the funds to spare, did not know where to begin. Some did not approve of spending local revenues on recreation for a transient population. Industrial employers likewise were holding back, afraid that labor unions would construe their initiative as paternalism of the company-unionism variety and haul them before the National Labor Relations Board.[76]

The hesitation was also psychological because, as FSA Administrator McNutt observed, the notion that one could contribute to the defeat of totalitarianism by manning a civilian worker's canteen simply did not stir the popular imagination. In all fairness, however, where localities, employers, and citizens had shown a willingness to act, they had sometimes been discouraged by the urban sprawl aggravated by the federal emergency housing program and by bureaucratic paralysis.[77] George Hjelte, superintendent of the Los Angeles Department of Recreation, testified, "The industrial population is spread all over the map, and it is a question of how, although the industrialists are willing to aid in providing recreation, they can make their aid effective." As to bureaucracy, in San Diego, where Lanham Act funds were used to build a new development of 4,000 homes, housing authorities were reluctant to reserve space in each project for recreation, despite a provision in the law requiring that 3 percent of a public housing project's space be preserved for community purposes.[78]

With a crisis fast approaching, McCloskey's problem was twofold: first, to mobilize and use efficiently the existing re-

75. "Field Policy in Industrial Communities," unpub. memorandum from Mark A. McCloskey to Field Recreation Representatives, Dec. 10, 1941, in NARG 215, OCWS Records.
76. "Minutes of the Regional Coordinators' Meeting," Apr. 28–29, 1941, *ibid.*
77. Charles E. Reed, "National Trends in Defense Recreation," *Recreation* 35 (Feb. 1942), 658, and McCloskey, "Recreation in Defense Communities," 323.
78. "Minutes of the Regional Coordinators' Meeting," Apr. 28–29, 1941, in NARG 215, OCWS Records.

sources of state and local recreation agencies; and second, to introduce federal funds for new operating programs in communities unable to bear the additional expense. In pursuit of the latter course, McCloskey had to be careful not to convey the impression that the OCWS was usurping a jurisdiction traditionally reserved for local government and private initiative—all the more because the President's own mind was attuned to recreation's roots in the local community.[79] Fortunately, dwindling financial resources minimized vigorous local opposition to federal intervention in the congested production centers, while the National Recreation Association (NRA) temporarily relaxed its policy that recreation was exclusively a local concern.

Not everyone suddenly welcomed federal funds with upturned palms, for in truth the NRA continued to harbor reservations about its own decision and admonished localities to carry their fair share of the recreation expense. Only in this way could the principle of local autonomy be maintained and the scope of federal activity contained. "We *do* want our government to be responsive to the needs of people in American communities, but the concern of the government should include helping the community, first of all, to square up to its own responsibility to meet the local recreation or defense problems," declared NRA President Charles E. Reed.[80]

To encourage cooperation, McCloskey decentralized control by hiring professional recreationists, sending them out into the field, and supporting them with specialized assistance and funds so that they were constantly aware of the sustaining and sympathetic interest of headquarters.[81] In a lengthy memorandum of December 10, 1941, McCloskey instructed his staff to assist local officials, at their request, both to canvass a community's needs and help establish recreation programs. He further emphasized that they must approach recreation as a neighborhood

79. "Franklin Delano Roosevelt's Messages to the National Recreation Congresses," *Recreation* 39 (May 1945), 85.

80. Reed, "National Trends in Defense Recreation," 694.

81. See "Recreation: Excerpts from Dr. Strong's Report on One Year of Recreation," unpub. report, Jan. 1, 1941, in NARG 215, OCWS Records.

153

and community-wide function, drawing into their planning a representative cross section of the population.[82]

After a slow start, the Division of Recreation's program, *viewed solely as a temporary emergency undertaking,* was well received, especially in the sorely pressed congested production centers. In its first year of operation, the division authorized 250 projects in 227 cities and towns. Thereafter progress in meeting recreational needs accelerated. FSA Administrator Watson B. Miller testified in 1946 that the division had assisted more than 2,500 communities to develop varied programs. The FWA, after certification by the OCWS, constructed more than 450 recreation buildings for military and civilian war workers, at a cost of more than $30 million. Complementing the federal effort were hundreds of state, local, and voluntary recreation programs. Most importantly as a harbinger of future action, over three hundred new towns and cities had established legally constituted, tax-supported community recreation systems, while twenty-three states organized departments of recreation.[83]

Beyond the immediate challenge, McCloskey had been confident that a new spirit of community forged by shared wartime experiences—a sense of common identity and purpose—would emerge from the recreation program to become a model for the nation. If his September 10 instructions to the staff had any broader connotation, they assuredly were intended to establish within city neighborhoods a framework for community renewal. This was a long-standing but hitherto unfulfilled dream of New Deal humanitarians, and it was certainly the meaning attached to them by the recreation staff. As one ranking official wrote, "The emphasis of the work of the Division of Recreation is on building community resources, community backing, and an expanding community understanding of the place of recreation in community life—so that our people may live fully and vigor-

---

82. See "Field Policy in Industrial Communities," Dec. 10, 1941, in *ibid.*

83. Miller's testimony may be found in *Development of Community Recreation Programs for the People of the United States,* Hearings before a Subcommittee of the Committee on Education and Labor, United States Senate, on S. 2070, May 13 and 27, 1946, 79th Cong., 2d sess. (1946), 4–5.

ously not only during the war but during the peace which will come when it is over.[84]

Apart from the public service bureaucrats, the program appealed to professional recreationists and to many planners. For several years the former had been promoting recreation's role in a modern, urban-industrial society, but with mixed results. The war gave their cause a much-needed lift, for recreation could be a useful instrument for combating disorganization in communities where transients abounded. Howard Braucher, editor of *Recreation,* the organ of the NRA, wrote about its potential for reconstructing community spirit in a nation grown weary of depression and war. Like McCloskey, he also believed the process must commence in the neighborhoods of each municipality. "How shall we have a sense of world community except as we have somehow gained a sense of local community, of local neighborhood?" he inquired. Recreation was the talisman for generating the new postwar community synthesis in our cities. "Those who play together, sing together, make things together, attain in its truest sense a community feeling. The sense of community begins right down in the neighborhood as people share their joys and sorrow," Braucher affirmed.[85]

A trite sentiment, perhaps, but it was widely felt. City planner Mel Scott, executive director of the Citizen's Planning Council of San Jose, asked the readers of *Recreation* to observe the "neighborhood of tomorrow" unfolding in that California city. "The future is now aborning," he quoted from one publicity brochure. "An expanding community is in the making. The opportunity to create something new and better is at hand." New recreational facilities, including community centers for teenagers, parks, playgrounds, and bicycle paths, figured prominently in the planning process, especially in upgrading essentially sound middle- and working-class neighborhoods. The same

84. "Excerpts from Dr. Strong's Report," and FSA, OCWS, "Blueprints for Tomorrow's Recreation," *Recreation Bulletin* 91 (Dec. 18, 1944), 1, in NARG 215, OCWS Records. Also, *New York Times,* Oct. 24, 1941.
85. Howard Braucher, "Building the Community," *Recreation* 39 (June 1945), 113.

facilities would also be extended to lower-class districts. If creature comforts were to provide the material foundation upon which to build a purposive and spirited community, then San Joseans would enjoy the same amenities as citizens elsewhere.[86]

In quest of this new community synthesis, the wartime recreation program could be used to nurture the positive middle-class values deemed indispensable for enhancing the *quality* of urban life. Louise S. Cobb, chairman of the Berkeley, California, defense recreation committee, was one of those who held this view. A survey of the activities of recreation committees in similar smaller cities across the nation had persuaded Cobb that wartime cooperation was demonstrating anew the value of community organization. She expected that the committees would continue to function beyond the war period, serving as advisory bodies to planning boards and providing the latter with useful current data on neighborhood recreational needs. From modest beginnings, the committees would grow to play a vital role in bringing the "good life" to all communities. "The greater understanding of the factors that made for the 'good life' in our cities should bring that good life nearer to us all," she declared.[87]

Encouraged by the Division of Recreation, cities engaged in filling wartime priorities were also thinking of peacetime recreation. Of necessity, however, much of the impetus for recreation planning—perhaps most of it as the end of the fighting drew closer—originated in a serious concern to avoid a new thirties-type depression. Proposals to better the urban environment through recreation often melded with plans for extensive public works programs to make jobs available to returning veterans. Thus in 1940 San Francisco's Recreation Commission had adopted a ten-year plan calling for the expenditure of $7,484,078 for construction of a little theater, junior museum, new day-camp sites, playgrounds, parks, and recreation centers. Four years later the plan was revised to serve as the nucleus of an extensive public works program. Chicago's City Planning

---

86. Mel Scott, "Neighborhoods of Tomorrow," *Recreation* 39 (Sept. 1945), 324–25.
87. Louise S. Cobb, "Wartime Recreation Councils in Small Cities," *ibid.,* 37 (Mar. 1944), 686.

Commission also included parks and playgrounds in its $59 million shopping list of public works.[88]

Several cities emulated the examples of Charlotte and Dallas in drafting master plans that incorporated recreation as an essential aspect of urban living, but few were as comprehensive or ambitious as Detroit's $270 million blueprint for public works construction. Apart from its anti-Depression tone, the most interesting aspect of the Detroit plan was its proposal to fit recreation into metropolitan *regional* planning in order to create an urban-rural continuum. Once again, planners were turning to the maximum use of the natural heritage of lakes, streams, and wooded areas that dotted the city and surrounding environs to improve the quality of urban life. This flurry of civic activity prompted Martin H. Neumeyer of the University of Southern California, a professor of recreation, to observe that specialists in recreation had "far more requests than they can handle from cities and towns seeking guidance in planning for the future."[89]

The Failure of Social Engineering

If the cities were not to disintegrate into a jumble of mutually antagonistic and self-seeking entities after the war, New Deal liberals, especially the public service bureaucrats of the ocws, realized that the dislocated urban populations must be anchored to common sets of symbolic representations of community, to common cognitive and moral assumptions about the larger society in which they were enmeshed. Urban dwellers needed to develop a social solidarity that would outlast and transcend the momentary dangers, dissolve class and, hopefully, racial antagonisms, and nurture a civic intelligence that would see beyond the myopic world of municipal politics and lead to a greater emphasis on democratic decision making. The war seemed to demonstrate that the old spirit of the universal obligation to serve was not dead. The "neighborly public spirit" of the war might

88. See "Blueprints for Tomorrow's Recreation," 1-2.
89. George F. Emery, "Detroit is Ready," news clipping from *The Detroiter,* Oct. 9, 1944, in NARG 215, ocws Records; Martin H. Neumeyer, "National Trends in Recreation," *Recreation* 38 (Jan. 1945), 539.

157

be used to achieve the spirit of affectionate community that was disappearing in the age of urban sprawl.[90]

Child-care facilities, recreation centers, neighborhood and city-wide programs of social protection, and better nutrition were intended to increase worker productivity, to assimilate the uprooted migrant, and to comfort the long-time resident whose status was being challenged by hordes of strangers. In the hands of liberal humanitarians, these programs also were expected to become the building blocks of the new community spirit that was to revitalize urban America—to nurture what Daniel P. Moynihan was talking about elsewhere when he called for "a public architecture of intimacy, one that brings together in an experience of confidence and trust . . . and restores to American public life the sense of shared experience, trust and common purpose that seems to be draining out of it."[91]

As victory drew closer, however, evidence appeared that voluntary associations and programs were ultimately imperfect means for redefining community in the urban context. The progress of the venereal disease control program illustrated this deficiency clearly: despite all the talk and propaganda, only sporadic efforts were made to examine and deal with the causes underlying either commercial prostitution or other forms of sexual promiscuity. Except in a few isolated instances, federal funds were not available for work of this sort. The original program of treatment had provided for rehabilitation in the form of social counseling and retraining, but under wartime pressure later treatment was so accelerated that there was no time to do this before the patients were discharged.[92]

Worse still, most experts feared that the incidence of infections would increase sharply in the period of demobilization. OCWS-Social Protection Division Director Thomas Devine reported in 1945 to the American Social Hygiene Association that the prognosis was bleak. The division had just completed an

90. See William Anderson, "National-State Relations During the War," in United States Department of Agriculture Graduate School, ed., *What We Learned in Public Administration During the War* (Washington, D.C., 1949), 67.
91. Quoted in Vance Packard, *A Nation of Strangers* (New York, 1972), 291.
92. Tooker, "Venereal Disease—Far from Beaten," 551.

analysis of the degree of cooperation in 247 cities among each of the following agencies: police, adult and juvenile courts, health departments, and welfare agencies. The result was "a pretty poor record concerning a vital community problem, the solving of which depends upon complete and carefully planned working relationships between agencies."[93]

In the aftermath of the D-Day invasion, there were apprehensions concerning the postwar federal presence in other community activities, such as recreation and child care. Howard Braucher, editor of *Recreation,* sounded the tocsin in October 1944, urging his fellow citizens to develop their own local leadership rather than rely upon the federal government. "We want in America growth in living that is native to the soil of each locality," wrote Braucher. "America has no place for Kultur."[94]

Poor communications at the intergovernmental level, jurisdictional conflicts within the federal bureaucracy, and the reappearance of an ideologically focused opposition also precluded continuing postwar federal involvement in child care. Whether funding had come through OCWS or the Lanham Act, the wartime child-care program never lived up to the expectations of its sponsors, and this was used as an argument to justify cutting off federal expenditures once the war ended.[95]

Most of the discontent centered on the Lanham Act, the unpredictability of its funding procedures creating confusion and ill will between federal agencies and state and local governments. The changeable nature of regulations had discouraged some localities from applying for funds, while others withdrew their requests when informed that they would have to meet 50 percent of the cost of the program—a sum they were led to believe the federal government would absorb in its entirety. State officials working to promote day-care programs were especially critical of the practice of distributing federal monies to the cities directly, instead of going through the appropriate

---

93. *New York Times,* Sept. 23, 1945; Devine, "Our Strength Is in United Action," 512.

94. Howard Braucher, "Culture or Kultur?" *Recreation* 38 (Oct. 1944), 338.

95. *Wartime Care and Protection of Children,* 64, and Philip B. Fleming to Fritz G. Lanham, Sept. 9, 1943, NARG 215, OCWS Records.

agencies. They preferred the grant-in-aid system made familiar under the Social Security Act, since with direct grants they had no means of assuring the maintenance of standards in local day-care operations.[96]

The persistence of bureaucratic infighting for administrative control of the program gave economy-minded legislators and conservatives the opening they were seeking. In March 1943 a coalition of Southern Democrats and conservative Republicans knocked out a provision in the Deficiency Appropriation Bill earmarking an additional $2,973,000 for child care. To compensate for the loss of funds, Senator Elbert D. Thomas, a New Deal Democrat of Utah, introduced a more comprehensive "War Area Child Act." The bill would have made nearly $20 million per year available to state welfare and educational departments for child care for the duration of the war and the first six months of reconversion. By working through the state bureaucracies, Thomas hoped to neutralize much of the criticism and, indeed, gained the support of one humanitarian-conservative, Senator Robert A. Taft, Republican of Ohio.[97]

Unfortunately, a provision to consolidate administration of the program in the Office of Education and the Children's Bureau immediately encountered opposition from FWA officials who resented having their agency left out of the program. Testifying before the Senate Committee on Education and Labor, they subtly but unmistakably manipulated conservatives' fear that the administration intended to use the defense emergency to institutionalize wartime social welfare programs.[98]

So persuasive were the FWA bureaucrats that anti-New Deal legislators successfully pigeonholed the bill until Congress adjourned. The remarks of Senator Walter F. George, Democrat of Georgia, were highly indicative of the growing sentiment to terminate as quickly as possible wartime programs (like child care) that could conceivably help reconstruct urban society. "A very serious question arises as to how far the Federal Govern-

96. *Wartime Care and Protection of Children,* 65, *passim.*
97. *New York Times,* Feb. 26, 27; Mar. 11, 13; June 9, 26, 1943; *Congressional Record,* 78th Cong., 1st sess., 89 (June 29, 1943), 6724–26.
98. *Wartime Care and Protection of Children,* 34, 45.

ment or any agency of the Federal Government should have control of the child life of the country," he declared. "I do not indulge in the optimism with which my friend from Utah regards this as a war baby and a war activity. There will be too much pressure ever to permit its curtailment after the war is ended."[99]

George's observation was correct, of course. As victory approached, New Dealers and other liberals, aware that Lanham Act funds would run out forever after October 31, 1945, did seek to extend the child-care program into a permanent instrument of community social engineering. Democratic Congresswoman Helen Gahagan Douglas, a staunch New Dealer from Los Angeles, told her colleagues: "The end of the war does not mean the end of social-service work if that social-service work is needed." The Child Welfare League of America recommended that its day-care division "stimulate plans for postwar planning for a comprehensive program of services for children . . . at local, state and federal levels, such programs to be integrated with the regularly established agencies including health, education and welfare."[100]

On the other hand, George's remarks also struck a responsive chord among conservative voters, Democrats and Republicans alike, who feared that New Dealers were trying to foster child-rearing concepts antithetical to family life. Thus the associate superintendent of schools of New York City told a meeting of the National Conference of Catholic Charities: "If this trend is allowed to continue unchecked, it can result only in the dissolution of the family, and in the family only are developed the basic traditions of democracy."[101]

Confronted by voter opposition to further social engineering and the general hostility of Congress toward New Deal welfare programs, the Thomas bill never again surfaced. By 1945 the future of the child-care program depended on how important the citizens of the localities felt it to be and on the willingness and

99. *Congressional Record,* 78th Cong., 1st sess., 89 (June 3, 1943), 6791–92.
100. *Ibid.,* 79th Cong., 1st sess., 91 (Sept. 24, 1945), Appendix, 3998–4002.
101. *New York Times,* May 3, and Nov. 14, 1943.

capacity of the states to bear its cost. With the exception of working mothers whose children were already enrolled, public interest in continuing the federal wartime program as a vehicle for postwar community renewal, even under state and local auspices, was disappointing.[102]

Unhappily, many of the local wartime child-care committees succumbed, along with the local defense councils, to public apathy. Otherwise, they might have offered themselves as focal points both to evaluate the program in relation to future needs and to formulate recommendations to their cities and states. In few communities in 1945 were such activities in the offing.[103]

102. *Ibid.,* Sept. 14, 26, 1945.
103. *Ibid.,* Jan. 30; Feb. 27; Mar. 1, 1946.

V. Urban Conservation and the NRPB

From its inception in the Depression-haunted thirties the National Resources Planning Board (NRPB) was inextricably caught up in the problems of the American city. Ample evidence of a continuing interest in the urban aspects of living was seen in the organization of the Urbanism Committee and its landmark report *Our Cities: Their Role in the National Economy,* in the supplementary reports on municipal government, city planning, and land use policies, and in the special studies of housing, public works, and transportation.[1] It is perhaps less well known that the NRPB continued to extend its activities in the area of neighborhood conservation and rehabilitation planning during the period of defense preparations in 1940–41, and that it experimented with new programs for urban redevelopment during the war itself.[2]

Between 1941 and its demise in 1943, the NRPB proceeded along four parallel but complementary paths. These were (1) the canvassing of informed opinion about the federal role in the postwar reconstruction of American cities; (2) establishing liaison with other federal agencies, planning bodies, and private institutions committed to reform of the urban environment;[3] (3) sponsoring studies bearing on specific aspects of urban problems,

1. National Resources Committee, Urban Section, *Our Cities: Their Role in the National Economy* (Washington, D.C., 1937).
2. The study of urban problems was a parallel but secondary development to the emphasis on the river basins and rural land planning which had President Roosevelt's strong support. Frederic A. Delano, a director of the NRPB and an advocate of regional planning, had worked with both the Chicago Plan and the Russell Sage Foundation's study of New York City and its environs. See David Cushman Coyle, "Frederic A. Delano: Catalyst," *Survey Graphic* 35 (July 1946), 252–54.
3. As of January 1937, there were 1,073 town or city planning boards in the United States, 933 of which were official and 84 unofficial. There were 128 zoning boards, and 515 cities which had no planning or zoning boards but had adopted some kind of zoning ordinance. See National Resources Committee, *Status of City and County Planning in the United States* (Washington, D.C., 1937), 4–6, 10–13.

such as metropolitan consolidation, new sources of revenue, and recreation; and (4) drafting a progressive urban planning procedure as a model for cities to emulate. An analysis of the last-mentioned item is fruitful, because it subsumed the first three and thereby affords some insight into the Roosevelt administration's policy toward the urban communities.[4]

One year before America entered World War II, President Roosevelt instructed the NRPB to undertake a study of what then was termed "post-defense planning."[5] Two urgent questions confronted the board's directors: First, how far should the NRPB go in seeking assistance of urban experts, private voluntary groups, and public agencies on specific problems; and second, should the planning confine itself to the immediate demobilization period or extend over a longer span of time. After considerable discussion, the directors agreed to make planning literature available to private parties but not especially to stimulate them to plan—a decision they eventually reversed.[6]

The directors also decided to conduct urban planning along two lines, namely, for the transitional period at the war's end (when returning veterans would be seeking employment) and for the decade after reconversion.[7] To this end they established an Urban Section, instructing it to take full advantage of the work of other governmental and private agencies in the field of urban rehabilitation and to think as boldly as the skilled and disciplined imagination of its personnel allowed.[8] For the directors of the NRPB and municipal experts recognized that the government could permit neither a sharp break nor a temporary

4. The NRPB immediately narrowed the focus of its inquiry because of dwindling funds, congressional hostility to planning, and the hope of achieving quick, dramatic results. It built upon rather than duplicated the work of other agencies.

5. The board's authority to function in this sphere flowed from the Federal Employment Stabilization Act of 1931. See Samuel I. Rosenman, comp., *The Public Papers and Addresses of Franklin D. Roosevelt,* 13 vols. (New York, 1938–50), III, 335–38.

6. See Louis Wirth, "Functions of the Urban Section," Oct. 16, 1942, National Archives (NA), Record Group (RG) 187, Records of the National Resources Planning Board (NRPB), Urban Section Files. Cited hereafter as NRPB Records.

7. Cf. "Post War Agenda," Feb. 3, 1942; Luther Gulick to Charles Eliot, Dec. 5, 1941, in *ibid.* See also the following reports: *After Defense—What?; After the War—Full Employment;* and *Better Cities* (Washington, D.C., 1941–42).

8. Cf. Louis Wirth, "The Background and Organization of the Urban Section," Aug. 19, 1942, in NARG 187, NRPB Records.

lag to occur between the civilian defense program and the post-war reconstruction of cities.

The war, declared Louis Wirth, professor of sociology at the University of Chicago, offered an unparalleled opportunity for each city to mold the quality of life within its boundaries more nearly in accord with its resources and aspirations. He noted that the abrupt dislocations attendant upon mobilization and migration had rendered communities more sensitive to older, neglected urban problems and that the concern of municipal officials for the postwar economic well-being of their cities could be used to good advantage. The NRPB might encourage them to approach urban rehabilitation in the broader context of community conservation rather than using city rebuilding as a vehicle for simply promoting full employment for returning GIs.[9]

For these reasons Wirth proposed that the board should reexamine and bring up to date the 1937–38 findings of the Urbanism Committee. More precisely, the Urban Section should establish an agency to channel funds to metropolitan areas, devise new budgetary procedures, experiment with eminent domain to facilitate site acquisition for redevelopment purposes, and articulate a national minimum standard of living for all citizens. The last would include housing, income, and social services. Finally, Wirth urged the NRPB to encourage greater citizen participation in planning and implementing the program.[10]

It would be an exaggeration to say that Wirth, a pioneer in the field of urban ecology, was the intellectual godfather of the NRPB's urban policies, but there is no question that his writing shaped its thinking.[11] The most notable expression of Wirth's influence was the joint proposal of Charles S. Ascher and Frank W. Herring, both staff members, requesting the board to authorize six demonstration experiments to test a markedly new approach to urban planning. With an initial allocation of $50,000, their objective was to evolve "a progressive planning procedure that can serve as a base for long-term programming

9. *Ibid.*
10. *Ibid.*
11. "Notes on National Resources Planning Board Urban Planning Committee," n.d., in *ibid.*

165

and for post-defense deployment of men and materials in city rebuilding.''[12] They hoped to attain a new level of sophistication in urban planning by treating the city not simply as an artifact but by integrating social, economic, and cultural factors into the planning process. When these factors were woven into a continually revised long-term capital program, Ascher and Herring expected to demonstrate that planning was "a continuous process, not a one-time undertaking that results in a 'master plan' to be put in a pigeon-hole."[13]

The experimental projects were to serve in the first instance as the yardstick for critically appraising other neighborhood redevelopment programs seeking federal assistance and as a catalyst for generating an integrated series of local projects. The first stage, which would last only a few months, was to culminate in an outline plan for overall development. Before and during the physical planning, and as a basis thereof, the planners expected to target the goals of economic, social, and cultural development and produce a practical blueprint to attain them. The plan itself would remain in skeletal form, being changed from time to time as required by changing objectives or local conditions.[14]

The emphasis throughout was put upon local action and responsibility, with a corresponding deemphasis on strong central direction from Washington. This was intended, as in the case of other New Deal programs, to reverse the concentration of control in the federal government and minimize opposition. The decision was predicated on the realistic assumption that private citizens, private organizations, and local public officials possessed the knowledge, good judgment, and experience to manage some segments of the planning better than outside technicians. Federal agencies would supply what data they had, and the technicians would offer expert assistance, but the initiative and personnel to conduct the day-to-day planning had to come from the local community.[15]

Before submitting the proposal to the board's directors,

12. "A Proposal for Progressive Urban Planning," Nov. 7, 1941, in *ibid*.
13. *Ibid*.
14. See the typewritten memorandum, "Urban Planning Procedure," n.d., in *ibid*.
15. *Ibid*. Also Robert B. Mitchell to Staff, Aug. 17, 1942, in *ibid*.

Ascher and Herring systematically cultivated the support of other federal officials, planners, and professional organizations. Walter H. Blucher, executive director of the American Society of Planning Officials, Hugh Pomeroy of the Virginia State Planning Board and future director of the Urban Land Institute, Frederick S. Bigger, the forward-looking head of the Pittsburgh City Planning Commission, and Dean Arthur Comey of the Harvard University School of Architecture endorsed the idea of demonstration projects.[16]

A few professional planners had doubts about the project's feasibility, but these were recorded in confidential letters to board members and passed largely unnoticed by the general public. Alfred Bettman and Ladislas Segoe of Cincinnati worried that popular participation in each stage of the planning process would dilute the quality of the plan and thus erode respect for the profession. Bettman, especially, feared that progressive urban planning was no more than a fad which, if mismanaged, would set back the cause of city planning in the United States. Segoe suggested that the Urban Section scale down its ambitious plans and, in lieu of demonstration experiments, settle for a program of clinics to instruct city officials in the daily application of planning techniques.[17]

Despite the criticisms, Herring and Ascher were optimistic that the Urban Section could produce a progressive planning manual (based upon the successful demonstration projects) that would be used by hundreds of localities across the United States. They did not minimize the obstacles and problems confronting them; these included a dearth of experienced personnel relative to the demands of postdefense city rebuilding; the absence of institutionalized planning commissions in most cities; the choice of project cities; the degree to which local officials were willing to cooperate with federal agencies and the NRPB's agents; the writing of a manual that would enlighten city officials ignorant of planning concepts; and the ability to persuade urban leaders

16. *Ibid.*
17. Alfred Bettman to Charles Eliot, Feb. 12, 1942; Robert B. Mitchell to Charles S. Ascher, Mar. 26, 1942, in *ibid.*

167

that the principles laid out in the handbook worked in practice. They were confident, however, that the Urban Section, under the direction of Robert B. Mitchell, author of neighborhood conservation and redevelopment plans for the Federal Home Loan Bank Board, could surmount these barriers.[18]

Mitchell's background certainly indicated a knowledge of urban problems. A university graduate and authority on housing, he had entered government service with the advent of the New Deal. As an official of the Federal Home Loan Bank Board in 1940 he had organized federal and municipal authorities into a cooperative program to rescue the shabby but fundamentally sound middle-class Baltimore neighborhood of Waverly from urban blight.[19] He also was responsible for preparing an elaborate study in neighborhood rehabilitation undertaken in cooperation with the University of Chicago and the Chicago City Planning Commission. The Woodlawn experience had alerted him to the community planning concepts espoused by Professor Wirth. In 1941, at the request of the Urban Section, Mitchell drafted a tentative statement of procedure that the unit would follow in the demonstration projects.[20]

Toward the close of 1941 the board agreed to permit the Urban Section to conduct the demonstrations with the cooperation of local municipal leaders. Speed was all-important, for the directors wanted the project to commence in February 1942—a

18. See Charles S. Ascher, "Recommendations for the Urban Program," June 12, 1942, in *ibid.*

19. Applicability of Mitchell's experience in Waverly to the extreme manifestations of urban decay in cities like New York, St. Louis, and Philadelphia was open to question. For, as the Federal Home Loan Bank Board report indicated, this predominantly residential district of Baltimore was not a slum nor were the homes substandard—they merely needed minor repairs and painting. Waverly was not the microcosm of the small American city as the report claimed; the experiment was valid only for other neighborhoods of identical composition and problems. See *ibid.* and Federal Home Loan Bank Board, *Waverly, A Study in Neighborhood Conservation* (Washington, D.C., 1940), esp. 8, 11, 16, 30, 53–55, 67.

20. The salient points of the Mitchell-Bacon statement of procedures included the selection of six demonstration cities, assignment of project consultants in sympathy with the aims of progressive planning, delineation of aspects of the procedure to be executed by local officials and those requiring skilled professional attention, gathering of current data, and formulation and dissemination of a statement of procedure. See "A Proposal for Progressive Urban Planning," Nov. 7, 1941, in NARG 187, NRPB Records.

168

deadline that proved impossible to meet given the fledgling condition of the urban unit.[21]

It was not until the spring of 1942 that the Urban Section began the spadework to ensure a successful demonstration experiment. Ascher drafted a confidential memorandum to guide the staff. The document rested upon three asumptions: that urban conservation and development constituted the "fourth dimension" in the board's work; that the fact of the city should be recognized in all matters pertaining to national planning; and that, since urban considerations permeated all the board's general approaches to planning, "the urban unit must be free to champion the cause of cities throughout a wide range of subjects."[22] The progressive urban planning procedure was clearly intended to attain these objectives.

With the director's permission, the urban unit had also begun to examine, as part of its process of self-definition, the obstacles to postwar urban redevelopment and how to eliminate them. In line with its "total approach" to urban planning, it assembled an interdisciplinary team of specialists and encouraged them to break new ground. Thus Ralph Temple, a lawyer, began drafting a new definition of the traditional sovereign power of the state (with respect to eminent domain, taxation, and the police power) for the social control of urban land use; Edwin H. Spengler, a Brooklyn College economist, investigated alternative sources for financing local units besides the property tax; Alvin H. Hansen and Guy Greer, economists, studied the implications of urban land acquisition and the funding of urban redevelopment for a full-employment economy; and V.O. Key, Jr., a Johns Hopkins political scientist, considered the problems of readjusting urban governmental machinery to facilitate planning and land acquisition control.[23]

Supervising their efforts was Mitchell, who refined the proce-

21. "The Interdepartmental Urban Planning Committee" [1941], and Charles Eliot to Regional Chairmen and Counselors, Jan. 2, 1942, in *ibid.*

22. Charles S. Ascher, "Proposed Program for Urban Conservation and Development, 1942–1943," n.d., in *ibid.*

23. Robert B. Mitchell to Charles Eliot, Nov. 2, 1942, and the accompanying memoranda of Spengler, Hansen, and Key, in *ibid.*

169

dure the urban unit ultimately followed. He instructed the field agents to capitalize on the existing data and to organize local resources for particular segments of the experiment. "We are really proceeding on the assumption that 'planning is a continuous process' and that no plan will or should be considered final. If we can get the local people into the habit of thinking of their plans in this way, I believe we can increase the chances of planning being integrated into the municipal function as a living process," he observed.[24]

Mitchell expected each agent to remain in a given community for as long as was required to complete the comprehensive planning outline and to organize the local planning function "so that it will continue as a permanent process of the community." The agent's task was to (1) determine the extent of the planning area; (2) estimate the future economic and cultural growth of the community against the plan; (3) develop both a general and hypothetical land use-population density plan; (4) evaluate the present major street pattern and the transit, utilities, railroad, and other service systems and extrapolate from them future requirements; (5) centralize and coordinate the developmental plans of local government and private enterprise and evaluate them against optimal land use and demographic patterns; (6) classify the neighborhoods according to condition (i.e., decadent, declining, static, improving, and good); and (7) collate all the information and integrate it into a comprehensive outline plan. Lastly, Mitchell invited suggestions for cities to be designated demonstration experiments.[25]

After Congress severely reduced the board's appropriation for fiscal 1942, the Urban Section scaled down the original calculation of nine experimental projects to three and designated the remainder as "area studies," in which the federal government would offer formal recognition and token assistance to local groups wanting to conduct their own intensive planning. Thus Mitchell was placed in the position of having to select only

24. Mitchell to Ladislas Segoe, Mar. 7, 1942, in *ibid.*
25. *Ibid.*

cities in which the project was likely to succeed—and quickly. Under these circumstances, the section drew up a new set of criteria, more exacting than the directors had sketched. The guidelines rested on two fundamental premises: (1) certain cities could utilize the funds most efficiently to yield the quickest results, and (2) since the preponderance of urban development had occurred in the East and Midwest, the distribution of projects ought to be weighted there.[26]

There were other criteria governing the choice of sites. The staff agreed, for example, to give priority to communities whose demographic, economic, social, and cultural data were current and readily accessible and to cities having regional problems in economic layout or political administration. The negative criteria were more rigorous. Population was a controlling factor— no city below 10,000 or above 150,000 was eligible; the Urban Section might conduct experiments in declining communities, but "not more than one in places such as Scranton, Pennsylvania, which seem to have a pretty hopeless future as they now are," nor in more than one satellite part of a metropolitan region. Certain categories of communities were excluded altogether—cities artificially boomed or revived by the defense program; those in which local leadership was antagonistic to federal planning and the New Deal; and communities already blessed with efficient and productive planning organizations.[27]

It is regrettable in retrospect that the budget reduction, congressional pressure, and failure to adhere strictly to the guidelines compromised the total impact of the planning procedure as a tool for other cities to utilize. The selection of Buffalo as the demonstration project in Region 2 elucidates this point. Under the criteria set forth above, New York, Philadelphia, and Baltimore—cities that experienced urban blight in extremis— were excluded from consideration because they were too large and their problems too complex to yield the swift results desired.

26. Cf. Mitchell to Carl Feiss, July 16, 1942, John Miller to Herbert S. Fairbank, Oct. 19, 1942, and John W. Hyde to Morton L. Wallerstein, Mar. 13, 1942, in *ibid.*
27. "Criteria for Choosing Cities for Demonstration Projects" [1942], in *ibid.*

For similar reasons, the war-swollen urban complex of Norfolk, Newport News, Hampton, and Portsmouth was ineligible.[28]

Given the guidelines, Albert C. Schweizer, a technician, pointed out that the logical site in Region 2 was Wilmington, Delaware, which had a population of 112,000 and a tentative master plan. He wrote up a convincing brief in support of his choice, noting that the city offered diverse and large-scale manufacturing, a strong planning commission, and the prospect of staunch local support. Schweizer played as his trump cards Wilmington's proximity to the District of Columbia, which made it possible for the Urban Section to monitor closely the progress of the precedure, and the presence of John Hyde, who knew the city's needs and was eager to direct the experiment. Violating its own criteria, the section instead selected Buffalo. Later, because of unfavorable local conditions there, it had to reduce its commitment and redesignate it an area study.[29]

Schweizer also recommended other cities as potential experiments, but they suffered the fate of Wilmington. Waterbury and Torrington, Connecticut, for example, were centers of industry, business, and aggressive agriculture representative of New England as a whole. They offered a combined population of 127,000, sympathetic public officials, a funded full-time planning engineer, and the nearby resources of the Yale University Planning Group. In Region 4, Jackson and Ann Arbor, Michigan, both urban satellites of Detroit, were possibilities. Jackson was a city of 49,000 population, with diverse manufacturing interests, and was quite typical of communities that appeared in numerous statistical tabulations. Its one serious drawback was that neither Schweizer nor Mitchell had a clear impression of the local political situation or the attitude toward planning. Ann Arbor, on the other hand, possessed a vigorous planning commission and an intelligent mayor, and it was eager to participate. The University of Michigan School of Architecture was

28. United States Department of Labor, *The Impact of War on the Hampton Roads Area* (Washington, D.C., 1944), chs. i, v, vi.

29. Albert C. Schweizer to Robert B. Mitchell, July 17, 1942, NARG 187, NRPB Records. On Buffalo, see NRPB, Region 2, *Preliminary Report: Niagara Frontier Area, War and Post-War Planning* (unpub. report, June 1941), 1–61, in *ibid.*

also enthusiastic to test the procedure in order to determine whether it had applicability for the Detroit metropolitan area.[30]

The city fathers of Birmingham, Alabama, bolder and more desperate, conducted a highly intensive but ultimately futile lobbying campaign to have their city designated a demonstration experiment. Located in Region 3, which extended from South Carolina along the Gulf Coast to Louisiana, the city had a population in 1942 just a shade under half a million. The war had brought to the hitherto quiet city a floating population of whites and rural blacks to work in the steel mills. The sudden influx of newcomers aggravated an already existing housing shortage and placed a strain upon transportation, health, educational, and recreational facilities.[31]

Birmingham officials, in lieu of preparing comprehensive plans for the city's future, speculated about the number of citizens who would remain after the war and the extent of services the community would have to provide for them. Upon learning of the board's progressive planning experiment, they approached the Urban Section for assistance. Mitchell and Schweizer concluded that Birmingham offered the kinds of problems that might provide an interesting test of the procedure but refused to commit themselves. Schweizer explained, in a veiled reference to the racial problem, that there were "indications that local direction of the survey would not be entirely satisfactory, would unduly prolong the test, and might not carry out the experiment in the manner originally intended."[32] The Urban Section decided instead to assist the city in organizing its planning authority but to concentrate its own resources elsewhere.

Mitchell, acting for the board, ultimately settled on Corpus Christi, Salt Lake City, and Tacoma as the most promising communities in which to test the progressive planning procedure. At its best—in Corpus Christi, a community that had achieved big-city status through a succession of booms in shipping, chemicals, oil, and war industry—the demonstration experiment embodied

---

30. Schweizer to Mitchell, July 17, 1942, in *ibid.*
31. *Ibid.* Also, Mitchell to John Archer, Mar. 24, 1942, in *ibid.*
32. *Ibid.*

173

the principles of coordinated, continuous, and, in the eyes of the board, democratic planning.[33]

As with other cities once the nation went to war, Corpus Christi had had to defer its normal public works construction, its building of streets, sewers, and utilities, and its new city hall, library, and school.[34] With the assistance of the Urban Section, however, city officials attempted to carry this Texas coastal community beyond the "city beautiful" and "city engineering" stages into a comprehensive design for work, play, and decent living. By planning for the orderly development of its public works and studying proper location and design, they hoped to foster what had always been lacking in the daily struggle to catch up with the rapid growth of the city.[35]

Members of the chamber of commerce, city councilmen, planning commissioners, and the *Caller-Times* wanted a plan that would provide direction to economic and industrial development and a pattern for the quality of urban living they deemed desirable. "For the first time," commented the chairman of the city planning commission, "Corpus Christi was consciously designing its own future. For the first time, planning was based on a true coordination of plans—economic, social, physical."[36] Complying with their request, the Urban Section dispatched Sam B. Zisman, one of its best technicians, to work with the local people in organizing the program and lending technical assistance. Zisman at no time attempted to draw up the plans for the city; rather, he aided Corpus Christi in doing its own planning.[37]

33. For the origins of the Corpus Christi project see Sam B. Zisman to Mitchell [Aug. 1942?], in *ibid.*

34. Corpus Christi had been established from the plan of 1930 prepared by Major Edward A. Wood, city planning engineer of Dallas. It was fairly typical of its time— heavily loaded on the zoning side—and was the basis for the city's original zoning ordinance. Although an improvement over the old, it fell far short of being a comprehensive city plan. At the same time, the city rejected various sections of the Washington-Arneson Master Highway Plan of 1939. See "Corpus Christi Reconnaissance Report," Oct. 3, 1942, in *ibid.*

35. Corpus Christi *Caller-Times,* June 2, Aug. 25, and Nov. 15, 1942.

36. Quoted in Sam B. Zisman, "Cities in Action," *Survey Graphic* 32 (Oct. 1943), 412.

37. Robert B. Mitchell to Charles Eliot, Sept. 10, 1942, in NARG 187, NRPB Records.

The first step in the procedure was to organize the entire community. Mayor Arthur C. McCaughan directed all municipal departments to contribute up-to-date statistics; the school board, housing authority, library, and real estate boards resolved to collaborate with the planning commission in developing programs and providing clerical assistance. The industrial committee of the chamber of commerce provided leadership in working out the plan for economic and industrial development. Over the months, its members met regularly, drawing in business, financial, and labor interests, marking out the problems to be tackled, surveying the resources of the city and its surrounding region, and defining long-range goals. It professed to give high priority to training programs that would result in full-employment opportunities for minority groups (principally Chicanos and blacks) and to housing, adequate consumer income, and regional economic development. Thus the pattern of individual and economic development became as much a part of the plan as did street paving or slum elimination.[38]

Local service and citizens' groups also joined in analyzing needs and proposing programs. The school board, for example, instituted studies of new schools and recommended improvements in the existing plant. It also worked closely with the recreation people, coordinating plans for schools with those for parks and playgrounds. The director of the housing authority, the real estate board, and private agencies grappled with the thorny question of a city-wide public housing program. They gave strong emphasis to the redevelopment of slums and blighted areas that cut through the heart of the city. Complementing their work were committees on health, welfare, and institutions organized under the supervision of the Council of Community Agencies. The engineering department brought its plans for streets, sewers and drainage systems, and water supply into the picture, while the police department drafted blueprints for a badly needed modern safety center.[39]

At each stage of the procedure, the planning commission at-

38. "The Corpus Christi Planning Demonstration," May 12, 1943, in *ibid.*
39. *Caller-Times,* Oct. 12, Dec. 2, 7, and 15, 1942.

175

tempted to employ to good advantage the resources of neighboring educational institutions and government agencies. The University of Texas conducted demographic studies; the department of architecture at Texas A&M analyzed waterfront patterns, and the Texas College of Arts and Industries initiated faculty studies of agricultural and industrial problems. The highway study required cooperative planning between the local and county engineering departments, the State Highway Department, and the Public Roads Administration. And the design for a major new airport to serve Corpus Christi spurred collaborative efforts on the part of local officials and the Civil Aeronautics Authority. The whole program was thus to be a demonstration of cooperation between private enterprise, private institutions, and public agencies.[40]

Toward the close of the demonstration in March 1943, over thirty agencies and 600 citizens were meeting, exchanging information, exploring problems, and projecting plans. At the center was the planning commission, coordinating the separate programs and driving toward the development of a comprehensive plan. The experience had significance beyond this appreciation of a coordinated plan. Zisman afterward claimed that the project had enlisted a wide democratic participation, that political difficulties and old prejudices had a hard time elbowing into the work, and that the citizens of Corpus Christi retained a hardheaded realism about how much they had accomplished and how far they still had to go.[41]

The experiment at its worst failed conspicuously in Tacoma, a nineteenth-century railroad community to which the war had given new impetus. In entering Tacoma, the Urban Section violated some of its own criteria, ignored others, and neglected to do its homework. It clearly understood very poorly the leadership problem in the community. The mayor was the most dynamic and enthusiastic local booster of the project, but his interest in improving the community was constantly frustrated by subordinate commissioners who either disapproved of his

40. *Ibid.*
41. Zisman, "Cities in Action," 412.

methods and specific proposals or feared he would set a city manager above them. The commissioner of public works, who appointed members to the planning commission, retaliated by refusing to cooperate with Art McVoy, the NRPB's field agent, or to call a meeting of the planning commission.

For his part, the mayor weakened his hand by insisting that planning be done on the quiet so that afterward he could spring it on the people. This tactic made it impossible for McVoy to identify his backers, to explain what he hoped to accomplish, or to bring local groups into the planning process.[42] McVoy's appearance in Tacoma occurred at the wrong time psychologically and politically. Understandably, he wrote to Mitchell: "I think if I had it to do over again, I would attempt to find out all the complexities of local politics before attempting to start applying the program."[43]

The record elsewhere in the case of the experimental projects and the area studies was mixed, as the urban unit modified its approach in accordance with particular geographical settings or in response to different emphases in a number of problems. In Denver and Buffalo, for example, the staff confronted fundamentally large metropolitan complexes and had to engage in planning for the metropolitan region.[44] In these urbanized areas the land-use plan was primarily *urban* land use in which the plan for industry focused upon decentralization rather than dispersion. The situation was quite the reverse on the Wasatch Front, which embraced Salt Lake City and its environs, where the board had to contemplate the requirements of both the urban core and the more rural hinterland.[45]

The Wasatch Front required a regional plan in which rural, mining, and urban land uses were interlocked. The industrial plan, for example, had to accommodate not only population density, housing, and urban size but also the reconversion of

42. "Progress Report," n.d.; Mitchell to John D. Spaeth, Jr., and to Eliot, Sept. 18 and Nov. 9, 1942, in NARG 187, NRPB Records.
43. Art McVoy to Mitchell, June 9, 1942, in *ibid.*
44. See NRPB, *National Resources Development Report for 1943,* House Doc. 128, pt. 2, 78th Cong., 1st sess. (1943), 74–75.
45. Zisman to Mitchell, Sept. 3, 1942, in NARG 187, NRPB Records.

war plants to civilian uses, the development of local processing industries, the agricultural program, ranching, the mining of metallic and nonmetallic resources, trade, the availability of public services (government, church, and education), and transportation (as transfer and service points for the national highway and air systems). At each stage of the planning, the Urban Section also had to take cognizance of the integrating force of the Mormon church in the social and cultural development of urban life.[46]

After the initial delay, the Salt Lake City experiment progressed smoothly, unlike the Buffalo area study that was plagued by foot-dragging and other obstacles. Albert C. Schweizer summed up the New York situation for Mitchell, following extensive conferences in September 1942 with NRPB representatives. He concluded that the board should not sink its resources into the area study because of the unfavorable atmosphere within the city.[47] Buffalo, unlike the demonstration experiments and most area studies projects, had experienced a mass in-migration of blacks seeking war-created jobs and opportunities. The rapid growth of the black population from 17,694 to 30,000 between 1940 and 1944 exacerbated tensions with the older, white ethnic (mainly Polish) communities. Sterling Albert, regional director for the National Housing Agency, informed Schweizer that local real estate interests and some Catholic church leaders, motivated either selfishly or from lack of sympathy with the New Deal's social objectives, had organized to block the public housing program.[48]

The volatile element of racism had received almost no consideration when the Urban Section first broached the question of progressive planning in Buffalo. Worse still, there was a very real doubt that local officials in the Buffalo-Niagara Frontier area were interested in planning. David Diamond, a former

46. See *ibid.*
47. Schweizer to Mitchell, Sept. 25, 1942, in *ibid.*
48. *Ibid.* See also the remarks of John J. Coffy in American Municipal Association, *Proceedings of the Twenty-second Annual Meeting* (Chicago, 1945), 23. The black population figures are taken from Municipal Research Bureau, *Just A Moment,* Bull. 678 (Buffalo, N.Y., Jan. 27, 1944), n.p.

Corporation Counsel and judge, believed that the "planning interest centers in [a] small group and 98% of [the] intelligent population doesn't even vaguely know what the word planning means."[49] The city's transportation system, moreover, was chaotic. The New York Central Railroad, headquartered in New York City, acted as an absentee landlord. From what Schweizer could discern, the railroad evinced absolutely no interest in transportation planning and looked upon Buffalo as "just a way station between more important cities."[50]

Not all the difficulties originated with the local officials, however. John D. Spaeth, Jr., the NRPB's technical director, had instituted studies of three substandard neighborhoods, implanting some doubt in Schweizer's mind whether "he was willing to abandon his own tactics in favor of the procedure advocated by the Urban unit." Thus by the winter of 1942, the NRPB's participation in the Buffalo-Niagara Frontier area project was in complete disarray, and Mitchell was disgusted.[51]

Buffalo, unfortunately, procrastinated well into 1943 before establishing an active planning body. The Committee on Post War Problems was established to parallel the county's Niagara Frontier Post War Planning Commission. The relationship between the two agencies was described best in a bulletin of the Municipal Research Bureau dated March 1943: "It is important to the Buffalo taxpayer that he is not charged with what is of no real benefit to the city, whatever the benefit to the Frontier or other portions thereof." Adding insult to injury, the Common Council appropriated a niggardly sum to conduct planning—an amount so small that the Buffalo planning body experienced a real hardship in hiring a full-time director.[52]

More seriously, the largely negative attitude of both local officials and private citizens militated against progressive planning. An anonymous writer to the *Buffalo Evening News*

49. *Just A Moment,* Bull. 678; *Buffalo Evening News,* Nov. 14, 1943.
50. Schweizer to Mitchell, Sept. 25, 1942, in NARG 187, NRPB Records.
51. See *ibid.,* and Mitchell to John Miller, Nov. 2, 1942, in *ibid.*
52. See William Ludlow to Morton L. Wallerstein, Apr. 28 and May 5, 1943; Mitchell to George S. Duggar, Jan. 4, 1943, in *ibid.* Also, *Buffalo Evening News,* Mar. 8, 15, 1943, and *Just A Moment,* Bull. 631 (Buffalo, N.Y., Mar. 4, 1943), n.p.

summed up the prevailing attitude accurately when he observed: "The economic postwar plans should be secondary to our efforts to overpower the enemy. Let's give our main support toward getting this war over, otherwise we may be like the woman in the story who 'counted her chickens before they were hatched' and in her greed dropped the eggs."[53]

If the board's city planning experiments and area studies were not wholly the success their enthusiasts proclaimed, neither were they the failures New Deal critics were eager to believe. The progressive planning procedure had accepted the functional interdependency of city and suburb, acknowledging that the basic problems of the core area originated in large measure in the flight of the productive middle class to the fringe and the expensive fragmentation of governmental and social services within the metropolitan region.[54] It spurred communities to act to stem the flight of industry by seeking alternative sources of revenue (e.g., the gasoline levy) to the real property tax.[55]

Also, the thrust of the neighborhood conservation and urban rehabilitation program brought the NRPB into close contact with other agencies, such as the Urban Land Institute, property owner groups, and taxpayers' associations, which were aggressively interested in housing and planning projects. As Charles Abrams, Mel Scott, and other scholars have observed, it was in the developing programs of government, organized realtors, and their allies that the tentative outlines of the urban redevelopment statutes of the several states in the 1940s and the salient features of Title I of the Housing Act of 1949 were located.[56]

The final product of the Urban Section's action was the compilation of the progressive planning manual, written in simple, nontechnical language. *Action for Cities: A Guide for Commu-*

53. *Buffalo Evening News,* Nov. 14, 1943.
54. Cf. John Friedmann, "The Concept of a Planning Region—The Evolution of an Idea in the United States," in John Friedmann and William Alonso, eds., *Regional Development and Planning* (Cambridge, Mass., 1964), 500–1.
55. See, for example, Edwin H. Spengler, "Memorandum on Urban Taxation," Feb. 1, 1943, in NARG 187, NRPB Records.
56. Charles Abrams, *The City Is the Frontier* (New York, 1965), 74–79, 257–58; Mel Scott, *American City Planning Since 1890* (Berkeley, 1969), 365.

nity Planning was intended to offer the kind of help interested and intelligent citizens and officials needed to develop planned programs for their communities.[57] Its value as an instrument for coping with the postwar redevelopment problems of even small and medium-sized cities was questionable, however, because the principles enunciated therein were not closely adhered to in practice. The incomplete development of the economic study for Corpus Christi, the city in which the Urban Section claimed its greatest success, is illustrative. Zisman reported in 1943 that the manual had not been followed "to any appreciable extent." In his view, "it was not satisfactorily organized, was over-detailed in many places. It was not really tested by the industrial technician who preferred to follow his own lines of thinking and approach."[58]

Despite its limitations, *Action for Cities* forced planners to look beyond the exclusively physical dimension of urban planning. Urban Section officials, for example, categorized American cities according to socioeconomic and cultural status, age of residents, mobility, health, and other services. It would be an exaggeration to say that they were acquainted with the modern tools of the social scientist for analyzing specific urban problems (e.g., multiple regression analysis or determinants studies), or that their plans adhered strictly to economics of scale, but they had gained experience and compiled raw data to make future analyses a distinct possibility. In this sense, the war years were a seedtime in which city planners, government officials, and social scientists approached the city as a functional organism whose ills were eradicable given the application of certain procedures.[59]

The NRPB, moreover, had expanded upon the Depression experience to provide new models for federal aid to the cities in the form of human, technical, and financial resources. Mitchell

57. *Action for Cities: A Guide for Community Planning* (Chicago, 1943), Div. 520.

58. Sam B. Zisman, "Corpus Christi Project—The Development of the Economic Study," n.d., in NARG 187, NRPB Records.

59. For the application of such tools see Roy W. Bahl, *Metropolitan City Expenditures* (Lexington, Ky., 1969).

believed the experiments had introduced, however rudimentar-
ily, the democratic concept of community participation in the
planning process. If one equates the "community" with the
local civic-business-realty leaders, then the observation is accurate. For Mitchell *had* secured the endorsement of the city's
political, economic, and social establishment in Corpus Christi
and elsewhere well in advance of the selection of the site. Thus
in the Texas community the mayor, the president of the largest
bank, the head of the Southern Alkali Corporation, representatives of the extractive industries (oil, gas, and fishing), the real
estate board, and the Junior Assistance Club, who were interested in redeveloping the central part of the city and preserving
land values, each pledged the support of his particular constituency. The NRPB's agents, in turn, were sensitive to the interests of those whom it relied upon for assistance.[60]

On the other hand, the needs of other segments of the community (Chicanos, blacks, the unorganized and inarticulate)
seem to have been ignored with relative impunity. The largely
WASP elite slighted the "Mexican" chamber of commerce and
black civic groups. Insensitive to their wishes, the power structure transmitted its decisions through the Commissioner of
Water and Gas and the principal of the all-black high school.
The result in Corpus Christi was to institute the now familiar
practice of demolishing inner-city ghettos, uprooting ethnic minorities, and replacing them with high-rent commercial and residential dwellings occupied by well-to-do-whites.[61]

Further weakening the "democratic" aspect of community
participation was the fact that once the city fathers and boosters
made their bid to have Corpus Christi selected as the demonstration site, there was no meaningful avenue for the expression of
dissatisfaction with the planning process. George Kunkel, for
example, threw the editorial support of the *Caller-Times,* the
city's largest newspaper (circulation 49,000), behind the project

60. Mitchell to Charles Eliot, Aug. 27, 1942, and Zisman to Mitchell, Aug. 21,
Oct. 31, 1942, in NARG 187, NRPB Records.
61. Zisman to Mitchell, Sept. 26, Dec. 13, 1942; Zisman to Ervin K. Zingler, Jan. 14,
1943, in *ibid.*

and, with Zisman, prepared a carefully orchestrated public relations program to counteract adverse publicity.[62]

If there was opposition to planning, it was thoroughly muted. War-induced regimentation, a housing shortage, lack of local funds, and the opportunity to be among the first to tap the federal treasury for urban redevelopment funds (which, in turn, promised to create new jobs for returning veterans) stilled dissent. This too contributed to a pattern that was to become familiar after the war, namely, the use of federal funds to expand housing for the middle and upper classes with proportionately fewer funds to finance public housing for the lower classes, which needed it most urgently. Again the evidence from Corpus Christi is illuminating. Finley Vinson, the director of the local housing authority, in his final report did not touch upon the problems of financing postwar public housing or the role of the Federal Public Housing Authority.[63]

How much postwar urban planning was stimulated as a direct consequence of the NRPB-sponsored experiments is uncertain. Not very much during the war years, it would appear, or at least no more than would have occurred in any event. Here, too, the experience of the board's field agents in Corpus Christi is instructive. Zisman reported in April 1943, shortly before terminating the project for lack of funds, that many of the studies (including the surveys of social and cultural problems, school, medical, and housing needs) still were incomplete. He attributed the delay to the fact that various groups "still had not completely captured the concept of planning as something more than survey and analysis" and to their "reluctance to set sights high, a tendency to think only of immediate and existing shortages."[64]

Elsewhere, the NRPB paid casual attention to independent, privately financed urban planning projects, as in the example of

---

62. See "Report on Publicity and Public Relations—Corpus Christi," Dec. 31, 1942, in *ibid.*
63. See "Progress Report No. 1," Sept. 28, 1942, and Bernard J. Smith to Jacob Crane, Mar. 16, 1943, in *ibid.*
64. Zisman, "Corpus Christi Project, Progress Report No. 12," Apr. 19, 1943, in *ibid.*

Fortune magazine's sponsorship of the Syracuse plan, and co-operated indirectly with the Federal Housing Administration's Tri-Cities project in Tennessee and Virginia. But a series of polls conducted between 1942 and 1944 by the *American City* indicated that while most cities in all size categories said they were thinking about postwar planning, a relatively large percentage conceded that they had no professional body, or even plans to establish one. Nor were they laying aside reserves to finance postwar improvements, although the fiscal position of the cities was probably better than at any time since 1929. Moreover, a disturbingly large number of cities admitted that they were waiting for, or anticipated, a federal handout, despite the mounting hostility to federal postwar expenditures in Congress and the nation.[65]

The promising work of the board, particularly its initiative as the leader in postwar urban redevelopment and neighborhood conservation, was short-lived. Congressional critics of planning and the New Deal, fiscal conservatives, rural Democrats and Republicans, and interest groups such as the National Association of Real Estate Boards seized upon the comprehensive plan of social security which the NRPB had submitted in two previous annual reports and voted in 1943 not simply to phase out the board but to obliterate its activities. Over the years these foes had come to resent the efforts of the NRPB, a public agency, to operate as though it were a private advocate of a public policy.[66]

A few friends rallied to the board's defense, but they were

65. See *Action for Cities,* Divs. 540–42; "Syracuse Tackles Its Future," *Fortune* 26 (May 1943), 120–23; Paul Oppermann, "The Tri-Cities Planning Project," *American Institute of Planners Journal* 8 (July-Sept. 1942), 11–17; and the series "How Cities Are Planning for Post-War Municipal Improvements," beginning with vol. 57 (Nov. 1942), 35–37, in the *American City.*

66. The reports in question were *Toward Full Employment* and *Security, Work and Relief* (Washington, D.C., 1942). The arguments against the board were summarized in a staff memorandum (1943?), "Arguments Against the NRPB Program," in NARG 187, NRPB Records. See also *Congressional Record,* 77th Cong., 2d sess., 88, pt. 9 (Mar. 8, 16, 1943), Appendix, 1212–13, 1673–76, pt. 9 (May 19, 28, 1943), Appendix, 1827–29, 1969–70; "A Congressional Short Circuit?" *Planning & Civic Comment* 9 (Apr. 1943), 20; Robert A. Walker, *The Planning Function in Urban Government* (Chicago, 1950, 2d ed.), 364–65; and James T. Patterson, *Congressional Conservatism and the New Deal: The Growth of the Conservative Coalition in Congress, 1933–1939* (Lexington, Ky., 1967).

184

never large enough in number or influential enough politically to make a difference. Senator Robert M. La Follette, Jr., of Wisconsin, for example, told his colleagues that it would be a "tragic mistake for a country confronted with what everybody acknowledges to be the greatest problems that any country has ever faced to take a meat ax and chop down or badly slash activities which are studying some kind of program with which to meet the terrible problems of the post-war period."[67]

That the board and the Urban Section had become fatally embroiled in the conflict between a conservative Congress eager to reassert its legislative prerogatives and an aggressive Chief Executive is beyond dispute. Yet the erosion of confidence in the NRPB also stemmed from other factors. These included the wartime resurgence of states' rights and the board's apparent failure to make a startling contribution to the war effort. There was also more than a kernel of truth to the observation of planner George Duggar that the board had been weakened by its friends. From the first, Charles E. Merriam and Charles Eliot, the NRPB's guiding lights, had never resolved the dilemma whether the NRPB should be a research, propagandizing, operating, or advisory agency. This confusion over aims and objectives ran fuguelike throughout the board's numerous activities and involved it in the bureaucratic infighting that plagued other New Deal agencies.[68]

Apart from its political and institutional weaknesses, there is some doubt whether the board's sponsorship of the demonstration experiments engendered any real, long-term accomplishments. The Urban Section succeeded in convincing over a hundred smaller cities to establish their own planning councils, but the ultimate influence of its urban policy fell far short of expectations. True, the section had devised new models for federal aid

---

67. *Congressional Record,* 77th Cong., 2d sess., pt. 9 (May 19, 28, 1943), Appendix, 1828, 1970. See also "The Threat to the National Resources Planning Board," *American City* 58 (Mar. 1943), 5.

68. George S. Duggar, "Experiment in Planning," *Task 5* (Spring 1944), 19; Norman S. Beckman, "Federal Long-Range Planning," *American Institute of Planners Journal* 26 (May 1960), 93; Scott, *American City Planning Since 1890,* 408–9; "How States Are Preparing for the Post-War Period," *Planning* (Chicago, 1944), 121.

to cities by proposing to furnish human, technical, and financial resources, but it overlooked basic problems of the poor. And despite the aspirations of Robert Mitchell toward greater "democracy" and citizen involvement in planning activities, the emphasis on "elitism" that existed in planning in the 1930s and 1940s persisted. The federal consultants continued to work with established interest groups, such as chambers of commerce. Moreover, the National Housing Agency's (NHA) displacement of the NRPB as the center of urban study in the federal government also blunted the influence of the latter on postwar urban policy. The Urban Section had ranged far and wide in its examination of American life and cities. Not only had it perceived the community as a composite of numerous diverse elements, but it had also attempted to place the city in a national context. The NHA, as historian Mark Gelfand noted, had a much more limited perspective, viewing the city simply as a place to construct— or not to construct—homes. This difference was crucial and had enormous consequences for postwar urban America.[69]

Thus Congress's savage destruction of the NRPB in 1943 was unfortunate. The nation forfeited an opportunity, however limited in scope and impact, to undertake the physical, social, economic, and spiritual reconstruction of American cities, thereby leaving the problems of the thirties and forties to persist more stubbornly into the present.

69. Mark Gelfand, *A Nation of Cities: The Federal Government and Urban America, 1933-1965* (New York, 1975), 102-4.

VI. British and American Postwar Planning: A Study in Contrasts

Even in the darkest days of the war when the outcome for the democratic nations was less than promising, Americans fixed one eye on the peace that was to come. Urban planners, architects, and economists optimistically anticipated that the postwar years would be a time of physical renaissance for the cities: a time to eradicate blight and rehabilitate the decaying business district of the central city; a time to develop entire metropolitan regions, with proper land-use controls; and a time to bring to fruition the vision of the good urban life.

Urban renewal was the sine qua non of postwar community revitalization. This was the informed judgment of many New Deal liberals, such as Louis Wirth, chairman of the Illinois Defense Council. "If we are able to salvage even a part of the war-born capacity for concerted community action for the peace to come, the cities may thereby find the strength and the means whereby to deal with some of their most serious problems which have hitherto defied solution," he told his colleagues in 1943.[1] Given their expectations, urban specialists had to decide when to initiate planning activities for the postwar period and which model(s) of urban land use were likely to be most beneficial to achieving their objectives.

The timing of the redevelopment planning and the appropriate strategies were important because they precipitated a debate that, as time passed, divided the planning profession, realtors, civic officials, and legislators, and because they had serious consequences for postwar urban reconstruction. Ernest F. Goodrich, chairman of a special committee on the war effort of the

1. Louis Wirth, "The Urban Community," in William F. Ogburn, ed., *American Society in Wartime* (Chicago, 1943), 75.

American Institute of Planners (AIP), sparked the controversy in 1942 when he proposed to relegate postwar urban planning to "a sort of after-regular-hours occupation." The first priority, he maintained, was to improve the organization of the nation's resources for waging war—a recommendation that was severely criticized by other members, including Carl Feiss of Denver, who countered that the AIP must conduct both tasks simultaneously.[2]

The indivisibility of wartime mobilization and postwar urban planning, accepted by the British as a matter of course, eventually carried the field. Richard Graves, executive secretary to the League of California Cities, told his colleagues in the American Municipal Association that wartime and postwar urban planning could not be compartmentalized: "they are not separable; they are inevitably and inextricably interrelated, because what we do to solve our immediate problems or to solve the problems of the period of demobilization will inevitably determine to some extent at least what we are able to do with long-range planning."[3]

In addition, the timing of postwar urban planning was critical both psychologically and tactically because, as Louis Wirth told the International City Managers Association, war fixed its own goal whereas peace was built on less determinate objectives. "What compelling motive shall guide us in reconstructing and replanning our cities for the era of peace?" he asked. European cities would find their inspiration for reconstruction in the ruins that were all about them. "We must find our incentive in the vision of what we have in contrast to what we might have; in the difference between the actual and the possible."[4]

Further weakening the Goodrich committee's recommendation was a growing awareness that big labor, big business, and big agriculture had pledged to their constituents that they would

2. "Are Pleas for Post-War Plans Premature?" *Planning & Civic Comment* 8 (July 1942), 15–17; "The Planners' Contribution," *Journal of the American Institute of Planners (JAIP),* 8 (Oct.-Dec.1942), 27–32.

3. "Letter to the Editor," *American City* 57 (July 1942), 65; American Municipal Association (AMA), *Proceedings of the Twentieth Annual Conference* (Chicago, 1943), 53; "Sweet Are the Uses of Adversity," *American Society of Planning Officials (ASPO) Newsletter* 8 (Aug. 1942), 65.

4. "The Cities' Most Serious Crisis," *American City* 59 (Nov. 1944), 5.

conduct postwar planning even as the fighting continued. Their primary interest was in public works programs to avoid a repetition of the thirties' Depression and not in urban renewal as a desirable end in itself. In September 1942, however, Frederick P. Champ, president of the Mortgage Bankers Association, observed that the time was ripe to begin studying the question of urban renewal: "The property in that fifth of the urban United States, now under the 'dead hand' influence of blight, will have to be rehabilitated sooner or later if the American city is not to suffer really serious disintegration, and it looks as though it will be the nation's most immediate and important postwar job." Then he added: "It certainly holds the greatest employment potentialities."[5]

The fear of being left at the gate, as well as dread of a postwar renewal of the struggle with the cyclical economic forces that had plunged the nation into depression, were in the final analysis the strongest spurs to action. As Clarence Stein, the influential author of *Toward New Towns for America,* noted, this argument ended the debate as no other could. Professional city planners and architects hurled themselves energetically into postwar urban planning, reaffirming their dedication to service, research, and experimentation. As professionals whose talents were committed to the city, they wandered up and down the nation, lecturing, writing, studying, and exhorting. They converged upon city councils, state legislatures, and Congress, bearing witness to the urgency of immediate planning to ensure the cities' future.[6]

Because the war had come to their shores first and more destructively, the British were alive to the importance of postwar planning and reconstruction earlier than their American allies. In October 1940 the government appointed Lord Reith, formerly of the British Broadcasting Corporation, to head a revi-

5. "Mortgage Bankers' Head Urges Attack on Obsolete Zoning Laws and Building Codes," *ibid.,* 57 (Nov. 1942), 71. See also *Congressional Record,* 77th Cong., 2d sess., 88 (Feb. 2, 1942), 898–99, and *ibid.,* 88 (Mar. 10 and May 15, 1942), Appendix, 936, 1853.

6. Clarence Stein, "Preparedness for Post-War Urban Redevelopment," *American City* 57 (Feb. 1942), 67–69.

189

talized Ministry of Works and Buildings. Four months later Reith announced from the floor of the House of Lords that the government had officially accepted the principle of planning as national policy. Winston Churchill articulated this shifting national sentiment in 1943 in an address delivered at the Lord Mayor's luncheon in London, saying: "Just as in time of peace, plans for war and measures for defense ought to be at readiness in every prudent state for a sudden emergency, so in time of war we must make sure that confusion and chaos do not follow the victories of the armies or stultify the surrender, unexpectedly early by the enemy. The policy of waging war till victory would be incomplete and, indeed, spoiled if it were not accompanied by a policy of food, work, and homes in the period following the victory for the men and women who fought and won."[7]

With official encouragement, a sense of vital urgency born of the blitz and thirty years of ineptitude entered the literature of British planners. They were more advanced in public awareness and professional boldness than their American counterparts, and their volume of output alone was enough to inspire admiration and respectful envy. Individuals, private agencies, and governmental bodies grappled with the functional requirements of agriculture, healthy living, modern industry, and convenience of communication. Whether it was Arthur Greenwood's Committee on Reconstruction Problems, the Nuffield College Social Reconstruction Survey, or PEP (Political and Economic Planning), counterpart of the American National Planning Association, they were valiantly challenging the decentralizing influence inherent in the development of automobiles and electric power. In urban reconstruction their avowed purpose was to prevent speculative profit in land and to devalue slums. Catherine Bauer, a leader in the national housing movement in the United States, perceived in the British models a stimulus to American urban planners. "And we need it," she declared, "not only because we also face crises in land-use, but because this nation may undergo a period of deep reaction, during which American

7. "Winston Churchill Urges Post-War Planning and Housing," *ibid.,* 58 (Dec. 1943), 67.

progressives will have to seek strength and inspiration wherever they can find it, abroad if not at home."[8]

The reports of three expert commissions during 1940–42, which quickly became benchmarks in the evolution of British land-use planning, aroused considerable interest and controversy on this side of the Atlantic. The original impetus for a reconsideration of the whole subject in Great Britain had come from the Barlow Report on the Location of Industry and the Distribution of the Industrial Population, in 1940. It was followed soon thereafter by the Scott Report on Land Utilization in Rural Areas and the Uthwatt Report on Compensation and Betterment. Of the three, the Barlow Report—with its sweeping judgment that rapid urbanization and industrialization had culminated in a "disastrous harvest of slums, sickness, stunted population, and human misery"—was the starting point for a new conception of the planned use of land. Its recommendations for the redevelopment of blighted urban areas, for the dispersal of industries and congested populations from such areas, and for the provision of a reasonable balance of industrial employment throughout the nation set in clear perspective the requirements of a better condition of life and work. The Barlow Report's portrayal of the problem as urgent and incapable of solution without the assumption of control by a central authority, one invested with initiative and responsibility, brought about a general acceptance of the principle of national planning.[9]

The Scott Committee, appointed in October 1941, was a direct outgrowth of the dispersal proposals of the Barlow Commission. Its recommendations, presented to the Commons in August 1942, were founded upon an exhaustive analysis of both the gross impact upon agriculture of a large increase in physical construction in the countryside and the policies necessary to revitalize the rural areas to enable them to absorb urban encroachment without drastically changing their life-style. In the course of the investigation, two findings emerged. First, planning must

8. Catherine Bauer, "Planning Is Politics But Are Planners Politicians?" *New Pencil Points* 25 (Mar. 1944), 67.

9. *Royal Commission on Distribution of the Industrial Population,* Cmd. 6153 (London, 1940). Cited hereafter as *Barlow Report.*

be a matter of balancing the national advantages in deciding the use to which a given parcel of land should be put. Second, decisions must be in the hands of a central authority having an adequate complement of legal and executive assistance.[10]

In January 1941, nine months before the Scott Committee was formed, Lord Reith had nominated Augustus A. Uthwatt, of His Majesty's High Court of Justice, Chancery Division, to head an Expert Committee on Compensation and Betterment. Composed of two lawyers and two surveyors experienced in land and legal matters, the committee received a mandate to advise the government on steps to be taken "now or before the end of the war" to prevent the work of physical reconstruction, notably in blitzed areas, from being prejudiced by the high price of land.[11] The government asked the committee to examine (1) the possible means of stabilizing the value of land required for development or redevelopment; (2) any extension or modification of powers that would enable the public to acquire such land on an equitable basis; and (3) alterations in existing law to facilitate land acquisition. The Uthwatt Committee submitted an interim report in April 1941, which analyzed prices and speculation in land, and a final report in September 1942 which contained several proposals for the reconstruction of developed and undeveloped land. The latter document was consistent with the Barlow and Scott reports in asserting that the purely individualistic, laissez-faire attitude toward land ownership and use must be abandoned, and that broad reconstruction depended upon national planning in which a central authority exercised initiative and control.[12]

Although the Uthwatt and Barlow reports were in many respects complementary documents, the former went considerably beyond the latter in the alterations it would have wrought upon

10. *Report of the Committee on Land Utilization in Rural Areas,* Cmd. 6378 (London, 1942). Cited hereafter as *Scott Report.*
11. "The Uthwatt Report," *Architectural Forum* 77 (Nov. 1942), 49–51.
12. The report also took cognizance of the tasks that local and regional planning bodies might undertake under the aegis of the central board. See *Final Report of Expert Committee on Compensation and Betterment,* Cmd. 6386 (London, 1942). Cited hereafter as *Uthwatt Report.*

British society and land-use patterns. The Uthwatt Report went into the controversial issue of public and private ownership and recommended that the way out of the confusion produced by the existing practice of "compensation and betterment"[13] was to bring all land affected by planning resolutions into a single ownership. In this manner, shifts of land value brought about by planning could occur without the disruptions that inevitably took place where land was held in multiple ownership. The report had recommended that the state acquire development rights in all land outside built-up areas with fair compensation at prewar values (i.e., March 31, 1939); that all land should be deemed from a fixed date to be covered within the planning ordinance; that planning authorities be vested with the power to purchase war-damaged, obsolete, and unsatisfactory built-up areas needing redevelopment, the land so acquired being leased to private developers and not sold outright; and, lastly, that the procedure for compulsory acquisition of land be speeded up.[14]

The Uthwatt Report stopped short of proposing nationalization of all land, particularly as the solution to the problem of "floating value," but as the American economist Edwin H. Spengler noted, it did appear to represent a significant change ideologically in British thinking. The wartime damage, the urgency of reconstruction, and a prevalent desire to provide tangible recompense for the sufferings of its citizens had created in Britain a mood of expectancy that gave an exceptional timeliness and relevancy to the reports.[15]

After some initial procrastination the government made the reports the cornerstone of postwar town planning policy. Parliament gave life to the Central Planning Authority when it es-

13. It was generally agreed that compensation was payable where private property was adversely affected. However, the mechanism for recovering betterment from owners whose property was enhanced in value was defective. This problem had handicapped any firm regulation of land use or any positive guidance of development. See British Information Services (BIS), comp., *Town and Country Planning in Great Britain* (London, 1949), 8-9.

14. Charles M. Haar, ed., *Law and Land Use* (Cambridge, Mass., 1964), x, 6; Lloyd Rodwin, *The British New Towns Policy* (Cambridge, Mass., 1956), 18-19.

15. Edwin H. Spengler, "The Uthwatt Committee Submits Its Final Report," *JAIP* 8 (Oct.-Dec. 1942), 16.

tablished in 1943 the *Town and Country Interim Development Act,* the first of a series of such legislation. For the first time, all land was put under planning control, and the planning authorities were vested with new powers of enforcement.[16]

Henry Strauss, Parliamentary Secretary for Planning, explained the significance of the changes in progress in an address to the national meeting of the Town Planning Institute of Great Britain, in 1942. "The acceptance of the principle of national planning means at least this: never again will it be possible for a Minister in either House, when some scandalous destruction of town or countryside or reckless squandering of our inheritance is brought to light, to disclaim all interest and responsibility, and to treat the matter as the exclusive affair of the local authority of the area in question. It is the affair of the nation," he observed.[17]

Strauss's speech, which was reprinted in *American City,* had a profound effect upon American planners, who were themselves seeking to substitute a controlled form of land use for the previous century's laissez-faire attitude toward development. "The international crisis has given a new intensity to our thinking about the future of cities," declared the NRPB in its annual report. "In Great Britain the impetus seems to be the desolation wrought by enemy bombers; it has led already to organization for post-war rebuilding of cities. . . . And even though the United States hopes to be spared the rain of death from the sky, there is the same ferment at work here: the determination that the communities of the future must be nobler embodiments of the democratic respect for the worth of the individual, if our war effort is to be justified."[18]

In a similar spirit, the editor of *Public Management* commented: "Reports from Britain indicate that plans are already

16. For the provisions of the historic *Town and Country Planning Acts* of 1944 and 1947 see BIS, comp., *Town and Country Planning in Great Britain,* 17–25, and Rodwin, *British New Towns Policy,* 21.

17. Henry Strauss, "In the Midst of War, England Plans for Better Post-War Communities," *American City* 57 (Oct. 1942), 41.

18. National Resources Planning Board (NRPB), *National Resources Development, Report for 1942* (Washington, D.C., 1942), 100–1.

being laid for a program of planning to rebuild English cities after the war on a scale that dwarfs all past achievements in urban planning." Then he asked the critical question that was in the minds of United States planners and urban liberals: "Must American cities wait until they, too, have been bombed and burned before awakening to the urgent need for comprehensive planning and rebuilding?"[19]

The answer was no, for as Walter Blucher of the American Society of Planning Officials (ASPO) perceived, the war had also created an opportunity for the United States to set its own cities in order. "The excuse of 'present emergency' must not be used as an evasion for sound planning. Our cities, states and the country as a whole will be here long after the present emergency has passed; rather than serving as justification for bad planning, it might be better used as a justification for obtaining some of these improvements which are so needed in our American communities but were not available heretofore," he declared.[20] Carl S. Stein, counsel for the New York State Board of Housing and member of the slum clearance committee of the Citizen's Housing Council, agreed. Alluding to the British experience, he told a Columbia University seminar on urbanism that this country, fortunately, had no civilian casualties and no precious structures to rebuild as a result of war damage: "The problem with us is whether we have the intelligence, imagination, and, above all, the will to devote resources that will not have to be devoted to repairing war's devastation to the cure of a disease which, though not acute and not dramatized by bombing, is becoming progressively more dear."[21]

The tradition of American planners and public housing enthusiasts looking abroad to Europe for new inspiration and fresh approaches to perennial urban problems was not unique in

19. "Post Defense Planning," *Public Management* 23 (Sept. 1941), 258. See also New York *Herald Tribune,* Apr. 6, 1941.

20. Walter H. Blucher, "City Planning for National Defense," *American City* 55 (Sept. 1940), 5.

21. Carl Stern, "Urban Redevelopment," in *Discussions on Urbanism: Reports of a Series of Seminars held by the Planning and Housing Division, School of Architecture, Columbia University, Jan. 8–Apr. 23, 1943* [reprinted from *Pencil Points* (1943), 25]. Cited hereafter as *Discussions on Urbanism.*

the 1940s. By the first quarter of the twentieth century, there had come into being in the United States and Great Britain striking historical parallels in the legislative control of land use. Britain's first *Town and Country Planning Act* in 1909, for example, antedated American legislation, but it typified contemporary thinking in this country as expressed at the National Planning Conferences and other early discussions in the legal stratagems of zoning. The first British legislation in town planning with any teeth—the 1932 act—coincided with the passage of state enabling legislation modeled upon Herbert Hoover's Standard Zoning and Planning Enabling Acts of 1926 and 1928. In the realm of housing, Henry S. Churchill, architect with the Resettlement Administration and a consultant to the New York State Division of Housing, observed: "Our present ideas of housing and the community that housing implies derive from the English—from Robert Owen, Ebenezer Howard, and Raymond Unwin."[22]

To Europeans generally, the United States with its size and resources had offered the perfect locale to implement regional planning schemes. American cities were untrammeled by tradition and the old centers of population that severely restricted the scope of urban planning in Europe. Thus Ebenezer Howard, architect of the English garden city, enthusiastically proclaimed to members of the International City and Regional Planning Conference, meeting in New York City in April 1925, that: "Possibilities lie before us which the Americans will do more to point out to the other nations of the world than has ever entered into the minds of any of us. Yes, there are possibilities of creating not only new towns, but new regions, of creating a new civilization which will surpass ours."[23]

In the tradition of this Anglo-American connection, United States planners turned to British as well as American sources for ideas about postwar urban reconstruction and community renewal. Just as the British cities of Coventry, Plymouth, and

22. Henry S. Churchill, "Housing and Community Planning," in *ibid.,* 11.
23. National Conference on City Planning, *Planning Problems of Town, City and Region* (Baltimore, 1925), 8.

196

London crumbled under the weight of Nazi bombings, so too they saw American cities decaying from internal corrosion. "Our own cities, as yet not threatened by devastation from above, are disintegrating in a different way—slowly, peacefully, but surely," observed Frederic A. Delano, head of the National Resources Planning Board (NRPB), in 1941.[24] Urban decay and loss of community were advancing in direct proportion to the decentralization of population and industry throughout the metropolitan areas of the nation's largest cities. If permitted to go unchecked, these phenomena boded ill for the future. "A greater danger lurks ahead, that the whole supporting bases of our great metropolitan areas will be so weakened by war, high taxes, and class conflicts that the structure of our highly specialized urban society of today will begin to crack and finally collapse as did the urban civilization of the Roman empire," warned Homer K. Hoyt.[25]

True, the causes of decay were starkly different, but prominent officials in both countries acknowledged that to truly win the war they would also have to win the peace. This meant fulfilling the promise of democracy embodied in the Atlantic Charter by affording to each of their citizens the opportunity to live decently in revitalized communities, at better than prewar levels. Charles S. Ascher of the NRPB, a specialist in the problems of the urban community, eloquently summed up this viewpoint when he stated: "We can seize what may be a unique opportunity to remold our cities, to provide a creative, healthful and satisfying living and working environment for a people afforded economic security by full employment."[26]

Of the three landmark British documents, the Uthwatt Report with its new conception of broad public control over land use seemed to offer the most promising tool for freeing American cities of urban blight. Ralph Walker, a partner in the New York architectural firm of Voorhees, Walker, Foley and

24. Frederic A. Delano, "Must Urban Redevelopment Wait on Bombing," *American City* 56 (May 1941), 35.
25. Quoted in Charles S. Ascher, "Better Cities After the War," *ibid.,* 57 (June 1942), 55.
26. Quoted in *ibid.,* 57.

Smith, praised the document as "an extension in philosophy of eminent domain," while Luther Gulick and E.N. Thompson, who had undertaken a comprehensive study of all British planning activities on behalf of the NRPB, described the report as "an extremely important document and one calculated to have large long-run influence, not only in Britain but perhaps as a precedent in other democracies facing the land-use and acquisition question." Planner Carl Stern advocated a similar *comprehensive* study of urban land use in the United States.[27]

Despite their own enthusiasm for the British reports, American planners were uncertain of their reception by United States policy makers. A substantial part of the philosophy running through the report had already received recognition and some degree of acceptance, principally among liberal New Dealers, but, cautioned urban economist Edwin H. Spengler, "It remains to be seen whether public opinion in favor of national planning is sufficiently strong to make possible the introduction of controls that would go this far in the reduction of authority and private initiative."[28] Carl Stern put the matter even more succinctly. "How far in this country we shall follow the English suggestions will be affected by what *we* deem necessary in our American scheme to protect the various interests in urban communities," he noted.[29]

In contrast to the audaciousness of its British counterpart, Catherine Bauer thought much of the American planning literature "narrow, negative, dull or opportunist." There was truth in this observation, but among the chaff the interested reader could find grains of wheat—articles whose authors advocated land-use concepts quite similar to those explicated by British

27. Ralph Walker, "The Planner's Position in Society Today," in *Discussions on Urbanism,* 3; Luther Gulick and E.N. Thompson, "Post-War Planning in Great Britain," Feb. 1942, unpub. confidential report, National Archives (NA), Record Group (RG) 69, Records of the Public Works Reserve.

28. Spengler, "The Uthwatt Committee Submits Its Final Report," 49–50; Philip H. Cornick, "Further Comments on the Uthwatt Committee Report," *American City* 57 (Dec. 1942), 53.

29. Stern, "Urban Redevelopment," in *Discussions on Urbanism,* 29. See also Robert B. Mitchell to Jonathan Daniels, Feb. 15, 1943, NARG 187, Records of the National Resources Planning Board.

planners. Clarence Stein, for example, argued that Americans would have to revise many of their beliefs about city planning, land use, and the role of government and private enterprise.[30] The National Economic and Social Planning Organization's (NESPO) own attitude paralleled at certain points several of the recommendations found in the British reports. In *Guides for Post-War Planning,* the NESPO discussed the need for a controlled (but nonregimented) economic and social environment in lieu of the laissez-faire land-use policies characteristic of the era. Metropolitan regional planning, the obligation of farmers to maximize land use, and the return to the public domain of land ill fitted for cultivation sounded very much like the British proposals.[31]

In a second pamphlet, *Urban Redevelopment and Housing,* Guy Greer, the senior economist of the board of governors of the Federal Reserve System, and Alvin H. Hansen of Harvard University, widely known in scholarly circles as "the American Keynes," explicated their ideas for postwar urban redevelopment. The key element was borrowed directly from the British reports: the establishment of a central planning authority "charged with the direction . . . of all activities of the Government having to do with the structure of urban communities," which the authors branded "economic monstrosities." Besides making loans and granting funds for site acquisition in advance of eliminating slums and blighted areas, the central authority would extend technical aid to local planning bodies and approve their comprehensive redevelopment plans. Thus, in structure and functions—particularly the call for a central authority and the freeing of land in redevelopment areas from inflated assessed values—the Hansen-Greer proposals had parallels with the Barlow and Uthwatt recommendations, although the authors stopped short of embracing the latter unequivocally.[32]

30. Stein, "Preparedness for Post-War Urban Redevelopment," 67–69; Bauer, "Planning Is Politics," 67.

31. National Economic and Social Planning Organization, *Guides For Post-War Planning* (Washington, D.C., 1941), 1–31.

32. Guy Greer and Alvin H. Hansen, *Urban Redevelopment and Housing* (Washington, D.C., 1941), 7–18.

If a paper comparison could be drawn between the English and American experiences, Britain's Ministry of Town and Country Planning in 1943 bore certain superficial similarities to the National Resources Planning Board, which Roosevelt had established under the Reorganization Act of July 1, 1939. This was not entirely fortuitous; the evidence suggests that the British authorities had the NRPB in mind when they created their own planning agency. However, they also seemed to have misconstrued the status of the NRPB vis-à-vis the executive and legislative branches of the government, for they exaggerated both its influence and capacity to function as a central planning body within the federal framework. There is no doubt that the board's interest in cities and promotion of planning suggested that it aspired to become this type of agency—the urban counterpart of the Department of Agriculture—but in the two years prior to its dissolution the NRPB was in certain respects taking its cues from British planning developments.[33]

Thus when the board reviewed urban problems in light of post-defense requirements, it asked itself whether a need existed for a national urban program. The board replied in the affirmative, and its demonstration projects were intended to serve as models for such a national program. As the Gulick-Thompson report indicated, some of the approaches to eradicating urban blight paralleled British land-use concepts. Now that the pioneering stage of speculative land use in the United States had come to a close, community revitalization, both spiritually and physically, depended upon *comprehensive* metropolitan planning that would extend over several decades. Like the British, the NRPB believed this could best be conducted under the auspices of a central planning authority.[34]

In order to provide the physical setting wherein community renewal might be nurtured, it was essential to "unfreeze" urban land, making it fluid once again. "European cities discovered long ago that to control their own destinies and to realize the

33. Mel Scott, *American City Planning Since 1890* (Berkeley, 1971), 382.
34. NRPB, *Progress Report 1940–1941* (Washington, D.C., 1941), 3, 76.

patterns that they had set themselves they must on occasion be free to withdraw land on the fringes from disruptive exploitation or to dedicate it to development in accord with a balanced plan," declared the NRPB. Here again the board took a leaf or two from the British reports: "A search must be launched for ways of bringing to bear more effectively the trinity of sovereign powers: eminent domain, taxation, and the police power." One possibility was for the states to relinquish a part of their jurisdiction over land use to the cities, thereby enabling the latter to retain title to the land while leasing it to private enterprise for redevelopment.[35]

Unfortunately for the advocates of comprehensive urban planning, their objectives increasingly met with opposition as the war dragged on to its final cataclysmic end. Among the obstacles were popular apathy; a tradition of privatism in which the physical forms of the city had been set by a real estate market of profit-selling builders, land speculators, and large investors; and the competing goals of urban-based politicians. The latter had always claimed a unique capacity to judge the public interest, and they concluded that what the public needed was not grandiose schemes for rebuilding the cities (such as the British were proposing) but more limited and practical public works projects to guarantee full employment to returning veterans. In saying this, they wanted to be the actual deciders of policy; they wanted to exercise their influence continuously, at levels of generality sufficiently low so that *their* decisions rather than the opinions of outsiders might affect matters of interest to their constituents.[36]

Robert Moses, the guiding genius of the New York Port Authority and controversial member of the city's planning commission, was among the most vocal foes of comprehensive planning and the British model. A highly successful self-made man,

35. NRPB, *National Resources Development, Report for 1942,* House Doc. 560, 77th Cong., 2d sess. (1942), 101-7.
36. On the idea of "privatism" see Samuel B. Warner, Jr., *The Private City: Philadelphia in Three Periods of Its Growth* (Philadelphia, 1968), 3-4, and Alan A. Altshuler, *The City Planning Process: A Political Analysis* (Ithaca, 1965), 317.

he exuded contempt for the intellectual and the professionally trained expert, even as he employed their talents. In 1942, when critics denounced the proposal to build Stuyvesant Town, a mammoth privately owned urban renewal complex in densely populated Manhattan, Moses lashed out against them.[37] His choicest barbs were reserved for the proponents of comprehensive urban planning, however. "It is easy enough for starry-eyed planners to make pretty pictures of wholesale slum clearance," he declared. "The real job is to find responsible public officials who will do something concrete, if necessary, on a small scale, which will actually tear down the old tenements, widen the streets, and provide not only better living conditions for those lucky enough to get into the new houses, but facilities and improvements for an entire neighborhood."[38]

Moses's disdain of comprehensive planners comforted ideological conservatives, property-oriented businessmen and realtors, Republican congressmen from rural and suburban constituencies, and conservative Democrats. These foes of the New Deal perceived that the ambitious proposals for eradicating urban blight and creating a new community synthesis could only be realized through the generous exercise of public power, and this they believed was undesirable. A central planning agency's arrogation of functions, such as described in the Uthwatt Report and the reports of the NRPB, interfered with the values of liberty and property which were crucial to a democratic society. As evidence, they adduced that every grant of power to Washington since 1933 had increased the chance of its being abused; had caused bureaucracy and red tape to permeate the daily routine of citizens; and had stifled initiative and self-reliance.

To check this tendency, the conservative opposition was prepared to fight bitterly against comprehensive urban planning, which they equated with national economic planning, and to endorse instead the principle of locally initiated and financed public works planning. Their lack of confidence in their own ability

37. For the controversial history of the project see Arthur Simon, *Stuyvesant Town, U.S.A.: Pattern for Two Americas* (New York, 1970), esp. chs. 2, 3, 8.
38. See "City Planning: Battle of the Approach," *Fortune* 28 (Nov. 1943), 164–68, and *New York Times,* June 18, 1942.

to influence planning decisions rendered at the federal level was more than offset by their belief that local planning was more susceptible to manipulation.[39]

Thus Arthur Binns resigned the vice presidency of the Urban Land Institute after that body had endorsed in principle federal assistance for urban planning. Binns articulated the conservatives' brief against comprehensive urban planning by drawing an analogy between allegedly radical New Deal and foreign (chiefly British) social concepts. If the nation returned to the soft sentimentalism and slipshod thinking of the New Deal, or adopted the cradle-to-grave security advocated by British social planners (a reference to Lord Beveridge's 1942 report, *Social Insurance and Allied Services*), it would have sealed the final destruction of the American free-enterprise system, he wrote in the *National Real Estate Journal.* From an attack upon the welfare state Binns made a cosmic leap to an attack upon the institute's support for comprehensive planning.[40]

This Jeffersonian distrust of big government, centralized, impersonal, and remote, was shared by others. The editor of the *National Real Estate Journal* urged local real estate groups to thwart the influence of comprehensive planners and public housing supporters, whom he viewed as leftist ideologues, by undertaking public works planning, revising building codes, working out more equitable tax formulas, and initiating local programs to eradicate blight. Thomas E. Dewey, appearing in 1943 before the *Herald Tribune Forum* in New York City, also affirmed the primacy of local initiative and rejected the comprehensive planners' argument that the country needed a central planning authority similar to Great Britain's. In the reconversion period that lay ahead, he asserted, the states would be strong. "They alone will have survived the war without overburdening debt. They express the vitality and resurgence of a free people."[41]

The feeling that the Depression and federal wartime controls

39. "Post-War Planning," *American City* 58 (July 1943), 67.
40. Arthur Binns, "Vital Issues of the Day," *National Real Estate Journal* 44 (Aug. 1943), 34–35.
41. "Your Post-War Responsibilities," *ibid.,* 44 (Sept. 1943, 7; *Buffalo Evening*

had created a disequilibrium in the structure of federalism also crept into the speech of more judicious urban and federal officials. They supported comprehensive urban planning as long as it was conducted on a local basis, and they shied away from the establishment of a central planning body. Richard Graves, secretary of the League of California Cities, told a Chicago audience that the choice was either to destroy state and local government by federal regulatory predominance, or to evolve a system in which the federal government established broad policies but gave the states latitude in implementing them. He opted for a cooperative federalism that made the states once again "a vital part of the American system." Leon Keyserling, general counsel of the National Housing Agency, likewise supported an expanded role for the states before a Johns Hopkins University urban planning conference.[42]

Politics makes strange bedfellows, and wartime politics was no exception. Public housing lobbyists, an interest group basically in agreement with the social objectives of the New Deal, were also undecided whether planning initiative should emanate from local authorities or a central board. In an angry address in 1943 to an audience of Cleveland realtors, Bryn J. Hovde, president of the National Public Housing Conference (NPHC), indirectly criticized comprehensive planners for failing to appreciate the importance of good housing. The NPHC had a deeply felt humanitarian commitment to public housing which, Hovde noted, clashed with the ideas of comprehensive planners who viewed housing as simply *one* element (on a par with transportation, recreation, and educational facilities) in the total physical, economic, and social regeneration of blighted communities. Catherine Bauer, NPHC vice president, wrote, perhaps somewhat unfairly, that "in the sacred name of 'master plans,' 'bold reconstruction,' 'saving cities,' and whatnot, it is proposed to bail out with Federal subsidy the owners of slum and

---

News, Nov. 8, 1943. See also Homer K. Hoyt, "What Is War Doing to Real Estate," *National Real Estate Journal* 44 (Mar. 1943), 41–42.

42. See "Post-War Problems Facing City Governments," in *AMA Proceedings,* 49–50, and Johns Hopkins University, *Report of the Urban Planning Conference Under the Auspices of the Johns Hopkins University, 1943* (Baltimore, 1944), 230.

blighted property—not in order to rehouse their present tenants properly, but to stimulate another war of speculative over-building for the well-to-do and thus, it is naïvely hoped, to turn the tide of decentralization and preserve down-town property values based on high densities and even higher hopes."[43]

With liberals and comprehensive planners at odds, all that remained was to tie together into a neat package the arguments against comprehensive planning, planning initiated by a central body, and the application of European land-use concepts to the American urban environment. This Robert Moses did in one furious outburst in the summer of 1944, in a nihilistic assault upon comprehensive planning as a conceptual tool, planners as professionals, and the New Deal programs of Franklin D. Roosevelt. On one level of analysis, Moses's criticism was symptomatic of a deeply ingrained hostility toward both European cultural attitudes and ideas and nearly a decade of welfare statism. On another level, his emotional outcry represented an effort to eradicate a deeply rooted sense of inadequacy by ravaging not merely planning but the integrity of the planners themselves.[44]

According to Moses, American urban planners had allowed themselves to be duped by the "Beiunskis," an unfortunate term of derision he coined to describe refugees from totalitarianism. Draping himself in the flag, he asserted that their alien notions of planning and land use and their criticism of American society exceeded the gratitude owed to a nation that had given them shelter. Worse, he accused them of being individualists who wanted to destroy the community as it had evolved in this country—of wanting to tear it out by the roots, toss the pieces in the air, and start afresh in open country. By contrast, Moses noted that the patriotic conservative would find plenty of faults at home and be just as eager to remedy them, "but," he

43. Cf. the statement of Charles Abrams in "Authorities Seek Voice in War Housing Centers," *Public Housing Progress* 8 (Dec. 1942), 1–3; "Public Housers Answer Foe's Blast," *ibid.*, 10 (Jan. 1944), 1; Bauer, "Planning Is Politics," 67.

44. *Post-War Economic Policy and Planning,* Hearings before the Special Committee on Postwar Economic Policy and Planning pursuant to H. Res. 408 and H. Res. 60, United States Congress, House of Representatives, 78th Cong., 2d sess., pt. 6 (1944), 1780ff.

added, "he must be loyal to the institutions and to the local scene in which his lot is cast." This might seem simplistic to revolutionary planning sophists, Moses averred, "but truths, like ballads, are always simple."[45]

To whom specifically did Moses refer when he bandied about terms like "Beiunski," "revolutionaries," and "radicals"? His targets included Eero Saarinen, Walter Gropius, and Eric Mendelsohn. Each was foreign-born and -educated; each had received his initial professional acclamation abroad; each was a fugitive from totalitarianism; and each was allegedly attempting to foist alien concepts upon a free, democratic society. Saarinen, whom Moses acknowledged as one of the true giants of twentieth-century architecture, was a Finn who had founded the Cranbrook Academy of Art in Michigan. But he was also a man "who forsook his profession to become a revolutionary planner." Gropius's sin was in translating the Bauhaus architectural style to the University of Chicago via the Weimar Republic and Harvard University. Mendelsohn, a German Jew, had gained prominence for a modernistic style that allegedly clashed with native American designs. Besides this triumvirate, Moses scathingly denounced British "revolutionary" planners.[46]

Quoting selectively from *The City—Its Growth—Its Future,* a broad-ranging inquiry into the character and purpose of the metropolis that Saarinen had published in 1943, Moses attacked the theory of organic decentralization on the grounds that it led to an espousal of communal land ownership. Having dismissed Saarinen out of hand, he stooped to public ridicule to discredit Gropius. Citing the non-American origin of the Bauhaus style, Moses accused Gropius of "hurting our architecture by advocating a philosophy which doesn't belong here and fundamentally offers nothing more novel than the lally column and two-by-four timber." Once again he quoted out of context from Gropius's book, *The New Architecture and the Bauhaus,* to

45. "Mr. Moses Dissects the 'Long Haired Planners,'" *New York Times Magazine* 6 (June 25, 1944), 16.
46. *Ibid.*

demonstrate that comprehensive planners were propagating a style alien to traditional American architectural norms.[47]

The next victim to suffer the sting of Moses's barbs was Eric Mendelsohn, who had recently delivered a lecture before an enthusiastic audience at the University of California. In the course of explicating his vision of postwar urban society, Mendelsohn observed that technology had provided the cities and the nation with the tools to eradicate urban blight. What interested him particularly was the connection between traffic congestion and urban decay. Mendelsohn traced urban blight to the narrow streets of the downtown business district where automobiles and people intermingled randomly among tired and worn-out buildings. In the future, he predicted, "motor traffic will bypass the city area, or run as part of an independent speed network from end-stations and flying fields, underground, to the focal points of industrial, business and residential quarters, thus clearing the city of all surface traffic." Moses, in biting repartee, commented that this was "a cute trick if you can do it." He ignored the architectural journals which even then showed that futuristic concepts of high-speed expressways, subways, dockside landing ports, and municipal airports were on the planners' drawing boards. The basic technology was there; the only items lacking were money and the will—which, hopefully, the war's end would release.[48]

Moses also detected in Scandinavian practices a potential threat to native American land-use and property concepts, particularly where the landlord-tenant relationship intersected. He cited a recent article by John Graham, Jr., analyzing the housing practices of Stockholm. According to Graham, property owned by the municipality in the inner city could be sold to private enterprise at prevailing rates or at a figure lower than the market value if assurances were forthcoming that the land would be put to a social use. Moses shared the fear of conservative realtors that if government provided the seed money for

47. *Ibid.,* 16–17.
48. *Ibid.,* 17.

207

land assembly in blighted areas, it might also intrude into landlord-tenant relationships.[49]

Not surprisingly, Moses had to take cognizance of the British planners whose ideas posed the most serious potential challenge to historic American land-use concepts, especially the Uthwatt *Report on Compensation and Betterment,* which he castigated as "one of those little gems which blush unseen in the star-spangled galaxy lighting us from the midwife to the mortician." Moses was distressed by the inclination of usually responsible people in this country to seize upon its recommendations un-critically in their quest for a panacea for urban blight. He accused the editors of *Fortune* of propagating the erroneous belief that comprehensive planners ("the revolutionaries") were the "true strategists while the practical planners and doers are merely tacticians."[50]

Moses's anxiety was rooted in a misplaced fear that the doer, the self-made man of action, might be displaced by the academically trained professional and the innovative architect. Thus he drew a sharp distinction in discussing postwar municipal planning between "revolution and commonsense, between the subsidized lamas in their remote mountain temples and those who must work in the market place." The professors of city planning and urban architecture had already been seduced by the Beiunskis and were spreading the poison to their students and to influential politicians eagerly seeking an excuse to abandon proven land-use practices.[51]

The Beiunskis had also led astray one of the luminaries of American architecture, Frank Lloyd Wright, whom Moses described as "a brilliant but erratic architect and planner." Resorting to guilt by association, he observed that the designer of "Broadacre City" was widely regarded as the United States' greatest builder—*in communist Russia!* Similarly he attacked Lewis Mumford and Rexford G. Tugwell for seeking to subvert the traditional American values of individual liberty and the

49. *Ibid.,* 16.
50. Haar, ed., *Law and Land Use,* 82–83; "The Uthwatt Report," 49–51.
51. "Mr. Moses Dissects the 'Long Haired Planners,'" 17, 38.

sanctity of property. He quoted selectively from Tugwell's 1939 essay, "The Fourth Power," to show that the latter advocated a central planning authority whose functions were wholly alien to historic American practices and which, though similar in name, was vastly superior to Britain's Ministry of Town and Country Planning.[52]

The argument over whether European models of urban planning and land use were appropriate to the United States was quickly taken up by urban liberals and planners who recognized that Moses's official ties with New York City gave his allegations an air of respectability. Even otherwise indifferent New Yorkers bestirred themselves to protest his demagogic tactics. Alfred E. Kahn, neither a planner nor an architect, observed that the "revolutionary" land-use ideas against which the commissioner was railing sounded very much like those of John Stuart Mill and Henry George, "neither of whom was born in either Germany or Russia." Kahn declared that "one need not be either a foreigner or a revolutionary to argue that Mr. Moses may do a little too much park and road building and too little slum clearance." Another citizen observed that Moses's language approximated Nazi Germany's racial discussions of *Kultur,* particularly his use of that vulgar term, the Beiunskis. The only phrase the commissioner had omitted, he noted, was, "Why don't they go back where they came from?"[53]

The respected urban planner Carol Aronovici accused Moses of misrepresenting Saarinen when he implied that the Scandinavian advocated expropriation of private property. Aronovici was uncertain why Moses objected to American planners borrowing from enlightened European land-use practices that might help eliminate urban blight. He asked, almost rhetorically, whether it was conceivable that the commissioner was

52. Michael Hughes, ed., *The Letters of Lewis Mumford and Frederic J. Osborn* (New York, 1972), 4, 143; *New York Times,* Dec. 6, 1940, July 26, 1941, Feb. 12, 1942. Tugwell's ideas on planning may be traced in Rexford G. Tugwell, "Planning in New York City," *JAIP* 6 (Apr.-June 1940), 33-34, "The Fourth Power," *Planning & Civic Comment,* pt. 2, 5 (Apr.-June 1939), 1-31, and "The Principle of Planning and the Institution of Laissez-Faire," *American Economic Review* 22 suppl. (Mar. 1932), 75-92.
53. H.I. Brock, "In Defense of City Planners," *New York Times Magazine* 6 (July 9, 1944), 20, 35.

blind to the chaotic disorganization of American cities and their sagging community spirit; and he observed that New York, like several other metropolitan centers, was contributing to the problem by building superhighways which bypassed the congested core. In the end, Aronovici had to inquire whether Moses's real motive was not to secure exclusive control over the city's postwar planning.[54]

A few readers, more sensitive to shifting political winds, sensed that Moses's accusations, however unfair, might impair the credibility of professional urban planners with Congress. This was highly serious because Congress, in 1943, had authorized the creation of special committees to investigate the cities' role in postwar economic reconstruction. Kenneth Reid, editor of *Pencil Points,* the journal of progressive architecture, declared that "the serious thing about this attack, which makes it of national rather than local importance, is that it is really directed not at the individuals named but at the whole idea of planning."[55]

With uncommonly good sense, Dean Joseph Hudnut of the Harvard School of Design, who had been instrumental in bringing Gropius and Marcel Breuer from abroad to enrich his faculty, suggested that the time had come to reconcile differences. In a scholarly, low-keyed manner, he too chastised Moses for criticizing foreigners simply because they *were* foreign, but also for his faulty conceptualization of planning. Hudnut pointed out that Moses's chief failure was in not recognizing that all practice originated in theory and planning was the combination of the two. Furthermore, United States urban planning was derived from European origins; for example, in 1629 Governor Winthrop of Massachusetts had written to his English sponsor: "Send me, pray, a Frenchman that he may lay out our city for me."[56]

54. *Ibid.,* 20–21.
55. Kenneth Reid, "More Planning Is Wanted—Not Less," *Pencil Points* 25 (Sept. 1944), 43; *New York Times,* July 9, 1944.
56. Joseph Hudnut, "A 'Long Haired' Reply to Moses," *New York Times Magazine* 6 (July 23, 1944), 16, 36–37.

To acknowledge this foreign collaboration and welcome its continuance was to keep faith with the American tradition, Hudnut insisted. He then proceeded to demonstrate that New York City's recent exhibition of postwar building projects had borrowed creatively from European-inspired models. The modernistic design of many of the scale models enhanced rather than violated American architectural concepts. One school building possessed the clarity of composition of a Mendelsohn design; another—a hospital—was sketched as precisely as a surgical instrument and might have come from the atelier of Alvar Aalto, the Finnish practitioner of organic architecture. Several structures evoked the humanity and perfection of surface of a Saarinen creation. While the exhibition at several points demonstrated a high degree of coordination reminiscent of the Bauhaus style, the end product was thoroughly American. Hudnut was ready to concede that the exhibit "did not in any way reach the fundamentals of planning," yet it reaffirmed, "albeit in the tremulous language of architects in search of jobs, the very principle which the Commissioner had so vehemently rejected."[57]

Aside from architectural considerations, Hudnut feared that Moses's constant references to "destroyed property values" and "expropriation" were symptomatic of a deeply rooted fear of change. How else could one explain the commissioner's lumping together comprehensive planning, the New Deal, and communism? How else could Moses ignore the corpus of planning literature, including the Uthwatt Report, in which the phrase "just compensation" occurred more frequently than any other? Hudnut urged Moses to find common ground with the planners by integrating specific public works projects into long-range plans. As Hudnut observed, the blight besetting the great cities of America and Europe was not so unique as to require wholly separate philosophies or techniques of analysis or synthesis. "They are like products of the industrial revolution; all are new and all are without guidance. We wandered into this iron theatre together; we confront together its strange confu-

57. *Ibid.*

211

sions; and we shall find our way out together," he declared. "Together, I think, or not at all."[58]

The rapprochement that Hudnut sought never came to pass. Despite the vast amount of new construction during the war years and in the period of reconversion, the opportunity to incorporate European, especially British, concepts of land use into plans for revitalizing the physical structure of decaying inner cities was not readily accepted. Apart from Moses's style and tactics, which were in the worst tradition of demagoguery, the causes were complex. Few planners had the time, organizational capacity, or political acumen to respond in kind to the conservatives' criticism. Even if they did, they were by and large divided in their views on postwar urban planning, and their divisions reflected the divisions of the American people as a whole.[59]

Both Marshall Miller, director of Pasadena's city planning commission, and Mayor Woodall Rogers of Dallas had followed with growing alarm the division that crept into the professionals' discussions of postwar urban planning. The problem arose over whether comprehensive planning or more limited public works planning best suited urban America's needs. The latter was intended to provide jobs to returning veterans to cushion the shock of reconversion to a civilian economy. The former was defined as including the preparation of long-range physical plans encompassing land use, transportation, and public facilities; long-term financing; the coordination of all subsidiary plans by local governmental agencies; intergovernmental coordination; and the preparation of supportive regulatory and administrative measures. To succeed in carrying out these functions, of course, comprehensive planners needed to understand the overall public interest (at least insofar as it related to the plan) and to be aware of the effect of their actions upon that interest.[60]

---

58. *Ibid.*

59. NRPB, *National Resources Development, Report for 1943,* House Doc. 128, pt. 1, 78th Cong., 1st sess. (1943), 31–36; United States Chamber of Commerce, *Why Plan for the Post-War Period?* (Washington, D.C., 1943), 6–7.

60. Charles W. Eliot, director of the NRPB, writing to Alfred Bettman on March 30, 1943, concerning a bill for postwar urban planning then before Congress, observed:

Neither public works proponents nor comprehensive planners were willing to compromise their reading of urban America's needs, thereby creating professional, political, and personal conflicts that played right into the hands of the conservative critics of the New Deal. This had detrimental implications for the movement for postwar community and urban redevelopment. For other reasons, too, most of which were strongly embedded in the divergent historical tradition of the two nations, the British approach to land-use controls and planning had only limited applicability to American cities. In their enthusiasm many American planners, including comprehensive planners within the NRPB, underestimated the importance of these different perceptions of land, the differences in political and legal institutions, and the divergent attitudes toward social reform that prevailed in wartime Britain.

Unlike Britain, the United States did not suffer the destruction of a large percentage of its industrial plant and residential properties in wartime bombings, and hence did not have the same impetus for physical rebirth to redeem the devastation of battle. Here, this seems to have remained the private view of some professional planners and some, but not all, government officials; the ordinary citizen was more concerned about holding on to his wartime gains. Moreover, America—unlike Britain—never viewed land as a scarce commodity. The total area of the continental United States was more than fifty times that of England and Wales. If the abolition of the National Resources Planning Board in 1943 was indicative, no one during or immediately following the war felt a pressing need to have the most minute detail of land planning supervised by a central agency.[61]

Neither were Americans as concerned about protecting

"We have found such violent opposition to the phrase 'Master Plan' that I would strongly recommend not using that particular term." In NARG 187, NRPB Records. See also Woodall Rogers, "Cities Now and at War's End," in *AMA Proceedings,* 5–11; J. Marshall Miller, "Postwar Planning Administration," *Public Management* 26 (Nov. 1944), 337–41; and "Post-War City and Regional Planning," *American City* 58 (Feb. 1943), 5.

61. See the perceptive comments in Haar, ed., *Law and Land Use,* xi, xiii.

agricultural land from encroaching urbanization. Indeed, one of the federal government's problems after 1945 was to hold down production of agricultural surpluses. And far from considering it "endangered" (as in Britain), realtors, land speculators, and politicians viewed agricultural land adjacent to large metropolitan areas as being ripe for suburban development. Congressional support in the form of the GI Bill home loan program, which provided for long-term, low-interest monthly payments, manifested the government's conviction that the veteran should own his own home. The result was that a suburban housing boom was under way almost as soon as the nation disarmed and the economy had retooled for civilian production.[62]

Institutionally, too, there was a fundamental difference between Britain's unitary form of government with parliamentary supremacy and the American federal system, composed as it was of forty-eight semisovereign jurisdictions subject to the ultimate check of an independent judiciary. Regionalism, overlapping jurisdictions, interest-group pressures, the reemergence of the states as intermediaries between Washington and the cities, and congressional conservatism made it extremely difficult for the Roosevelt administration (assuming it was so inclined), acting through the NRPB or an equivalent agency, to effect legislation comparable to the *Town and Country Planning Acts.*[63]

The whole approach to land-use controls was different in the two countries. The historic procedure of the United States was for Congress or the states first to legislate the specifics of land use (not simply set forth a general outline), and then to act accordingly. The practice was generally more pragmatic in Britain, where detailed legislation was formulated for individual problems as they emerged in the exercise of broad powers conferred in advance. This difference was compounded by a conflict of attitudes toward excessive condemnation. In the United States condemnation as an expedient was traditionally circumscribed by ethical and political considerations, whereas in the

62. *Ibid.* See also Norval D. Glenn, "Suburbanization in the United States Since World War II," in Louis H. Masotti and Jeffrey K. Hadden, eds., *The Urbanization of the Suburbs* (Beverly Hills, Calif., 1973), 55.
63. Haar, ed., *Law and Land Use,* xii.

Britain of the forties the problem was simply one of money. Again, divergent attitudes toward the proper function of government played a part. In the United States, compensation was not payable to owners whose property lost value as a result of a planning decision. Under the police power in contrast to eminent domain, compensation for condemnation need not be paid, the controls being analogous to fire or structural regulations. In Britain in the early forties, Parliament established a massive compensation fund of £300 million.[64]

Stronger even than these reasons was the belief in the "American way of life" or, more accurately, the American economic system. True, Americans had altered many of their long-standing ideas about government intervention in response to the Depression of the thirties and the exigencies of global warfare, and yet strong prejudice against federal regulation of some segments of the economy still persisted. Land-use controls were one such realm in which unfettered freedom of enterprise was still cherished.[65]

Tied into this, of course, was a political environment in the United States distinctly hostile to planning, the social-reform ideology of the New Deal, and Britain's comprehensive social security program as articulated in the Beveridge report. Wartime America was not an encouraging place for experimentation, if the editors of *Fortune* may be believed. When the magazine asked its readers whether socialism would be good or bad for the United States, 40 percent said bad and only 25 percent said good.

Americans were more conservative than their British counterparts, most of whom were ardent for more social reform in the postwar era; but this may have been because Americans had something to conserve. Their view of the postwar world was one of apprehension, fearing a return to a thirties-type Depression that would rob them of their wartime gains. The counterattack against New Deal economic and social programs executed by the

---

64. *Ibid.*, xiii.
65. John Delafons, *Land-Use Controls in the United States* (Cambridge, Mass., 1962), 7, 12–14.

Seventy-seventh and Seventy-eighth Congresses (1942–45) occurred in an atmosphere antagonistic to planning of any sort. The concern was not with postwar organization, planning, or the plight of the cities; it was to protect the economic gains of the specific constituencies they represented. Unhappily, the Roosevelt administration also appeared to have only one policy: placating Congress in order to obtain its support for winning the war and the peace after it.[66] In this hostile environment, the interest of American liberals in British land-use concepts and models never progressed beyond the level of what British planners were thinking or saying.

66. See T.R.B., "Pressure Politics," *New Republic* 109 (Dec. 20, 1943), 884; Roland Young, *Congressional Politics in the Second World War* (New York, 1956), 9; Geoffrey Perrett, *Days of Sadness, Years of Triumph: The American People, 1939–1945* (New York, 1973), 353.

VII. The Frustration of Federal Redevelopment Legislation

One of the most significant lessons for employment stabilization to emerge from the Great Depression was the importance of advance surveys and investigations. The national defense emergency also required that the nation give thoughtful consideration to the preparation beforehand of plans for a public works program during the period of transition to a peacetime economy. Urban redevelopment served the interests of both community revitalization and peacetime prosperity, but from the outset federal redevelopment legislation was caught up in the controversy between long-range master planning and short-term public works construction and between congressional proponents of the New Deal and conservative critics.

In March 1941, upon transmitting the annual report of the National Resources Planning Board (NRPB) to Congress, President Roosevelt noted that cities were deferring vitally needed public works construction because of the defense emergency. Sidestepping the budding controversy between the exponents of master planning and public works, he simply observed that in the postwar period the cities would have to go forward with their programs.[1] Shortly thereafter Congressman Alfred Beiter, Democrat of Buffalo, New York, formerly an assistant to Secretary of the Interior Harold L. Ickes, spoke out along similar lines. Beiter was known as an advocate of urban redevelopment to avert a postwar depression. In Detroit in June 1942 he identified urban redevelopment with the goals of the Atlantic Charter and urged the members of the American Institute of Architects to involve themselves "seriously with the matter of planning preparations."[2]

1. *New York Times,* Mar. 4, 1941.
2. *Congressional Record,* 77th Cong., 2d sess., 88 (June 25, 1942), Appendix, 2455–57.

In response to Beiter's and similar admonitions, identical bills on the subject of postwar urban redevelopment were introduced in the first session of the Seventy-seventh Congress. These bills were framed not only to supplement existing federal authorizations for survey and planning work but also to provide funding for state and local planning. The merits of this procedure were obvious: the preliminary groundwork would be undertaken by agencies that regularly drafted such plans, but on a more systematic basis, and a measure of coordination would adhere to the program.[3]

Typical of the early postwar urban redevelopment bills was H.R. 5638, which Beiter introduced as an amendment to the Employment Stabilization Act of 1931. Its basic feature was to authorize the appropriation of a revolving fund in the Executive Office to enable federal, state, and local agencies to prepare detailed plans and specifications for a shelf list of public works projects. The general principle underlying this legislation received wide support initially from many governmental, planning, business, and labor organizations. As the bill passed through the legislative mills, however, it became immediately apparent that planning for postwar urban redevelopment was nearly as controversial as public housing. Urban redevelopment raised important constitutional questions, required public subsidies, confronted elected officials with troublesome issues of public policy, and challenged city planners to reexamine the merits of long-range versus more limited public works programs.[4]

The strongest endorsement of the Beiter bill came from Alfred S. Bettman, chairman of the legislative affairs committee of the American Institute of Planners (AIP). Bettman's support, however, was qualified because fundamentally he disliked the "shelf list" approach to redevelopment and thought the wording of the bill was vague at certain key points. He wrote that there was "no evidence of consciousness of the comprehensive

3. National Resources Planning Board, *National Resources Development, Report for 1943,* House Doc. 128, pt. 2, 78th Cong., 1st sess. (1943), 37.

4. Senator Robert F. Wagner's bill (S. 1617) approximated Beiter's approach to postwar urban planning. See *ibid.,* 36–37. Also, John Miller, "Planning for Victory, 1942," *Planning & Civic Comment* 9 (Jan. 1943), 1–9.

or master planning of the municipality or urban areas as one of the purposes of the bill,'' a defect which provoked ''the justifiable fear that the most urgent and fundamental of the classes of planning may be ignored or minimized in the administration of the statute.'' [5]

Despite its imperfections, Bettman gave his support to H.R. 5638 because he viewed it as a stepping stone to a comprehensive model statute governing postwar urban land use and control. Nonetheless, his reservations raised fundamental issues that had plagued others: whether urban problems were essentially local in nature and whether they should be resolved by private enterprise alone or by the private sector in combination with local municipalities and state governments; whether the federal government had legal or moral commitments to the cities in areas such as planning, redevelopment, and housing; whether the federal government, if it intervened at all, should operate upon the cities directly or through the intermediary of the states; whether postwar planning was primarily an executive or legislative function; whether the financial condition of government at war's end would permit urban renewal and, if so, which level of government was in the best situation to bear the cost; and where, in the broad spectrum of postwar programs, did the administration's urban policy stand.

H.R. 5638 received a sympathetic hearing before the Labor Committee, which in February 1942 placed it on the House's calendar for early consideration. When the bill came to the floor of the House in mid-February, the hostility of ''Win-the-War-First'' congressmen, fiscal conservatives, anti-New Deal Democrats, and Republicans was loosed upon it. With memories of Pearl Harbor still fresh, the war understandably dominated their thinking. It was also—and ominously—clear that the forces which bound together this coalition were a deep-seated distrust of planners and planning, expansion of New Deal social programs, and further accretion of power to the executive branch. The arguments of two congressmen, Representatives

5. ''Planning Legislation: Review and Recommendations,'' *American Institute of Planners' Journal (AIPJ)* 9 (Jan.-Mar. 1943), 5.

Everett Dirksen, Republican of Illinois, and William M. Whittington, Democrat of Mississippi, were typical and presaged the growing rift between Congress and the President on the question of postwar planning.[6]

Adorned with his usual hyperbole, Dirksen's protest was rooted in solid ground because the Beiter bill had been drafted somewhat hastily, and its wording was loose. H.R. 5638 contained no definite sum of money for implementing its purposes, nor did it have exact guidelines for the federal planning agency to follow; neither did it specify in detail the nature of the work to be undertaken nor set a terminal date for its completion. In a word, the bill bore all the earmarks and deficiencies of a crisis atmosphere. Dirksen's recommendation, that the Beiter bill be sent back to committee for rewriting, had a certain validity.

By contrast, Whittington's objections were rooted in an ideological and emotional distaste for the New Deal and any form of planning. He especially feared that the Beiter bill would institutionalize the National Resources Planning Board, giving it carte blanche funds that would make it independent of the House Appropriations Committee. This reason was not as well known as his officially expressed fear that the bill would duplicate the work of other federal agencies and detract from the war effort.[7]

Unfortunately, neither Beiter nor the architects of similar legislation were able to parry their opponents' thrusts with any degree of confidence. Talk about the postwar future of the cities seemed premature while the Japanese occupied Wake Island, Manila was being bombed, and Bataan was under siege. The most Beiter could promise to appease critics was that the central planning agency would cooperate with local authorities and not divert engineers from the war effort. This did not satisfy opponents, who voted down the bill in the House by a very wide margin (252 to 104). In the Senate, the bill never even came to a

6. *Congressional Record,* 77th Cong., 2d sess., 88 (Feb. 19, 1942), 1488–91.
7. *Ibid.* See also "Washington News Letter," *American Society of Planning Officials (ASPO) News Letter* 8 (Mar. 1942), 26.

vote. Beiter's response, understandably, was one of disappointment and bitterness.[8]

The defeat of H.R. 5638 and similar legislation in 1942 was just one manifestation of a growing rift between the legislature and the executive in the Seventy-seventh Congress, and it temporarily set back the federal government's involvement in redevelopment planning. Beyond this, the Seventy-seventh Congress marked the end of a decade in which the Democrats possessed an unchallengeable majority in both House and Senate—large enough to obscure sharp divergences within the party. When the Congress assembled in January 1942, Democratic representation in the House had shrunk to 222, while Republican strength had risen to 208. Seven of the eight new members of the Senate were Republicans, putting the tally at 38 to 57. In both houses, party lines were so tightly drawn as to make any defection a serious matter. Thus the narrowness of the Democratic majority afforded an opportunity for exercising leverage upon the administration by any small group of dissident Democrats wishing to capitalize on it, a fact which guaranteed that any urban redevelopment legislation in this and future Congresses would have rough sledding.[9]

The year 1943 was transitional both in the fighting and the discussions about postwar hopes and policies. In the war, as historian James McGregor Burns has pointed out, it was not one of desperate defense like most of 1942, but not yet the year for all-out attack, and certainly not the year for victory. On the planning and legislative fronts the progression was equally tentative: urban planners approached the new year and a new Congress in a hopeful context, laboring for the reconstruction of the cities even as the war insatiably consumed the nation's energies.

8. Senator Wagner had pointed out that Congress was given the opportunity to take the initiative in postwar urban planning but had done nothing. See *Congressional Record,* 77th Cong., 2d sess., 88 (May 28, 1942), Appendix 1969–70, and *ibid.* (June 25, 1942), Appendix, 2456.

9. See J. Donald Kingsley, "Congress and the New Deal," *Current History* 4 (Mar. 1943), 27–28; John Robert Moore, "The Conservative Coalition in the United States Senate, 1942–1945," *Journal of Southern History* 33 (Aug. 1967), 368–76; V.O. Key, Jr., *Southern Politics in State and Nation* (New York, 1949), esp. chs. 16, 17.

In this endeavor they received encouragement from the administration and, initially at least, from realtors, businessmen, and public housing lobbyists.[10]

President Roosevelt, for example, used the occasion of the twentieth annual conference of the American Municipal Association (AMA) in 1942 to speak about the quality of life in postwar urban society. Praising the association for its contribution to defense mobilization, Roosevelt then turned his attention to the need to plan for the postwar period in order to realize the benefits for which so many Americans were making sacrifices. "It is not enough to assemble a list of public works projects or to put them in blueprint form. Plans must be based on an analysis of the physical conditions that necessitate improvement, on the social and economic needs of the community that will make such projects of permanent value, and must be implemented by a practical program in terms of finances, manpower, and material through which blueprints can be translated into construction at the first available opportunity," the President declared. The federal government had an obligation to assist the cities, he noted, and was seeking a consensus from the municipalities on which courses of action to pursue.[11]

Roosevelt's approach to postwar urban reconstruction flowed from several basic assumptions. The city was more than an artifact or physical container; it was an organic entity in which government bore a responsibility for the social and economic well-being of its urban population. The initiative for comprehensive planning and reconstruction should be primarily local, with the federal government granting subsidies to initiate planning. In endorsing cooperative federalism, the President was also making no distinction between comprehensive planning for human welfare and the physical improvement of local communities. Postwar planning was to encompass more than new highways, improved bridges, and impressive public buildings—these were the practical results, to be sure, but in Roosevelt's estima-

10. James M. Burns, *Roosevelt: The Soldier of Freedom* (New York, 1970), 282, 300, 331–55.

11. American Municipal Association, *Proceedings of the Twentieth Annual Conference* (Chicago, 1943), iii. Cited hereafter as *AMA Proceedings.*

tion the reasons for undertaking them were a far cry from the "city beautiful" movement or the "bigger and better" era of the 1920s. His emphasis upon local initiative was intended to persuade the cities and states to cease their traditional bickering and to undertake realistic, practical planning.[12]

The President's words had their intended impact upon the AMA delegates. One after another, ranking municipal officials rose to endorse his sentiments, sometimes employing embarrassingly purple rhetoric. Mayor Woodall Rogers of Dallas, for example, exhorted his colleagues in language reminiscent of the great landscape architect Daniel Burnham to think boldly, comprehensively, and realistically while preparing urban redevelopment plans.[13]

As Rogers was urging his listeners to adopt order, beauty, and planning as their beacons, Herbert A. Olson, the AMA vice president, expressed the hope that ancient divisions might be submerged in a show of national wartime unity. He noted that several organizations not usually found in agreement with the AMA—specifically the Urban Land Institute, the National Association of Real Estate Boards, and the United States Chamber of Commerce—had made overtures to cooperate on the problems of postwar planning. This was a sign of progress, but Olson cautioned his audience and the organizations concerned that they would not be able to resolve the problems of postwar urban society on an ad hoc basis. "We are all in the same boat, and so I am glad today that the lion and the lamb are starting to get into the same place," he declared.[14]

By mid-year, however, a note of uneasiness crept into the deliberations of those busily drafting blueprints for postwar urban reconstruction. *Fortune* magazine reported in November 1943 that the fragile truce had definitely been shattered and that planners, realtors, urban politicians, and public housing lobby-

12. See Robert A. Walker, *The Planning Function in Urban Government* (Chicago, 1950, 2d ed.), 346–47; Walter H. Blucher, "Has the Technique of Planning Changed?" *ASPO News Letter* 15 (Apr. 1949), 33.
13. See Rogers's comments, "Cities Now and at War's End," in *AMA Proceedings*, 5–11.
14. *Ibid.*, 67.

ists were fighting one another in an effort to shape urban policy to their own particular ends. Before *Fortune*'s report there was other evidence to suggest that Olson's optimism was premature. The controversy over comprehensive versus public works planning was flaring anew, and in June 1943 the retiring president of the American Water Works Association felt compelled to dissociate planning (which he assured his colleagues was both "democratic" and "thinking ahead") from New Deal collectivism. In August 1943, the editor of the *National Real Estate Journal* warned fellow realtors that the fight "against the ideologies of the public housers is not yet over, and may not be over for a long time to come."[15]

The Seventy-eighth Congress, which convened in 1943, mirrored these divided opinions, but the most highly publicized legislative battles were fought over the vital wartime issues of inflation, labor and manpower shortages, food and agricultural subsidies, and taxation. The press largely ignored the legislation pertaining to postwar urban planning that jammed Congress's calendar.[16] Broadly speaking, the bills fell into three categories: some, like the Lynch bill (H.R. 1898), which was a recasting of the original Beiter bill, approached redevelopment from the single perspective of public works and were, more properly speaking, intended to avert a postwar economic slump; others, like the Thomas bill (S. 953), embodied a comprehensive city planning technique, utilizing the "master plan" to treat the city both as physical artifact and social organism; the largest number, following the example of Congressman Dirksen's bill, would have wrested control of postwar urban planning from the executive by establishing a joint congressional committee responsible to the legislature. Most of these bills were unceremoniously interred in the Rules Committees of the House and Senate and never saw daylight, but in the debates attending those which did come to the floor another cohesive link was

15. "City Planning: Battle of the Approach," *Fortune* 28 (Nov. 1943), 164–68; "Unity in the Home Building Industry After the War," *National Real Estate Journal* 44 (Aug. 1943), 7.

16. Rhoda D. Edwards, "The Seventy-eighth Congress on the Home Front" (Ph.D. diss., Rutgers Univ., 1967), chs. 3–6.

forged in the chain binding conservative Republicans and anti-New Deal Democrats.[17]

Of the various redevelopment bills, only those in the second category, which were drafted by planners, economists, and realty bodies, made any effort to cope with one of the major obstacles to urban renewal: the legal and fiscal problems of land assemblage. The Thomas bill (S. 953) of April 1943, embodying the comprehensive formula of Hansen and Greer cited earlier, was a good example of this. Reprinted with several changes by the committee on education and labor, the bill proposed to establish a federal Urban Redevelopment Agency (URA) with authority to make loans at 1 percent interest to municipalities for the acquisition and redevelopment of real property. To qualify for a long-term low-interest loan, the bill stipulated that a municipality must *first* have a planning agency, a master plan, and detailed project area plans. To placate public housing critics the bill also stipulated that the master plan give "consideration" to the problem of rehousing families displaced by redevelopment, one of the first instances of an awareness of the special problems of families uprooted by urban renewal. One aspect of S. 953 was quite unique and seemed to be patterned after British land-use practice: the land acquired for redevelopment with federal monies had to remain permanently in public ownership—it might be *leased* to a prospective redevelopment corporation, but for no more than thirty years.[18]

The Thomas bill was the closest approximation to the comprehensive planner's ideal, consistent with historic American land-use practices. It carried through the administration's assumption that redevelopment was to be primarily a local matter. The establishment of a federal agency to administer funds for the initial planning and land assemblage was not viewed as a violation of the principle of localism because the URA's functions fell considerably short of those of Britain's Ministry of Town and Country Planning. Indeed, by 1943, given the states'

17. Catherine Bauer, "Urban Redevelopment: A Critical Review of Five Post War Plans," *Public Housing* 9 (Jan. 1943), 2, 5.

18. "Pending Bills on All Housing Are Summarized," *ibid.*, 10 (Aug.-Sept. 1944), 2, 12.

and cities' inadequacies, all but the most diehard business and real estate bodies had reluctantly come to accept the necessity of limited federal participation to give the redevelopment process a starting push.[19]

Meanwhile, on June 4, 1943, Senator Robert F. Wagner introduced the "Neighborhood Development Bill" (S. 1163), written under the auspices of the Urban Land Institute, the city planning arm of the NAREB headquartered in Washington. Wagner indicated that he was introducing the bill by request—to advance the discussion of postwar urban reconstruction—and was not wedded to it in its pristine form.[20]

The "Neighborhood Development Bill" was similar to the Thomas bill in most respects, except for the more pronounced role it assigned to private enterprise, land developers, and builders in the redevelopment process. It encouraged their entry by permitting the outright sale or lease of all or any part of the assisted land. The bill also utilized already existing federal machinery in place of a central planning body such as the URA. Thus, the administrator of the National Housing Agency (NHA) was to have an initial appropriation of one billion dollars to enable states and municipalities to purchase and assemble large sites in blighted areas. A community qualified for a loan by presenting to the NHA a developmental plan listing local objectives in traffic, public transportation, utilities, recreational facilities, and neighborhood structures; a detailed plan for urban renewal and land use; and a proposal for the relocation of persons in areas designated for clearance and redevelopment. Private enterprise—realtors and businessmen—clearly favored S. 1163 over the Thomas bill because it limited the federal government's role to paying the otherwise prohibitive costs of land assemblage while they enjoyed the fruits of the redevelopment.[21]

Hugh Potter, president of the Urban Land Institute, made it very clear that the future of private enterprise itself was at issue in postwar urban redevelopment. On two separate occasions in

19. *Congressional Record,* 78th Cong., 1st sess., 89 (Apr. 2, 1943), 2836.
20. "To Aid Cities in Acquiring Land for Private or Public Redevelopment," *American City* 58 (July 1943), 38–39.
21. *Congressional Record,* 78th Cong., 1st sess., 89 (June 4, 1943), 5357.

226

1943, before a Citizens Conference on Planning in Omaha and before the United States Chamber of Commerce's Conference on Urban Problems in Washington, D.C., Potter asserted that given a favorable political climate private enterprise could perform the major part of rebuilding American cities and, in any event, should have the *first* opportunity to do so. The federal government's role should be narrowly confined to putting up the money for site acquisitions because of inflated land values. The institute's Washington-based lobbyist repeated this theme in the pages of the *National Real Estate Journal.*[22]

To Potter's chagrin, some of his conservative colleagues missed the more subtle implications of the Wagner bill for federal participation and accused the institute, in the words of Vice President Arthur Binns, the chairman of its housing committee, of "steadily moving away from private enterprise." This accusation precipitated a vigorous quarrel among the private realtors who composed the institute, and soon all the anti-New Deal, anti-public housing venom spewed forth across the pages of the *National Real Estate Journal.* Ironically, Binns had been an early proponent of S. 1163, on the assumption that public enterprise could be shaped to support private enterprise. He soon became disenchanted, however, and feared that the legislation would create "the greatest centralized control of the life of the cities ever proposed in our history" and advance the cause of "national socialism."[23]

Binns ultimately reached the point where he could no longer support the bill and resigned in order to lobby against it and to purge the institute of the public housing virus. He aligned himself with other foes of comprehensive planning and launched a slashing attack upon Potter, the Roosevelt administration, and the whole notion of positive government action. His criticisms were not to be dismissed lightly, for a Gallup poll in 1943 had

---

22. Hugh Potter, "The Need for Federal Action in Rebuilding Cities," *American Planning & Civic Annual* (1943), 175–79; Charles T. Stewart, "Wagner Bill Would Help Rebuild American Cities," *National Real Estate Journal* 44 (July 1943), 35.

23. "Is the Wagner Bill for Rebuilding Our Cities Desirable?" *National Real Estate Journal* 44 (Oct. 1943), 16–17. See also "Johnston Opposes Federal Aid," *ASPO News Letter* 9 (Dec. 1943), 101.

asked people in the United Kingdom and the United States whether they wanted reforms after the war. In Great Britain, 57 percent answered "yes." In the United States, 58 percent answered "no." Americans were weary of reform, George Gallup concluded.[24]

Potter recognized that the Urban Land Institute could not run back the calendar to the laissez-faire private-enterprise economy of the 1920s. Federal assistance in acquiring blighted properties in the inner city had become a sine qua non for redevelopment. The institute was simply accommodating itself to the new reality. The "Neighborhood Development Bill" was needed to cure advanced urban blight by limiting postwar construction on newer, undeveloped acreage to the detriment of the older central areas. As a conciliatory gesture, moreover, Potter observed that the institute had cooperated with the Association of Housing Builders in successfully lobbying Congress to refuse appropriations for public housing beyond what was needed to shelter defense workers. Properly administered (an oblique reference to Housing Administrator John Blandford, who repeatedly spoke in favor of private enterprise building postwar housing), the Wagner bill could protect local planning authorities from further centralization of control in Washington.[25]

Another serious threat to the legislation came from the center-left—from professional planners and public housing lobbyists who were fundamentally sympathetic to the administration's social policies. Supporters of public housing tended to equate rehabilitation almost exclusively with additional federally sponsored, low-cost housing, whereas the planners, adopting a more comprehensive perspective, viewed housing as only *one* element in the total physical, economic, and social regeneration of the city. This schism put urban reformers like Catherine Bauer, who was both an executive of the American Society of Planning Officials (ASPO) and vice president of the National Public Housing Conference (NPHC), in a particularly sensitive

24. Geoffrey Perrett, *Days of Sadness, Years of Triumph: The American People, 1939-1945* (New York, 1973), 352-54.
25. "Is the Wagner Bill . . . Desirable?" 17-20.

position. She ultimately chose public housing over comprehensive planning and spearheaded the liberal assault against both pieces of legislation. In her judgment the Thomas and Wagner bills contained three essential weaknesses: (1) they placed undue emphasis upon central city *re*-development, which would have benefited realtors and businessmen primarily; (2) they failed to recognize the need to coordinate a comprehensive public housing program with blueprints for site acquisition and land use; and (3) they gave *insufficient* consideration to the social responsibility of rehousing families displaced by redevelopment.[26]

Although not decisive in itself, the lobbying of public housing enthusiasts against the bills was counterproductive. The NPHC was exacerbating divisions within liberal ranks at a time when greater unity was essential to counter the increasingly regular operation of a conservative coalition in Congress. Walter H. Blucher, executive director of the ASPO, brought the disagreement between planners and housing enthusiasts into sharp focus in a 1944 address to the American Municipal Association. "At the present time," he observed, "we have two bills in Congress for federal aid to localities for urban renewal . . . and insofar as I can tell . . . there are several camps and each camp is more interested in cutting the throat of the other camp than in getting some unified agreement on the part of Congress or on the part of the states."[27]

Blucher's assertion that "a terrific amount of confusion" existed on the subject of urban renewal and housing was an unmistakable reference to the well-intentioned but misguided opposition of the NPHC. In his judgment their arguments merely compounded the confusion; he was just as anxious to relocate people in decent housing, but he did not want this problem to delay further redevelopment of the central district. He saw—as the public housing lobby did not—that the long-term pattern of metropolitan decentralization was creating blight in the inner cities. The dislocated remained behind while industry moved to

26. "NPHC Attacks 3 Errors in Post War Bills," *Public Housing* 9 (June 1943), 2, 7. See also Michael Hughes, ed., *Letters of Lewis Mumford and Frederic J. Osborn* (New York, 1972), 19, 27, 36.
27. Cf. *AMA Proceedings,* 23-25.

the suburban fringes; the wartime migration of population was masking the long-term secular trend. Blucher's solution was to build decent housing in the suburbs at prices workers could afford so that they could be nearer their places of employment, and, *at the same time,* to redevelop the central districts in order to lure white-collar workers *back* to the city.[28]

Even before the first session of the Seventy-eighth Congress recessed, agreement upon a single course of action had eluded policy makers and legislators alike. The facile optimism and expressions of national unity of 1942 had given way to intramural skirmishing, ideological outbursts, and uncertainty. The exponents of postwar urban planning were fragmented, and each fragment in turn was splintered many ways. Hostile legislators, incited by grievances over patronage, executive usurpation, a feeling that winning the war took precedence over all else, and fears of radicalism were asserting their independence. Republicans and conservative Southern Democrats responded to administration initiatives by jettisoning New Deal agencies, blocking presidential nominations, waging guerilla warfare against the Office of Price Administration, and only reluctantly adopting national gasoline rationing. They killed both urban redevelopment bills outright and in June 1943 forced the liquidation of the NRPB, without indicating any successor to coordinate national, state, and local urban planning. The absence of positive initiatives toward planning seriously disturbed Blucher, who asked: "What is the Congress of the United States doing, or what does it propose to do? What national planning is underway at the present time?"[29]

Indeed, there was very little. Foreign affairs were at the center of events. Domestic legislation was keyed to providing the minimum change and maximum sacrifice which fighting a global war allowed. Congress's hostility forced President Roosevelt to entrust coordination of public works planning and budgeting to Harold D. Smith, director of the Bureau of the Budget, and to

28. *Ibid.*
29. Roland Young, *Congressional Politics in the Second World War* (New York, 1956), 91–103, 107–8; Walter H. Blucher, "Congressional Planning for the Post-War Period," *ASPO News Letter* 9 (Nov. 1943), 89.

the Office of War Mobilization and Reconversion (OWMR), whose director, James F. Byrnes of South Carolina, was highly popular in Congress. These ad hoc actions satisfied no one, urban planners least of all. Smith's primary commitment was to reining in wartime inflation, while Byrnes interpreted his assignment very narrowly. Urban redevelopment was not given concrete consideration as an end in itself but only in relation to the broader problems of inflation, demobilization, and reconversion.[30]

Thus Congress and the administration both eschewed the comprehensive urban redevelopment strategies of 1943. Alarmed by inflation and executive aggrandizement, haunted by the specter of a postwar depression, Congress especially reacted by forsaking the more dramatic and possibly more effective tool for eradicating urban blight. George H. Field, an administrative assistant in the Federal Housing Agency (FHA), perceived the significance of the legislature's action in a speech delivered in 1944. "As we all know," he observed, "the Federal Government has carried a tremendous burden during the war, and steps are now being taken to reduce the federal expenditures to peacetime levels as soon as the military action will permit."[31]

Field, like many other observers, anticipated that Congress would at least appropriate seed money under Title V of the "War Mobilization and Reconversion Act" to stimulate local planning.[32] On January 17, 1945, President Roosevelt transmitted a request for $78,115,000, on behalf of FWA Administrator Philip Fleming, to the Democratic Speaker of the House, Sam Rayburn of Texas. Neither Field nor administration officials were prepared for the virulence of the opposition to what they

30. See Margaret Hinchey, "The Frustration of the New Deal Revival" (Ph.D. diss., Univ. of Missouri, 1965), 11.
31. "Post-War Public Works Planning, Title V, War Mobilization and Reconversion Act of 1944," in American Municipal Association, *Proceedings of the Twenty-first Annual Conference* (Chicago, 1944), 45–48. Cited hereafter as *AMA Proceedings 1944.*
32. Congress had responded to the Baruch Report by passing the "War Mobilization and Reconversion Act," on Sept. 20, 1944. Under Title V, limited federal funds were to be made available to the states for planning public works projects as an anti-depression measure. See "Baruch Report Urges Prompt Planning of Public Works," *American City* 59 (Mar. 1944), 5, 61; Paul V. Betters, "New Federal Actions Affecting Cities," *ibid.,* 59 (Oct. 1944), 5.

231

considered was a modest proposal. Critics of the New Deal, such as the editor of the *Engineering News Record,* a McGraw-Hill trade publication, contended that the granting of planning funds would lead inexorably to pressures for federal construction money, which was detrimental to a free-enterprise economy.[33]

The opposition was so effective that first the House and later the Senate gutted the Independent Offices Appropriation bill. In lieu of the $78 million requested, Congress allotted a paltry $17.5 million to encourage municipal and state planning. However, it steadfastly refused to commit itself to appropriations for actual construction. A spokesman for the United States Conference of Mayors was so visibly distraught that he declared the sum might better be eliminated completely. Harold S. Buttenheim, editor of the *American City,* likened Congress's action to arming a battleship with three-inch guns.[34]

What had happened? How does one account for Congress's niggardly attitude in the face of substantial evidence that most cities and states were *not* making adequate preparations for the transition to peace? Who, if anyone, was at fault? The complex answers can partly be found in the actions of the special and standing congressional committees which in 1944 began to investigate postwar economic and urban problems. A reexamination of their activities and the political atmosphere in which they functioned discloses that Congress's action was neither precipitate nor dramatic but a culmination of long-held attitudes prejudicial to the postwar interest of urban America. Also, the persistent division of urban liberals into warring camps encouraged the critics of a progressive federal urban policy. As a result, the scope of planning at war's end remained no wider than the local community's interest.

The issues of postwar urban policy were fought and decided

---

33. *Post-War Economic Policy and Planning,* Hearings before the Special Committee on Postwar Economic Policy and Planning pursuant to H. Res. 408 and H. Res. 60, United States Congress, House of Representatives, 78th Cong., 2d sess., pt. 6 (1944), 1905.

34. *New York Times,* Jan. 18, 1945; "Post-War Jobs Through Public Works," *American City* 60 (Mar. 1945), 5; "Plan, Spend, and Build Boldly," *ibid.,* 60 (July 1945), 7.

in committee even before they reached the floor of Congress. Shortly after the Seventy-eighth Congress reconvened in January 1944, the House leadership established a special committee to receive all bills pertaining to economic policy and planning during the period of reconversion. The Senate followed suit later. The ostensible purpose of this decision was to forestall a deluge of postwar legislation that almost certainly would have delayed or impeded Congress's other business; but in fact, because of the complicated committee structure of the House and Senate and the jurisdiction which the regular standing committees had over various aspects of reconversion planning, *the special committees were not empowered to report legislation.* Thus, although the committees unearthed much valuable information, they functioned more as sounding boards for the members and witnesses who believed that the operation of a free economy should be reestablished quickly and with the least possible disturbance. The leadership's actions, then, had ominous implications not only for the advocates of comprehensive urban planning but also for public works construction and public housing—in short, for the proponents of virtually every program whose chief beneficiary was urban America.[35]

The composition of the committees guaranteed that urban liberals and New Dealers would have rough going. The chairman of the Senate's committee was Walter F. George of Georgia, the primary target of Roosevelt's unsuccessful purge of conservative Southern Democrats in 1938. George delegated the specific aspects of postwar urban policy to a subcommittee chaired by Robert A. Taft of Ohio. A Republican foe of the New Deal, Taft's conservatism masked a basically humanitarian instinct which had caused him to support low-cost public housing, unlike many other conservatives. In 1944–45 his compassion was not latitudinarian enough to encompass comprehensive urban planning, however. The House committee was scarcely more sympathetic to the problems of an industrial-urban society, being under the powerful domination of another administration foe, Democratic Representative William M. Colmer of

35. Young, *Congressional Politics,* 223.

Mississippi. The Colmer Committee was easily the more vigorous in hacking away at postwar urban planning and housing bills. It was pursuing the advice of Republican Hamilton Fish of suburban Westchester County, New York, who told his colleagues they had been given a mandate to wrest control of the legislative process from "radical young lawyers" so that Congress could "act on its own initiative as a separate and independent branch of the Government."[36]

In this hostile atmosphere the House committee convened in May 1944. One of the first administration witnesses to testify was Budget Director Harold Smith, the coordinator of public works planning and budgeting after the demise of the NRPB. Smith made a futile effort to allay conservative fears, declaring that executive planning had not been designed to encroach upon the prerogatives of the legislature but "to facilitate the work of Congress in formulating legislation." His words fell on deaf ears, because conservatives were convinced that Roosevelt really intended to revive the NRPB. Colmer, for example, conceded the need for action to bring the cities through the reconversion process. But his subsequent words and attitude carefully hedged his initial expansiveness, until it was unmistakable that what he really intended was to minimize presidential and federal intervention by stimulating *private* planning, funding, and construction.[37]

Colmer was not alone in this desire. Representative Charles S. Dewey, an Illinois Republican, also rejected the concept of a central body to coordinate municipal and state planning. He yearned nostalgically for a return to the good old days when life was simpler and less complicated. Dewey evidenced no comprehension whatever of the planning process. Elsewhere, in the Committee on Public Buildings and Grounds, which also was

36. *Post-War Economic Policy and Planning,* Hearings before the Special Committee on Postwar Economic Policy and Planning pursuant to Sen. Res. 102, United States Congress, Senate, 79th Cong., 1st sess., pt. 6 (1944–45), 1192; *Congressional Record,* 78th Cong., 2d sess., 90 (Jan. 26, 1944), 754–55; *ibid.,* 90 (Nov. 22, 1944), Appendix 4481–83.

37. House, *Post-War Economic Policy and Planning,* pt. 2, 321–22, 411; pt. 6, 1780–92.

investigating postwar policy, Carter Manasco, Democrat of Alabama, drew a dubious parallel between Nazi Germany and the planning movement in the United States.[38]

Several state and municipal officials shared the conservatives' hostility to an expanded federal role in reconversion, though not always for the same reasons. The executive secretary of Minnesota's Resources Commission feared that federal planning funds would establish new ties to the cities, further weakening state influence; others argued that the threat to withhold federal funds would be used to pressure the states to share their revenues with the cities. The secretary of the League of Minnesota Municipalities argued against both federal *and* state interference. "The best way for the states to assist cities is to give them adequate taxing powers," he declared.[39]

These men spoke essentially for rural and suburban America and did not reflect accurately the attitudes of the big urban centers and the United States Conference of Mayors. Throughout 1944 and 1945, in testimony before the congressional committees investigating postwar economic policy and the Public Buildings and Grounds committee of the House, mayors of major cities such as Chicago's Edward Kelly, St. Paul's John J. McDonough, Camden's George E. Brunnder, Denver's Ben Stapleton, and Kansas City's John B. Gage, and Miami's city manager, Arnold B. Curry, endorsed federal funding of urban public works planning.[40]

Besides the constitutional and political issues, much of the conservative opposition to a dynamic postwar urban policy originated in the belief that the cities (and states) would emerge from World War II in better fiscal shape than the federal gov-

---

38. *Ibid.,* pt. 3, 592. See also *Post-War Planning No. 2,* Hearings before the Committee on Public Buildings and Grounds, United States Congress, House of Representatives, Nov. 1943–Mar. 1944, 78th Cong., 2d sess. (1944), 219–23. Cited hereafter as Lanham Committee, *Hearings.*

39. House, *Post-War Economic Policy and Planning,* pt. 6, 1988, 2025–27. See also the American Institute of Planners' memorandum, "Federal Legislation for Aid to Urban Redevelopment within the States," in Senate, *Post-War Economic Policy and Planning,* pt. 9, 1621.

40. Lanham Committee, *Hearings,* 306; Senate, *Post-War Economic Policy and Planning,* pt. 9, 1608–9.

ernment. This conviction was central to non-Keynesians and was one of the cardinal tenets upon which the conservative coalition established its identity. Conservatives also feared that the appropriation of federal funds for planning was like the tip of an iceberg, intended to revive a broad spectrum of New Deal programs. Behind their fears was uncertainty whether the reconversion period would be marked by inflationary pressures or the deflation-unemployment cycle that many Keynesians anticipated.[41]

In either event, because of legislatively mandated tax and borrowing limitations several cities, including New Haven, Buffalo, Spokane, and Jacksonville, doubted whether they would have the wherewithal to finance renewal. Wall Street's *Daily Bond Buyer* reported that civic officials were proceeding cautiously in anticipation of a signal from state or federal authorities. A few took it for granted that Congress *would* enact some kind of federal funding program at the conclusion of the war, but others harbored misgivings.[42]

Alvin H. Hansen, special economic adviser to the Federal Reserve Board, assumed that the federal government would finance urban redevelopment. With this in mind, he had outlined the administration's options. It could (1) follow the Wagner-Thomas bills approach, whereby the federal government granted long-term low-interest loans to enable the cities to acquire sites; (2) guarantee municipal revenue bonds to finance self-sustaining projects; (3) grant tax write-offs to lure investors into the municipal bond market; or (4) make available other guarantees and tax incentives. The second and third options had drawbacks, encouraging building in the more profitable suburban areas rather than in the blighted sections of the inner city. As coauthor of the Thomas bill in 1943 he naturally preferred

41. Lanham Committee, *Hearings, passim;* Frank W. Horne, "Financing Post-War Improvements," *American City* 59 (Aug. 1944), 68–69. An ASPO survey indicated that few localities believed that they had funds available to conduct postwar planning, but they were expecting to receive federal funds. See Walter H. Blucher, "Can a City Solve Its Own Problems?" *ASPO News Letter* 10 (Feb. 1944), 13.

42. "How Cities Will Finance Post-War Projects," *American City* 58 (Dec. 1943), 47; Johns Hopkins University, *Report of the Urban Planning Conference Under the Auspices of the Johns Hopkins University, 1943* (Baltimore, 1944), 230–31.

the first option, but if this proved to be impractical for political reasons, Hansen supported the fourth, which had the merit of raising funds in the regular capital markets, thereby minimizing dependency upon the legislature.[43]

Hansen's funding scheme contained two aspects guaranteed to incur the ire of congressional conservatives and their allies. The proposal was potentially inflationary, while the introduction of the cash nexus forged a stronger link in the chain binding the cities to the federal government. Thus Eric Johnston, president of the United States Chamber of Commerce, railed before the Lanham Committee against federal subsidies, even as seed money for local public works planning. Representative Fritz Lanham, Democrat of Texas, agreed that federal planning money should not be forthcoming. "That responsibility is going to rest upon the local communities. If they do not begin to plan from their own resources, they are going to be the ones to suffer," he told Alan Johnstone, general counsel of the FWA.[44]

When Carl H. Chatters, executive director of the Municipal Finance Officers Association, testified before the Colmer Committee, sentiment against federal financing of postwar urban planning was already strong. Chatters conceded that the cities had reduced their aggregate indebtedness, but he observed that during reconversion the cities would be expected to shoulder the burden of new major capital outlays as well as pay higher governmental costs and wages. "We are going to get some shocks in the communities where the people think we are going to get back to normal as soon as the war is over, due to things that must be done that have been neglected in the immediate past," he predicted.[45]

One might have expected Chatters to speak favorably on behalf of federal funding because fewer than half the states had established a postwar municipal reserve. However, he adhered to

43. Alvin H. Hansen, "Urban Redevelopment," *Survey Graphic* 33 (Mar. 1944), 204–5. See also Senate, *Post-War Economic Policy and Planning,* pt. 9, 1611.

44. Lanham Committee, *Hearings,* 207, 219, 223, 519–23.

45. See the memorandum, "A Specific Program for Municipal Finances During the War and in the Post-War Years," in House, *Post-War Economic Policy and Planning,* pt. 8, 2518–20.

the cautious stance which the association had adopted before the Lanham Committee. The association had recommended that the cities continue to reduce their indebtedness and pursue pay-as-you-go policies. It was optimistic that the states would assume increased fiscal responsibility for urban problems by sharing revenues (notably automobile and gasoline taxes) with the cities.[46]

Unhappily for urban liberals, Chatter's testimony was not lost upon Colmer and his fellow conservatives, who interpreted the program as being anti-inflationary. It placed the burden of planning, financing, and construction upon local and state initiative and private resources, where it properly belonged. Although political and economic power, control over the spending of billions of dollars, and the opportunity to shape the physical and spiritual destinies of the cities for decades to come were at stake, urban reformers made little headway with the Colmer Committee in part because of their own dissension and disunity. To the concerned citizen who closely followed their testimony, the urban coalition seemed to lack focus in what it hoped to achieve, or it was attempting too much, or it was relying too heavily on the efficacy of exhortation, resolutions, and model redevelopment statutes. Worse still, it was unable to present a united front at a time when unity was crucial.

The exchange among Congressmen Richard J. Welch, Republican of California, and Walter Lynch of New York and FWA Administrator Philip Fleming illustrated the difficulty of achieving a liberal consensus. Welch and Lynch wanted to establish for the record the need of a central agency to coordinate planning initiatives during reconversion. After some prodding, they got Fleming to admit that few states and cities had established postwar planning organizations. Fleming attributed the procrastination not to an absence of money but to a lack of foresight and observed that even where planning bodies existed, "most of the programs have been just dreams, fancies, pictures of what they want." He refused to concede that a revived NRPB was desirable and noted that the FWA, by virtue of its

46. *Ibid.*, pt. 3, 586–95; Lanham Committee, *Hearings,* 683–85.

public works and highway construction experience, had both the organization and experience in dealing with the cities.[47]

Like any sharp-eyed bureaucrat, administrator Fleming must have calculated that a new central planning body would challenge the FWA's role in reconversion. To advocates of comprehensive redevelopment, however, Fleming's conception of urban planning was no more than "nuts and bolts" tinkering—some housing here, public works there, and roads everywhere.[48] Harold Buttenheim, for example, wrote in *American City* that an "unfortunate misconception of the differences between comprehensive community planning and public works planning" still persisted. Walter H. Blucher had little confidence in public works as an antidepression remedy, because "the total amount of public works in the plan stage, with financial arrangements and necessary land acquired, is pitifully small." He testified that comprehensive planning was essential, observing that it was "not possible to have a rational program of public works until a community knows what its overall needs will be."[49]

In an oblique reference to Fleming and critics of comprehensive planning such as Moses and Mayor La Guardia, Blucher observed that there were some urban officials "who believe the function of a community planning organization is the preparation of a public works program." The conception was erroneous, he observed, adding that the ASPO took the position that "the preparation of such a program is a final step rather than a first step." For this you needed *federal* stimulation in the form of seed money.[50]

The reason the federal government had to take the initiative was because the cities and states were not doing the planning

47. House, *Post-War Economic Policy and Planning,* pt. 2, 325–28.

48. *Ibid.,* pt. 3, 575–77.

49. Harold S. Buttenheim, "State and Federal Aid for Blueprinting," *American City* 59 (Sept. 1944), 5.

50. House, *Post-War Economic Policy and Planning,* pt. 3, 577–82. Blucher's views were received sympathetically by some but not all liberals. Dorothy Rosenman was one who criticized the shelf-list public works approach espoused by urban politicians like La Guardia and Robert Moses. See Mrs. Samuel I. Rosenman, "A Re-Appraisal of Urban Planning," in Arnold J. Zurcher and Raymond Page, eds., *Postwar Economic Society* (New York, 1944), 77.

themselves. They were supinely waiting for Washington to come to the rescue. As evidence, Blucher cited an ASPO survey indicating that 167 cities with a population over 25,000 had compiled lists of projects to be initiated during reconversion. The sum totaled $5.3 billion, but eight of the larger cities (including New York and Chicago) accounted for $4 billion. Even these statistics were misleading because in nearly every municipality planning still was in the formative stage: vital details of financing, site acquisition, and the like had not been worked out. Moreover, their approach suggested that there was as yet no great understanding of the planning function or of the importance of rebuilding blighted areas in accordance with a well-conceived comprehensive plan of community development.[51]

Anxious to get postwar planning off the ground but at the same time perceiving the committee's tight-fisted mood, Blucher offered a compromise whose minimal terms might be acceptable to everyone. He proposed that public works blueprints be drafted in the context of a comprehensive plan, but that Congress restrict matching grants and loans only to planning and site acquisition. In this manner, Congress, worried about inflation, would not have to commit itself to the indefinite appropriation of enormous sums or sums for actual construction. The latter task would be left to the cities and states to work out. In the spirit of cooperative federalism and to allay fears of federal encroachment upon state sovereignty, Blucher proposed that redevelopment planning be entrusted to the local communities, subject only to very broad federal guidelines. To his dismay even this relatively modest proposal brought down Colmer's wrath. The Mississippian retorted, "If that is done, we are going to find a lot of extravagant plans made by the communities at the expense of the Federal Government and plans that will never be executed when the communities find that they are going to have to put up all the money or any substantial part of it."[52]

Blucher's plea not only fell upon the closed ears of conserva-

---

51. House, *Post-War Economic Policy and Planning*, pt. 3, 577–82.
52. *Ibid.*, pt. 3, 583; pt. 6, 1719; Senate, *Post-War Economic Policy and Planning*, pt. 9, 1619–22.

tives, but also encountered vigorous criticism from urban politicians. The testimony of Mayor La Guardia, who appeared before the committee with several high-ranking New York politicos, illustrated how conservatives exploited the absence of unity, the confusion of objectives, and the working at cross purposes. Two realities conditioned La Guardia's thinking about the postwar city, namely, the nightmarish specter of widespread unemployment and depression among returning veterans and the presence of $100 million in blueprints on the city's public works shelf. With the planning already well advanced in New York City, La Guardia's real need was for federal funds to underwrite the construction. He had long since despaired of the state coming to the city's rescue; hence he testified on July 27, 1944, that Congress should appropriate funds to cover 75 percent of the cities' postwar planning cost *plus* 50 percent of the cost of construction.[53]

Both La Guardia and Commissioner Robert Moses coupled the petition for federal funds with a gratuitous assault upon comprehensive planners. In response to New York Congressman Walter Lynch, who was making a vain attempt to persuade them that comprehensive planning was desirable in certain circumstances, Moses declared: "I don't know what comprehensive plans are. If you mean this long-hair planning of ripping up cities, and doing them over again, that is preposterous." This gambit of dissociating themselves as "realists" from impractical comprehensive planners in order to secure federal monies failed totally. Colmer and other conservatives manipulated their arguments into stern lectures on orthodox fiscal policy which implied no federal funding. "There must be a bottom to the Government's meal barrel as well as to the individual's. If we are going to have a $300 billion indebtedness when the war is over, with a $7.5 billion carrying charge on it, is it not going to be a rather serious proposition for the Federal Government to go into a gigantic public works program?" Colmer responded.[54]

Conservatives also exploited the differing opinions within La

53. House, *Post-War Economic Policy and Planning,* pt. 6, 1719ff.
54. *Ibid.,* pt. 6, 1717–19; 1730; 1780–92.

241

Guardia's entourage on the merits of direct federal-city relationships. If there should be federal assistance, was the money to be delivered to the cities directly or channeled through the states? "Well, speaking for myself and 99.99 percent of the mayors, I would have it come direct," declared an angry Mayor La Guardia, whose long, bitter struggle to wrest funds from an upstate, rural-dominated legislature was well known.[55] Manhattan Borough President Edgar J. Nathan opposed federal intervention, fearing that financial inducements would erode the cities' moral fiber and sovereignty. Manhattan already had some $12 million in public works blueprints on the shelf and another $56 million in various stages of completion. Should a depression recur, Nathan could legitimately expect the federal government to intercede as it had done before the war; and if there were no depression, the borough would probably qualify for fewer funds, based upon any formula of need. Arthur V. Sheridan, the Bronx commissioner of public works, reaffirmed on constitutional grounds the role of the states in the federal-city relationship. While granting that New York City had unusual problems with the state, he still believed that federal monies should come through the state.[56]

Robert Moses, an ideological foe of the New Deal philosophy and program, was in the most anomalous position. He accused the Roosevelt administration of having gone "entirely too far in undermining municipal and State governments." Then, throwing consistency to the winds, he argued for federal funds on the grounds that this was an emergency situation. Unfortunately, the committee's conservative membership bought some of his arguments but not all of them. There was a crisis all right, asserted Congressman B. Carroll Reece, a Tennessee Republican, but it was in state and federal relationships and the threat of inflation. "If we start out on the assumptions that the States and the cities cannot finance projects, private enterprise cannot provide employment, and that the only alternative is the Federal Government, acceptance of that philosophy destroys their mo-

55. *Ibid.*, pt. 6, 1718.
56. *Ibid.*, pt. 6, 1732–35; 1824.

tive and undermines their determination to solve their problem. It seems to me that is a very discouraging aspect,'' he told Moses.[57]

With minor variations, the same scenario was enacted before the Senate committee exploring postwar policy issues. The exchange between Senator Taft and Alfred Bettman, an executive of the AIP, provides an excellent index of the strength of congressional sentiment for retrenchment. Speaking as chairman of the Housing and Urban Affairs Subcommittee on January 12, 1945, Taft argued that twelve years of deficit spending had virtually bankrupted the federal government. In his opinion, the odds were greatly against the cities' receiving financial assistance from this source, especially since there was little likelihood of the loans being repaid. This upset Bettman, who questioned Congress's priorities. He told the Taft subcommittee that if the cities' future well-being was important to the nation, it must not be treated as a residue after the many other important things were done.[58]

Taft, overly concerned about the price tag for slum clearance and comprehensive redevelopment, pointed out that so-called ''experts'' were unable to provide his subcommittee with concrete figures. Neither was he able intellectually or emotionally to accept Bettman's assertion that economic blight afflicted one-quarter of America's urban environment, or to believe that redevelopment in the long term would pay for itself in enhanced tax revenues, higher productivity, and fuller employment. In Taft's opinion, urban blight was not a matter of national concern. ''I don't see what interest the Federal Government has in the blighted area at all, why we are concerned with rebuilding all the cities of the United States,'' he continually reiterated to each of Bettman's pleas.[59]

The exchange between the Ohioan and Bettman showed unmistakably that Taft distrusted the centralizing tendencies of the New Deal. The latter stood for the world of organization that

57. *Ibid.,* pt. 6, 1780–93.
58. Senate, *Post-War Economic Policy and Planning,* pt. 9, 1612.
59. *Ibid.,* pt. 9, 1614–18.

threatened the individualistic values and belief in the centrality of "integrity" that was the core of his own creed. Standing squarely in the nineteenth-century liberal tradition, Taft viewed urban blight as a local community problem. However, another aspect of the same tradition was its generous and compassionate response to human welfare. Thus if Taft did not endorse redevelopment planning, he could—and did—sponsor public housing legislation. He drew a distinction between public housing and redevelopment, supporting federal assistance for the former. "I don't see why we are interested in any way in an urban redevelopment program beyond the housing question," he told Bettman.[60]

Thus it went before the Senate Subcommittee on Housing and Urban Redevelopment. Bettman's petition for federal sponsorship of redevelopment planning received the coup de grâce, particularly after another proponent of public housing, Senator Allen J. Ellender, a Louisiana Democrat, observed that he was also "inclined to the belief that the Federal Government should not step in and try to remedy the situation that you just described."[61] Ironically, Taft's and Ellender's opposition came back to haunt them one year later when five conservative Republicans on the House Banking and Currency Committee blocked consideration of the Wagner-Taft-Ellender postwar housing bill. The legislation, whose passage was virtually assured had it been permitted to reach a vote on the House floor, would have resulted in the construction of possibly 12,500,000 new homes over the next ten years.[62]

Retreat soon became rout. Congressional sentiment for retrenchment rendered it impossible to approach urban redevelopment along the lines comprehensive planners had advocated in 1943. The elections in 1944 had not weakened substantially the obstructive force of the conservative coalition, which received intellectual sustenance from the publication (also in 1944) of Friederich von Hayek's *The Road to Serfdom*. However mis-

60. *Ibid.*
61. *Ibid.,* pt. 9, 1619.
62. "House Committee Kills Housing Bill," *Public Housing* 12 (Sept. 1946), 1, 3.

interpreted or acclaimed by laissez-faire economists, Hayek's book, a ringing denunciation of economic collectivism and a strident plea for the restoration of individual liberty and economic decision making, touched a responsive chord in those Americans unable to cope with the complexities of a modern industrial-urban society.[63] To these Americans comprehensive urban planning, if they thought about it at all, was an exotic, foreign, and wholly inapplicable and inappropriate device.[64]

Fears and suspicions of national dominance, triggered by the centralizing tendencies of the New Deal, came to the forefront more strongly in 1944–45 than at any time since the start of the war. The editor of the AIP *Journal* observed that the winds of controversy were rising in Congress and will "doubtless blow harder before they subside." Congressman Walter Lynch asserted that Congress in its present mood would not pass a single grant-in-aid program until widespread unemployment ravaged the country.[65] A new round of wartime inflation in the winter of 1944, the surprise German offensive in the Ardennes, and preparations for the Yalta conference in February 1945 caused Roosevelt to put domestic policies of reconstruction, including urban renewal, on the back burner.[66]

---

63. Friederich von Hayek, *The Road to Serfdom* (Chicago, 1944), *passim*. Rather than attempting to refute Hayek, many liberal urban planners dismissed his arguments as self-evidently fallacious or did not respond at all. See Walter H. Blucher, "Planning and the Road to Serfdom," *ASPO News Letter* 11 (June 1945), 49, and Laurence M. Orton, "Editorial," *AIPJ* 11 (Winter 1945), 3–4.

64. Hugh R. Pomeroy, executive director of the National Association of Housing Officials, told the Taft subcommittee: "I find no deep urge that can justify me in saying that the Federal Government should assume the major part of the obligation of rebuilding the industrial areas and the business districts and the transportation systems of American cities." Senate, *Post-War Economic Policy and Planning*, pt. 11, 1739.

65. Orton, "Editorial," 3–4; Walter H. Blucher, "What of the Future?" *ASPO News Letter* 10 (Aug. 1944), 61; "Federal Aid to Public Works Not Likely in 1945, Says Lynch," *ibid.*, 10 (Nov. 1944), 86.

66. Hinchey, "Frustration of the New Deal Revival," 47–51, and *passim*.

Epilogue

Every great conflict constitutes a revolution producing violent torsions and sweeping changes. World War II was no exception, unleashing economic and social forces that had an enormous impact on American life long after the last bomb dropped. Mobilization propelled literally millions of men and women into urban defense centers. Millions of black Americans, too, left the farm, trekking north and west, testing the fruits and hardships, the opportunities and the frustrations of city life.[1]

Migration historically has been a dynamic factor in American urban growth, and so it was during World War II. The patterns of migration during the war years, however, were not inconsistent with those of earlier periods. They represented an acceleration of the population shifts resulting from basic forces that have operated in population distribution during much of our history rather than exceptions that could easily be reversed when the war ended. Thus the war slowed temporarily but did not reverse the long-term trend toward dispersal of population throughout the metropolitan areas of the United States.[2]

Although the full brunt of the war fell upon urban America, every hamlet, village, and town also experienced the conflict at first hand. The social cost to communities whose routine was disrupted was high, and the nation paid the price years after the return of peace. Family ties were painfully strained and in many cases broken altogether; juvenile delinquency increased; crimes against the person—murder, rape, assault—rose sharply. As one war year rolled into another, the overgrown communities showed signs of wear and neglect. By 1945 American cities—

1. Jack Goodman, ed., *While You Were Gone: A Report on Wartime Life in the United States* (New York, 1946), 7–8; James M. Burns, *Roosevelt: The Soldier of Freedom* (New York, 1970), 355.
2. Conrad Taeuber, "Wartime Population Changes in the United States," *Milbank Memorial Fund Quarterly* 24 (July 1946), 242.

even the land on which they rested—appeared more war-weary than the people themselves. They had stood the test, but they had not been built for such a strain.[3]

Public discussion of urban affairs, which had come to be established on the agenda of liberal reform in the Depression-ridden thirties, increased during World War II. Urban liberals believed that the wartime dislocations provided an opportunity to substitute for the speculative city building of the past a community planning method which approached physical changes in the context of the social situation of which they were a part.[4] To the extent that these liberals joined forces with community-oriented federal agencies, such as the NRPB and the OCWS, New Deal reform was not dead. On the contrary, there continued to exist a larger vitality to the reform impulse between the pre- and postwar eras than most participants realized and most scholars have acknowledged. During 1941–45, the cause of urban progress functioned within war-induced parameters.

Not all the reform efforts in housing, planning, and urban welfare proved fruitful of ultimate success, however. The belief that one could create a new community synthesis by means of recreation centers, clubhouses, and child-care programs was excessively optimistic. There simply was too much physical movement for individuals, even friendly ones, to create significant numbers of *enduring* personal relationships which could be related to a specific neighborhood within the city.

Indeed, the whole wartime milieu compromised the case for a national policy of urban reconstruction even before the war ended. The presence of a conservative coalition in Congress, a hesitant administration, partisan politics, and the reassertion of state prerogatives established definite boundaries to cooperative federalism that affected the cities adversely. The stormy careers of both the housing and planning movements were instructive

3. See, for example, "Mobile, Alabama: After the Storm," *Fortune* 33 (Mar. 1946), 108, and "Our Land Resources: War-Weary Cities," *Building America* 11 (Feb. 1946), 155–57.

4. See Lewis Mumford, *City Development: Studies in Disintegration and Renewal* (New York, 1945), 191, 193.

of both the aspirations of urban reform and its limitations given the enduring strength of conservatism in American society. Thus Congress, which had not appropriated the money required to attain the goals of its own housing program in the Depression, held the line on domestic fiscal spending during the war. The defeat of the Wagner-Ellender-Taft low-cost housing bill in July 1946 should not have occasioned any surprise.[5]

Similarly disappointed were the professional planners, who had hoped that a larger element of constructive creativity would emerge from the wartime experience. They had believed that rational men could consciously shape the physical and social environment of their communities rather than leave them to the speculative economic process. They perceived urban planning not as the displacement of reality, as critics charged, but the clarification and bringing of all its elements into harmony with human purposes. Unhappily, the scope of planning in 1945 remained no wider than a local community's interest.[6]

The reasons the planners' dreams were dashed so abruptly are complex, but among them must certainly be counted the divisions within the ranks of liberals themselves. The New Deal broadened the urban political spectrum in the thirties, but it had not eliminated factionalism within the urban polity. When the social welfare organizations that supported public housing looked at the cities, they saw the slums; when site planners and landscape architects looked at these same cities, they saw inappropriate street patterns, poor transportation facilities, obsolete business districts, and aging factories. Whereas public housing reformers viewed urban rehabilitation as just another tool for improving the housing picture, the planners dreamed of using the program to reshape American cities in a new image.[7]

Similarly, powerful private interests were cool to the rebuild-

5. Samuel I. Rosenman, comp., *The Public Papers and Addresses of Franklin D. Roosevelt,* 13 vols. (New York, 1938–50), VI, 1–6; *New York Times,* July 29, 1946. See also the testimony of John Blandford in *General Housing Act of 1945,* Hearings before the Committee on Banking and Currency pursuant to S. 1592, United States Congress, Senate, 79th Cong., 1st sess., pt. 1 (1945–46), 1259ff.

6. "Mobilizing for the Post-War City," *American City* 57 (Dec. 1942), 44.

7. Mark I. Gelfand, *A Nation of Cities: The Federal Government and Urban America, 1933–1965* (New York, 1975), 385.

ing of blighted areas, fearful that the exponents of redevelopment wished to impose numerous restraints on the firms undertaking reconstruction projects. Mortgage bankers and builders, with an eye on returning veterans as a house-hungry group eager to buy whatever they produced, resisted any proposals that might retard the pace of construction or lower their profits. Since comprehensive planning in their eyes encompassed nothing but red tape, annoying regulations, and higher costs, the private developers wanted no part of it. Consequently no aesthetic image, no notion of public purpose, no historical memory or respect for ancestral places was allowed to hinder private endeavor and individual initiative.[8]

Worse still, city planners of the forties were isolated from national politics and popular understanding. They were unable to persuade the Roosevelt administration to accept urban rehabilitation on its own merits as an integral part of the New Deal, distinct from the problems of unemployment, depression, and inflation. Similarly, they lacked the special kind of democratic leadership that would enable them to weld philosophic purpose, scientific fact, and popular initiative into a dynamic program. Their education had not prepared them for cooperative work with the citizenry who were their clientele. Thus they ignored the fact that neighborhood conservation involved a slow upgrading process devoid of dramatic qualities, which made it difficult to sustain popular interest. The main elements in planning, they forgot, also involved certain restrictions on existing liberties which could not be effected without a positive public opinion.[9]

To attain the objectives of comprehensive planning nationally would have required not only the cooperation of private enterprise but also decisive political action fundamentally reordering the structure of cooperative federalism. State and local governmental relations would have had to be reformulated to provide for metropolitan or city-region government. Interstate com-

8. *Ibid.,* 149.
9. See Catherine Bauer's review of Mumford's *City Development* which appeared in the *AIP Journal* 11 (Summer 1945), 40; Corwin R. Mocine to the Editor, n.d., *AIP Journal* 11 (Winter 1945), 32; Laurence M. Orton, "Editorial," *ibid.,* 4.

THE CHALLENGE TO URBAN LIBERALISM

pacts allowing greater flexibility for metropolitan self-determination would have had to be negotiated. This would have required the active encouragement of Washington, the consent of the state legislatures, and the willingness of municipalities to experiment. But when their plans were attacked in Congress, in the press, at the local level, and by entrenched interests (as they almost certainly would be if they contained any substantive content), the planners found themselves alone, fending off criticism with little outside help. By 1945 comprehensive planning was an idea without a program or movement, without effective political organization, without broad popular party strength behind it, and without leadership.

In attempting to assess the reasons urban liberals did not make greater headway during the war years in translating their enthusiasm and ideas into a national urban policy that would rank on a par with a national economic policy or a national foreign policy, one must finally consider another aspect of the federal system within which the reformers had to operate.[10] American federalism historically has made a virtue of decentralized decision making. To a degree not commonly appreciated by wartime critics of "growing federal control," the Roosevelt administration continued to pay homage to this ideal by carefully respecting the traditional division of national and local authorities. Thus federal wartime activity put more rather than less emphasis on state and municipal responsibility. The result was that in the midst of important centralization there also occurred tremendous noncentralization.

The process commenced with mobilization in 1941, when President Roosevelt decided that the restoration of state and local authority in their respective jurisdictions must be effected as soon after the war as was feasible. At the same time, Roosevelt also decided to leave most of the basic determinations of wartime programs to the states, acting through their municipalities and volunteer citizens' groups. These decisions com-

10. The federal system is discussed in Jane Perry Clark, *The Rise of a New Federalism* (New York, 1938) and Daniel J. Elazar, "The Shaping of Intergovernmental Relations in the Twentieth Century," in the *Annals of the American Academy of Political and Social Science* 359 (May 1965), 10–22.

ported fully with Roosevelt's own prepresidential career as state senator and governor of New York and his own understanding of the American past. The President believed that in structuring the American system of government the Founding Fathers had never intended national or presidential dominance in domestic policy. Their design rested upon a diffusion of power and responsibility intended to give important interests a veto over legislation that might affect them adversely.[11]

There was also a pragmatic basis for the President's decisions. For in spite of repeated warnings of impending war, the administration was not prepared either in 1941 or in the first months immediately following Pearl Harbor to establish quickly across the United States the bureaucratic apparatus that total war required. This meant that the states and municipalities —almost by default—retained a large measure of freedom of choice and such unity of purpose as was necessary to perform vital wartime functions. The latter demonstrated their complete loyalty to the national defense effort and relinquished to Washington full control over military policy, while enlisting willingly through their defense councils in all that needed to be done at home to prosecute the war successfully. Thus the arrangement that evolved from both ideological and pragmatic considerations, whereby the machinery, resources, and personnel of one level of government were utilized to implement the defense programs of the others, helped to foster cooperative federalism but also noncentralization.[12]

The fundamental problem of federalism during the war years was to establish a just and efficient division of labor among the different contributing and constituent units of government. As the foregoing account has indicated, the administration's initial approach to civilian defense was through the states, which already possessed a central secretariat in the Council of State Governments. Wisely, Roosevelt paved the way for this decision earlier by appointing Frank Bane, former head of the council,

11. See Howard S. Zavin, "Forward to the Land: Franklin D. Roosevelt and the City, 1882–1933" (Ph.D. diss., New York Univ., 1972), *passim*.

12. Charles E. Merriam, "Observations on Centralization and Decentralization: The Federal System in Wartime," *State Government* 15 (Jan. 1943), 3.

251

as federal administrator in charge of coordinating state and municipal planning for protection of the home front. This maneuver almost immediately returned dividends because Bane used his contacts with the council to persuade the governors to take action on defense matters on relatively short notice. State agencies and experienced civil servants were thus enlisted to perform national functions under federal direction. This stratagem, Roosevelt came to appreciate, facilitated economy (for wastefulness was one of the principal grounds of state and local criticism of the New Deal), reduced needless duplication of work and facilities, and left largely undisturbed the balance wheel of federalism.[13]

However much centralization was a requisite of military success, the administration quickly discovered that in matters directly affecting the home front it was more efficient to leave the actual implementation of basic protective measures to the states, cities, and regions. Washington worked out the broad guidelines of its civilian protection program with the help of input from state and city officials, but it delegated operation to the states, which farmed out the work to municipal governments and volunteer organizations. The national Office of Civilian Defense served mainly as a planning, coordinating, and stimulating agency. It supplied to the states and cities most, if not all, of the needed funds; but the basic program remained under state control.

The history of the OCD and its program of civilian protection illustrated two other facets of cooperative federalism worth noting. The first was the capacity of governmental units below the national level to perform their tasks efficiently even when leadership from the top was weak or misdirected. The second was the growing tendency of the federal government under wartime duress to enter into new contractual relationships with the states and, indirectly, the municipalities. Except in a few localities designated "Congested Production Areas," federal grants-

13. William Anderson, "National-State Relations During the War," in United States Department of Agriculture Graduate School, ed., *What We Learned in Public Administration During the War* (Washington, D.C., 1949), 67.

in-aid were increasingly routed to the cities through the state bureaucracies and supported a wide variety of activities: day-care centers for children, housing, school lunches, community recreational facilities, road and highway planning, and a municipal airport program.

The Council of State Governments in its annual report for 1945 aptly summarized the shifting intergovernmental relationship that was occurring during the war. Noting that the Roosevelt administration had chosen to emphasize coordination rather than centralization, the council declared: "Cooperative governmental programs, operated from the federal government to the states and from the states to the local governments . . . have worked, and have worked well, in an effective and economical fashion. These programs have met the needs as they have developed, and in operation they have been under the control of and responsive to the will of the people."[14]

This summation was accurate but was far from telling the whole story. For the President's decisions in 1941 made it inevitable that the war would bring about a resurgence of state initiative within the federal structure and a concomitant demand for a scaling down of New Deal programs that stood to benefit urban constituencies. As the Council of State Governments observed in 1948, the states were "no longer on the defensive in their relations with the Federal Government" but were becoming "increasingly active in the preservation of their dignity and rights."[15] This was a partial reversion to the pattern of federalism that had evolved before the thirties and suggested that despite the crises of depression and global war the structure of federalism was never truly free of tension.

With the advent of the New Deal, the states had come to view the growing practice of direct federal-city relationships (as symbolized by the omnipresent grant-in-aid) with a jaundiced eye, regarding it as a perversion of the Founding Fathers' intent and a threat to state sovereignty. Wartime exigencies offered them an

14. The Council of State Governments, ed., *The Book of the States 1945–1946* (Chicago, 1945), 8.
15. *The Book of the States 1948,* 63.

opportunity to reassert their authority as the primary agencies operating on the municipalities while also serving the cause of patriotism. Through relentless lobbying, the states made certain that federal funds for defense centers were channeled through the state bureaucracies, that the role of the United States Conference of Mayors in civilian defense activities was downgraded, and that specific clauses strictly limiting the exercise of extraordinary powers to the duration of the war found their way into virtually all national defense legislation. In this manner the states eroded the practice of the federal government dealing directly with the cities and reinforced the belief that, in coping with metropolitan problems, state autonomy was sacrosanct.

As the history of the civilian defense and other wartime programs has disclosed, Roosevelt not only acknowledged this situation but worked within the parameters set by the states and their conservative allies. Whether as a matter of priority or because he feared that he would not receive adequate support for his war program without a quid pro quo, the President postponed further expansion of the domestic New Deal while the nation was at war—a decision that boded ill for the postwar prospects of urban America. There was no public disclosure to this effect, but the President's actions were revealing. Through the report of the National Resources Committee in 1937 and the activities of the NRPB between 1941 and 1943, the administration had made a clear commitment to aid the cities in the form of planning for permanent improvement. Roosevelt gave verbal encouragement to urban liberals who endeavored to transform emergency wartime programs into a blueprint for urban reconstruction, but he did not give them any substantive assistance. His unwillingness to formulate and sustain a federal urban policy strengthened critics' belief that the administration did not put urban rehabilitation high on its list of postwar priorities.

As the war wound down, it also became clear that the Executive Office of the Presidency was incapable of thinking about urban reconstruction on its own merits. There was more than a kernel of truth in Rexford G. Tugwell's remark in the 1950s that

Roosevelt "always did, and always would regard the cities as rather hopeless."[16] The result was that congressional conservatives, egged on by realtors, builders, and bankers, responded to the administration's inaction accordingly. To the degree that they were effective, the case for a national urban policy and for neighborhood and community development was prejudiced against reformers long before 1945.

To be successful, federal planning for postwar urban society would, at the very least, have necessitated close intragovernmental and intergovernmental cooperation. Unfortunately, the administration's failure to clarify jurisdictional boundaries encouraged bureaucratic infighting that jeopardized the possibility of using wartime programs in the fight against urban blight. Each agency functioned as a separate fiefdom serving the interests of a particular constituency and ignored the broader social problem. In part, this was also a result of the administration's failure to define clearly realizable goals. Housing policy, especially, often worked at cross purposes. Despite liberal rhetoric, the emphasis of the New Deal's housing program in the thirties had been on homes for sale in the suburbs. The FHA continued to uphold the sanctity of the single-family home during World War II, even though the amount of actual construction was small. In the period of reconversion, its mortgage insurance system along with Veterans Administration programs helped to enhance suburban sprawl and an emerging middle class—despite the fact that the NHA and its constituent public housing unit clearly identified central city housing, particularly rental units, as the greater need.[17]

The FHA's lending practices, which continued into the postwar period, exercised a push-pull effect—pushing people out of the central cities because there was no way they could obtain

16. Rexford G. Tugwell, "Sources of New Deal Reform," *Ethics* 64 (July 1954), 266.

17. See Rosenman, "A Program to Break the Housing Log-Jam," *New York Times Magazine* 6 (Mar. 28, 1948), 38–42, and *Building the American City,* United States Congress, House of Representatives, House Doc. No. 34, 91st Cong., 1st sess. (1969), 99–102.

mortgages at reasonable rates, and pulling them to the insured safety of the suburbs. Such practices were especially detrimental to urban blacks and were a barometer of the degree to which the New Deal (and its successor the Fair Deal) accepted the racial prejudices of the larger society. The result was that the national housing policy of the New Deal turned out to be not a policy at all. There was no definition of the nation's housing goals, nor an integrated program based upon the concepts of a healthy neighborhood environment, structurally sound dwellings with full plumbing facilities, and access to essential services. Rather, as many urban liberals feared, it consisted of separate programs enacted piecemeal over two decades, each with different eligibility standards, definitions, guidelines, and regulations.

The liberals' definition of national standards for a decent home and suitable community environment might have been realized, but only if federal housing assistance to the states and municipalities had been linked more firmly to equality of opportunity and a comprehensive program to revitalize existing communities and develop new ones. On this score, Washington failed to live up to its role in the federal partnership. The congressional pulling and tugging over the housing issue, the community services program, and others—between liberals and conservatives, within conservative ranks, and between legislative and appropriations committees—did not encourage a bureaucracy that was timid and lacked robust faith in the programs and policies it was supposed to administer. Conservative congressional opposition weakened the will of the federal bureaucracy not only in low-cost housing but also in postwar urban renewal, rent supplements, leased housing, nonprofit housing, and many other community-oriented programs. In the absence of strong federal and state support, the ability of the cities to cope with substandard housing, blighted neighborhoods, and urban sprawl was limited to the relatively low level of their financial resources. Private enterprise concentrated its resources on the more lucrative suburban market.

By the same token, war-induced unity between Washington

256

and the states on matters pertaining to national defense did not extend to discussions of postwar urban reform. Both the federal government and the state legislatures retreated wholly or in part from their obligations to the cities as full-fledged members of the federal system. Conservatives believed that the New Deal, over the past fifteen years, had upset the equilibrium in government and that the time was ripe to restore to the states many of the functions assumed by Washington. They used the war as an excuse to thwart legislation for urban redevelopment, to cripple the public housing program, and to eliminate such community services programs as child-care centers. For all the conservatives' insistence upon state autonomy, the states did not take up the slack themselves. Operating under outmoded constitutions, many drawn up before the automobile age, the states resumed their essentially passive stance in the face of serious metropolitan problems. Eleven state legislatures had enacted redevelopment laws by 1945, but only two had appropriated the funds needed to put them into practice. The irony, of course, was that the states had emerged from World War II in a more favorable position financially than at any time since the start of the Depression.[18]

When Franklin D. Roosevelt died in April 1945, postwar domestic policy, particularly with reference to the cities, was in a state of arrested development. Publicly, the administration had held back from direct sponsorship of any legislation, as the President expended his diminishing time and resources on military strategy and foreign policy. If Roosevelt's legacy to his successor was a strong commitment to full employment and reviving the New Deal, Harry S. Truman also inherited the deceased leader's major domestic problems: a hostile conservative coalition in Congress, inflationary pressures in the economy, and state governments nostalgic for a return to the small, autono-

18. See Seward H. Mott, "Urban Redevelopment Legislation Analyzed," *American City* 60 (Aug. 1945), 83–84; Donoh W. Hanks, Jr., "Neglected Cities Turn to U.S.," *National Municipal Review* 35 (Apr. 1946), 173.

mous, preurban community. Guiding the nation past these obstacles imposed limitations upon what a new and inexperienced president could accomplish for the cities.[19]

19. This conclusion may be extended beyond the period of reconversion to include the years from 1947 to 1962. In examining the structure of the U.S. House of Representatives, David R. Mayhew estimated that at any time during this period Democratic strength had to number at least 260 to ensure passage of urban-oriented reform legislation and that the breaking point of the difficult labor questions (e.g., minimum wage and labor-management legislation) lay well above 280. At the peak of their strength during the Truman years, in the 81st Congress, the Democrats had a House delegation of only 263. Not surprisingly, they enacted only a modest reform program. See David R. Mayhew, *Party Loyalty Among Congressmen: The Difference Between Democrats and Republicans, 1947–1962* (Cambridge, 1966), 167.

Bibliographical Essay

It would be foolhardy—and probably gratuitous—to attempt to list every letter and report, every article, every monograph from which I have drawn raw evidence, valuable leads, and interpretative ideas or organizing principles. The footnote citations attest to some of the specific kinds of materials I used. I intend here to select and to discuss merely those materials, primary and secondary, that were most useful to me and presumably would be most helpful to the serious reader.

Personal Papers

The Charles Poletti Papers, Columbia University, include correspondence, clippings, and articles pertaining to the organization of civilian defense activities, and especially wartime housing, in New York State. Poletti was one of the founding members of the Public Housing Conference and, during the early war years, served as Lieutenant Governor of New York. The Dorothy Rosenman Papers, also at Columbia University, are important for ascertaining the views of the public housing lobby. The wife of presidential adviser Samuel I. Rosenman, she was head of the National Committee on the Housing Emergency.

The Franklin D. Roosevelt Library, Hyde Park, New York, contains the papers of numerous figures whose activities touched upon urban affairs at the national, state, and local levels. The papers of John Carmody, Wayne Coy, and Budget Director Harold D. Smith are useful for investigating the early bureaucratic difficulties of the housing and civil defense programs. Samuel I. Rosenman's Papers deal with the transition from the Office of Defense Housing Coordination to the formation of the National Housing Agency in 1942. The papers of Nathan Straus are indispensable for understanding the wartime

259

and postwar objectives of the United States Housing Authority (USHA). His correspondence with the President, Eleanor Roosevelt, and others presents the controversy between public and private housing in bold relief. Eleanor Roosevelt's Papers, which include correspondence, drafts of speeches, reprints of articles, and clippings, give detailed descriptions of urban civilian defense work and offer rich insights into the issues of urban reform, race relations, and housing. Mrs. Roosevelt's position as head of the Division of Volunteer Participation gave her a unique vantage point from which to observe Fiorello H. La Guardia's management of the Office of Civilian Defense (OCD) and to delineate the growing rift in the ranks of urban liberals on the question of postwar urban reform.

In contrast, the Franklin D. Roosevelt Papers are more guarded concerning the President's private views on such matters as urbanization, reform, and wartime politics. The incoming correspondence does present useful insights into the impact of defense mobilization and war on cities that were the focal points of industrial production. The Official File and the President's Personal File occasionally reveal glimpses into the President's relations with Congress.

The Fiorello H. La Guardia Papers, located in the Municipal Archives in New York City, are extraordinarily rich in correspondence, reports, and other data concerning civilian defense activities in large metropolitan areas. They also highlight La Guardia's own role as director of the OCD down to 1941. Unfortunately, the papers are not very accessible physically.

The Oral History Project at Columbia University contains transcripts of interviews relative to urban matters with leaders in many fields. Germane for their insights into urban reform, intergovernmental relations, and the problems of civilian defense are the reminiscences of James H. Landis and Governor Herbert H. Lehman of New York State.

Archival Records

The official records of the National Defense Advisory Commission (NDAC), an executive agency established in May 1940, are located in the Franklin D. Roosevelt Library. They contain the reports and studies, minutes, and correspondence of the commission and are useful for analyzing the early problems of industrial and civilian mobilization in the context of federal, state, and local relations.

In addition, each administrative agency of the federal government kept its own detailed and often voluminous account of its wartime activities. These records, arranged in the Archives by Record Group, are essential for understanding wartime urban America and federal thinking about the postwar period. They are stored in the National Archives in Washington, D.C., and in Suitland, Maryland, and are readily available to scholars. Housing, naturally, was a central concern of wartime federal bureaucrats, and the political and social dimensions of the housing problem may be traced in the records of the following agencies: the Central Housing Committee, a coordinating body Roosevelt had established in his first administration, the Division of Defense Housing Coordination (headed by Charles F. Palmer), the United States Housing Authority, the Housing and Home Finance Corporation, the National Housing Agency, and the Public Works Reserve. These provide not only important insight into the conflict between public and private housing but also much raw data in the form of surveys, investigators' reports, and correspondence for understanding the whole spectrum of urban problems both nationally and locally. These records should be supplemented with those of the Committee for Congested Production Areas, also in the National Archives.

Mobilization of the home front was the specific mandate of the USOCD, although other federal agencies participated to a greater or lesser degree. The records of the OCD, located in Suitland, Maryland, contain much valuable information on its predecessor, the Division of State and Local Cooperation of the Defense Advisory Commission. Together they chronicle the vicissitudes that beset civilian defense officials. For a more thorough understanding of the activities of its director, Mayor La Guardia, they should be supplemented with La Guardia's own papers, the Eleanor Roosevelt Papers, the reminiscences of

261

James H. Landis, and the relevant files of the Bureau of the Budget (Records Division of the Office of Management and Budget) in Washington, D.C.

The extent and limitations of federal interest in wartime and postwar urban planning are revealed in the records of the Urban Section of the National Resources Planning Board, successor to the 1937 Urbanism Committee. Its interest in the physical aspects of urban renewal should be examined in conjunction with the Federal Security Agency's Office of Community War Services' concern for the broad spectrum of urban social problems that afflicted the home front. The latter ranged from juvenile delinquency and venereal disease to the need for child-care centers and recreation facilities. Together they provide a valuable insight into the thinking of one segment of the federal bureaucracy about postwar urban society.

Other Published Sources

The number of government publications touching upon wartime urban America churned out by the Government Printing Office is extensive. These took the form of congressional hearings, agency annual reports, special studies, and census data. Wartime population shifts resulting from industrial mobilization are extensively investigated in the 42-volume compilation of hearings and reports, *National Defense Migration* (1940–42), by the United States House of Representatives. That same body later conducted an *Investigation of Congested Areas* (1945), an in-depth study of the major metropolitan centers of war production. These studies should be supplemented with the work of Gladys K. Bowles, *Farm Population: Net Migration from the Rural-Farm Population, 1940–1950* (1956).

The organization of civilian defense activities in urban areas was the subject of lively controversy. For the activities of the OCD see the hearings and reports of the United States House of Representatives on the several deficiency and supplemental national defense appropriations bills that it considered between

262

1941 and 1943. Criticism of La Guardia's handling of civilian defense both from conservatives and liberals may also be found in the joint House and Senate hearings pertaining to the *Reduction of Non-essential Federal Expenditures* (1941) and the special Truman Committee's *Investigation of the National Defense Program* (1941) for the United States Senate.

There is no adequate examination of the cities' legal position in American federalism, but the following government-sponsored and privately sponsored publications shed some insight into the delicate wartime balance among municipal, state, and national governments: *The Book of the States* (1940–1945), published by the Council of State Governments, the annual *Proceedings* of the American Municipal Association, and the collected essays by J. Donald Kingsley et al. for the Department of Agriculture, *What We Learned in Public Administration During the War* (1949). The records of the United States Conference of Mayors for the war years unfortunately no longer exist.

The National Resources Planning Board was the focal point of considerable federal activity in the fields of urban housing and urban planning. Beginning with its landmark report in 1937, *Our Cities—Their Role in the National Economy,* the development of housing policy may be traced in its annual reports (*National Resources Development Report . . .*) for 1941–43. These documents should be supplemented with the annual reports of the National Housing Agency for 1944 and 1945, the United States Senate's hearings on the *General Housing Act of 1945* (1945), and two important studies by the National Committee on the Housing Emergency, an advocate of public housing: *A Program for Action on Housing for Defense Workers and Families of Low Income* (1941) and *Recommendations for the Disposition of Federal War Housing* (1943).

In the sphere of postwar urban planning the board's activities may be followed in *Better Cities* (1942) and *The Future of Transportation: Rebuilding America* (1942). The board's thinking in the area of urban rehabilitation was heavily influenced by the Federal Home Loan Bank Board's *Waverly, A Study in*

Neighborhood Conservation (1940) and the land-use concepts of British planners. The latter's ideas were spelled out in a series of reports that established the groundwork for the famous Town and Country Planning Act of 1947: *Royal Commission on Distribution of the Industrial Population* (1940), *Final Report of Expert Commission on Compensation and Betterment* (1942), and *Report of the Commission on Land Utilization in Rural Areas* (1942). To understand more fully the arguments pro and con on postwar urban planning, the reader must also consult the extensive House and Senate hearings of 1944 and 1945, *Post-War Economic Policy and Planning,* the *Congressional Record* (1941–1946), and the United States Chamber of Commerce's pamphlet, *Why Plan for the Post-War Period?* (1943).

The Federal Security Agency's Office of Community War Services examined in great detail the social impact of the war and how urban communities were responding to the disruption of their normal peacetime activities. The results of its investigation were published in a number of pamphlets of which the following were most useful for analyzing the agency's long-term commitment to urban rehabilitation: *Citizens of Tomorrow: A Wartime Challenge To Community Action* (1943), *Teamwork in Community Services 1941–1946: A Demonstration in Federal, State, and Local Cooperation* (1946), and the *Proceedings of the National Nutrition Conference for Defense* (1942). These should be supplemented with three important Senate investigations bearing on the social aspects of community renewal: *Wartime Care and Protection of Children of Employed Mothers* (1943), *Wartime Health and Education* (1944), and *Development of Community Recreation Programs for the People of the United States* (1946).

Newspapers, of course, provided extensive coverage of the war and its multifaceted impact upon American society. For the purpose of illustrating particular points I found the following newspapers useful: the *New York Times,* the *New York Herald Tribune,* the *Boston Globe,* the *Buffalo* (N.Y.) *Evening News,*

264

the *Baltimore Evening Sun,* the Corpus Christi *Caller-Times,* and the two Norfolk, Virginia, dailies, the *Ledger Dispatch* and *Virginian Pilot.*

Secondary Works

There are many general studies of the United States during the war. Among the accounts that I found most useful for their bibliographies and valuable insights into political, social, and economic developments were James M. Burn's *Roosevelt: The Soldier of Freedom* (1970), Richard Polenberg's *War and Society: The United States, 1941–1945* (1972), and Geoffrey Perrett's impressionistic *Days of Sadness, Years of Triumph: The American People, 1939–1945* (1973).

Contemporary periodicals of both a professional and popular nature devoted many articles and in some instances entire issues to the impact of mobilization and war upon American society. The most obvious starting point from which to begin to examine urban developments is the *American City,* whose editor was the influential Harold S. Buttenheim. Wartime population shifts may be traced in the publications of the *Milbank Memorial Fund Quarterly,* the *Journal of the American Statistical Association,* the *Social Security Bulletin,* and the *American Sociological Review.* The problems of women and black defense migrants are discussed in *Independent Woman* and *Race Relations.* There is relatively little in print on the wartime migration of Chicanos to urban areas, but see the interesting dissertation of Robin F. Scott, "The Mexican-American in the Los Angeles Area, 1920–1950: From Acquiescence to Action" (University of Southern California, 1971).

Intergovernmental relations as they touched upon urban communities may be followed in the pages of the *Public Administration Review, State Government,* the *National Municipal Review, Public Management,* and the *Public Welfare News.* A provocative essay that I found useful in formulating my thoughts on this important subject is Daniel J. Elazar's "The

Shaping of Intergovernmental Relations in the Twentieth Century,'' in the *Annals* of the American Academy of Political and Social Science, 359 (May 1965), 10–22.

Civil defense activities may be pursued in the pages of the OCD's official publication *Defense* (later retitled *Victory*) and in the various issues of *Newsweek, Harper's,* and *Business Week.* The last three were particularly critical of La Guardia's leadership. For the influence of Britain's civilian defense program on American thinking see especially Eric H. Biddle's *The Mobilization of the Home Front: The British Experience and Its Significance for the United States* (1942), published for the University of Chicago's Public Administration Institute. Excellent background reading for an understanding of the complexities of civilian mobilization is Angus Calder's *The People's War: Britain, 1939–1945* (1969).

For the social impact of the war upon urban communities, especially family life, I relied heavily upon *The Child, Child Welfare, The Family, Survey Graphic, Recreation,* the *Journal of Social Hygiene,* the *American Journal of Public Health, Social Service Review,* the *Journal of Home Economics,* and the *American Home.* From them I gleaned a deeper insight into how urban dwellers responded to wartime pressures at the local community level and a deeper appreciation of the struggle to maintain wartime social gains into the postwar period. In addition, the following historical and sociological studies proved useful for understanding community problems: Francis E. Merrill, *Social Problems on the Home Front* (1948), William F. Ogburn, ed., *American Society in Wartime* (1943), Robert J. Havighurst and H. Gerthon Morgan, *The Social History of a War-Boom Community* (1951), and Lowell J. Carr and James E. Stermer, *Willow Run: A Study of Industrial and Cultural Inadequacy* (1952).

Housing was central to the discussion of postwar urban planning. The controversy over public versus private housing received a thorough airing in both *Public Housing,* the organ of the National Public Housing Conference, and the *National Real Estate Journal,* which spoke for the proponents of private enterprise. The politics of wartime housing was closely followed in *Architectural Forum,* the *Journal of Land and Public Utility Economics,* and the excellent monograph of Charles Abrams, *The Future of Housing* (1946). Similarly, the fate of urban planning may be traced in the *News Letter* of the American Society of Planning Officials, the *Journal* of the American Institute of Planners, *New Pencil Points, Planning & Civic Comment,* and the *American Planning & Civic Annual.* Sharpening my perception of the planning controversy were Alan A. Altshuler's *The City Planning Process: A Political Analysis* (1965), Mel D. Scott's *American City Planning Since 1890* (1971), an encyclopedic account commemorating the fiftieth anniversary of the American Institute of Planners, and Robert A. Walker's *The Planning Function in Urban Government* (second edition, 1950). Mark I. Gelfand's *A Nation of Cities: The Federal Government and Urban America, 1933–1965* (1975) provides an excellent overview of its subject and has a comprehensive bibliography.

Index

273

Twentieth-Century America Series

DEWEY W. GRANTHAM, GENERAL EDITOR

Each volume in this series focuses on some aspect of the politics of social change in recent American history, utilizing new approaches to clarify the response of Americans to the dislocating forces of our own day—economic, technological, racial, demographic, and administrative.

VOLUMES PUBLISHED:

*The Reaffirmation of Republicanism: Eisenhower and the
    Eighty-third Congress* by Gary W. Reichard
*The Crisis of Conservative Virginia: The Byrd Organization
    and the Politics of Massive Resistance* by James W. Ely, Jr.
Black Tennesseans, 1900–1930 by Lester C. Lamon
Political Power in Birmingham, 1871–1921 by Carl V. Harris
*The Challenge to Urban Liberalism: Federal-City Relations
    during World War II* by Philip J. Funigiello

This book has been composed on the Compugraphic phototypesetter in eleven-point English Times with two-point line spacing. Helvetica type was selected for display. The book was designed by Jim Billingsley and set into type by Metricomp, Inc., Grundy Center, Iowa. It was printed offset by Thomson-Shore, Inc., Dexter, Michigan, and bound by John H. Dekker and Sons, Inc., Grand Rapids, Michigan. The paper on which the book is printed bears the watermark of S. D. Warren and is designed for an effective life of at least three hundred years.